Essays and Studies 2016

Series Editor: Elaine Treharne

The English Association

The objects of the English Association are to promote the knowledge and appreciation of the English language and its literatures, and to foster good practice in its teaching and learning at all levels.

The Association pursues these aims by creating opportunities of co-operation among all those interested in English; by furthering the recognition of English as essential in education; by discussing methods of English teaching; by holding lectures, conferences, and other meetings; by publishing journals, books, and leaflets; and by forming local branches.

Publications

The Year's Work in English Studies. An annual bibliography. Published by Blackwell.

The Year's Work in Critical and Cultural Theory. An annual bibliography. Published by Blackwell.

Essays and Studies. An annual volume of essays by various scholars assembled by the collector covering usually a wide range of subjects and authors from the medieval to the modern. Published by D. S. Brewer.

English. A journal of the Association, *English*, is published four times a year by the Association.

English 4–11. A journal supporting literacy in the primary classroom, published three times a year

The Use of English. A journal of the Association, *The Use of English*, is published three times a year by the Association.

Newsletter. A *Newsletter* is published three times a year giving information about forthcoming publications, conferences, and other matters of interest.

Benefits of Membership

Institutional Membership

Full members receive copies of *The Year's Work in English Studies, Essays and Studies, English* (4 issues) and three *Newsletters*.

Ordinary Membership covers *English* (4 issues) and three *Newsletters*.

Schools Membership includes copies of each issue of *English* and *The Use of English*, one copy of *Essays and Studies*, three *Newsletters*, and preferential booking and rates for various conferences held by the Association.

Individual Membership

Individuals take out Basic Membership, which entitles them to buy all regular publications of the English Association at a discounted price, and attend Association gatherings.

For further details write to the Membership Administrator, The English Association, The University of Leicester, University Road, Leicester LE1 7RH.

Essays and Studies 2016

Writing China
Essays on the Amherst Embassy (1816) and Sino-British Cultural Relations

**Edited by
Peter J. Kitson and Robert Markley**

for the English Association

D. S. BREWER

ESSAYS AND STUDIES 2016
IS VOLUME SIXTY-NINE IN THE NEW SERIES
OF ESSAYS AND STUDIES COLLECTED ON BEHALF OF
THE ENGLISH ASSOCIATION
ISSN 0071-1357

First published 2016
D. S. Brewer, Cambridge

D. S. Brewer is an imprint of Boydell & Brewer Ltd
PO Box 9, Woodbridge, Suffolk IP12 3DF, UK
and of Boydell & Brewer Inc.
668 Mt Hope Avenue, Rochester, NY 14620–2731 USA
website: www.boydellandbrewer.com

ISBN 978-1-84384-445-7

A CIP catalogue record for this book is available
from the British Library

The publisher has no responsibility for the continued existence or accuracy of
URLs for external or third-party internet websites referred to in this book, and
does not guarantee that any content on such websites is, or will remain, accurate
or appropriate

This publication is printed on acid-free paper

MIX
Paper from
responsible sources
FSC® C013056

Printed and bound in Great Britain by TJ International Ltd, Padstow

Contents

Illustrations

Notes on Contributors

Mingjun Lu received her Ph.D. from the English department at the University of Toronto and her MA in global affairs at the University of Toronto's Munk Center. Her research interests include Renaissance English literature, transnational early modernities, comparative poetics, and global intellectual history. Lu has published several journal articles and translated books. Her recently published monograph is entitled *The Chinese Impact upon English Renaissance Literature: A Globalization and Liberal Cosmopolitan Approach to Donne and Milton* (2015).

Eun Kyung Min is Professor of English at Seoul National University. She received her Ph.D. in Comparative Literature from Princeton University. A specialist in eighteenth-century British literature and culture, she has recently completed a book manuscript entitled 'China and the Writing of English Literary Modernity, 1690–1770'. Her published work appears in such journals as *The Eighteenth Century: Theory and Interpretation, Eighteenth-Century Studies, Studies on Voltaire and the Eighteenth Century* (SVEC), *Social Text,* and *English Literary History* (ELH). She has received fellowships from the International Society for Eighteenth-Century Studies, Lewis Walpole Library, Clark Library, Radcliffe Institute for Advanced Study, and the Korea Research Foundation.

Peter J. Kitson is Professor of English at the University of East Anglia. He is the author of *Forging Romantic China: Sino-British Cultural Exchange, 1760–1840* (2013); *Romantic Literature, Race and Colonial Encounter* (2007) and (with Debbie Lee and Tim Fulford), *Romantic Literature, Science and Exploration in the Romantic Era: Bodies of Knowledge* (2004). He is currently working on a study of British writing about the Opium Trade and First Opium War.

Robert Markley is W. D. and Sara E. Trowbridge Professor of English at the University of Illinois and editor of *The Eighteenth Century: Theory and Interpretation.* He is author of more than eighty articles in eighteenth-century studies, science studies, and new media; his recent books include *Fallen Languages: Crises of Representation in Newtonian England* (1993), *Virtual Realities and Their Discontents* (1996), *Dying Planet: Mars in Science and the Imagination* (2005), and *The Far East and the English Imagination, 1600–1730* (2006). He has held fellowships from the National

Endowment for the Humanities, the Huntington, Clark, and Beinecke Libraries, and most recently at the National Center for Supercomputing Applications. His study of the contemporary science-fiction novelist, *Kim Stanley Robinson*, is forthcoming from the University of Illinois Press. The current President of the Society for Literature, Science, and the Arts, he is currently completing a book on understandings of global climate and literary culture during the Little Ice Age (c. 1500–1800).

Eugenia Zuroski-Jenkins is Associate Professor of English and Cultural Studies at McMaster University. She is the author of *A Taste for China: English Subjectivity and the Prehistory of Orientalism* (2013) and editor of the journal *Eighteenth-Century Fiction*. Her current research project, A Funny Thing: Prehistories of the Uncanny, is supported by a SSHRC Insight Grant.

Elizabeth Chang is an Associate Professor of English at the University of Missouri. She is the author of *Britain's Chinese Eye: Literature, Empire and Aesthetics in Nineteenth-Century Britain* (2010) and the editor of *British Travel Writings from China, 1793–1901* (2009). Her research interests include Sino-British relations in the nineteenth century, visual and material culture, and environmental studies.

Zhang Longxi holds an MA in English from Peking University and a Ph.D. in Comparative Literature from Harvard University. He has taught at Peking, Harvard, and the University of California, Riverside, and is currently Chair Professor of Chinese and Comparative Literature at the City University of Hong Kong. He was elected a foreign member of the Royal Swedish Academy of Letters, History and Antiquities in 2009 and a foreign member of Academia Europaea in 2013. He serves as an Advisory Editor of *New Literary History*, and an Editor-in-Chief of the *Journal of World Literature*. He has published more than twenty books and numerous articles in both English and Chinese in East–West comparative studies. His major English book publications include *The Tao and the Logos: Literary Hermeneutics, East and West* (1992); *Mighty Opposites: From Dichotomies to Differences in the Comparative Study of China* (1998); *Allegoresis: Reading Canonical Literature East and West* (2005); *Unexpected Affinities: Reading across Cultures* (2007); and most recently, *From Comparison to World Literature* (2015).

Q. S. Tong is University Professor of English in both the College of Liberal Arts and the English Department, Sun Yat-sen University, China.

Before he joined Sun Yat-sen University, he had worked at the University of Hong Kong for over two decades. He has published extensively, in both English and Chinese, on issues of critical significance in literary and cultural studies, criticism and theory, and the history of literary ideas, with special attention to the historical interactions between China and the West. His current work focuses on the Chinese language reform movement in the early twentieth century and its social and political consequences. He has served as advisory editor for a number of international journals including *boundary 2*.

Introduction: Writing China

PETER J. KITSON AND ROBERT MARKLEY

Two hundred years ago, in the early hours of the morning of 29 August 1816, William Pitt, Lord Amherst, unrested after travelling overnight, was apparently unceremoniously manhandled in an attempt to usher him physically with his two deputies, George Thomas Staunton and Henry Ellis, into the presence of the Jiaqing Emperor at the Summer Palace of Yuanming Yuan. Fatigued, separated from his diplomatic credentials and ambassadorial robes, Amherst and his deputies resisted, and left the palace in anger. It was reported to the emperor that Amherst's inability to attend was occasioned by illness, as was that of his two deputies. The emperor, discovering the ambassador was not ill, immediately dismissed the embassy without granting an imperial audience and rejected its 'tribute' of gifts. Amherst's party then began its long overland journey south to Canton (Guangzhou) where it embarked for home.

British accounts of the embassy lay its ostensible 'failure' to secure an audience not on the emperor, but on the scheming of senior court officials who had unwisely assured him that Amherst was preparing to perform the problematic ceremony of the full imperial *koutou* or 'kowtow' with its three kneelings accompanied by three knockings of the forehead for each prostration. After a process of negotiation Amherst instead offered to perform the compromised version of the ceremony that his more famous predecessor, Viscount George Macartney, had agreed to undertake for the Qianlong Emperor at Jehol in September 1793, kneeling on one knee and bowing his head thrice as he would before his royal master, George III. Indeed in an extension of the compromise the ambassador offered to perform this kneeling not once but three times with the full complement of nine bows of the head in total. The Qianlong Emperor had accepted a compromise in 1793; his fifth son and successor would not. The expensive items brought by the British as 'presents' for the Jiaqing Emperor, costing some £20,000, were not accepted, though afterwards, the emperor agreed to a very limited and symbolic exchange of a few items in his apparent recognition of the sincerity and obedience of the Prince Regent in sending this tribute. The embassy left Canton for home on 28 January 1817, suffering shipwreck and pirate attack on the return voyage, and visiting the deposed emperor Napoleon on St Helena (who told Amherst he was very foolish not to kowtow), arriving back in Britain on 17 August 1817.

The Amherst embassy was only the second British embassy to visit China. As Q. S. Tong reminds us, however, in his essay on Tibet in this volume, the first proper British mission to approach China was organized by Warren Hastings, Governor-general of Bengal, who sent George Bogle into Tibet in 1774. In 1788 the first embassy from Britain to the Qing court was aborted when its ambassador, Lt-Colonel Charles, died en route, and it was not until 1793 that Viscount Macartney finally arrived at the imperial court of the Qianlong Emperor. The Amherst embassy, twenty-three years later, was a crucial event in the lead up to the First Opium War of 1839–42. John Francis Davis, one of the several interpreters for the embassy, looked back in 1840 at the beginning of that historic war, predicting that the year

> was destined to present the extraordinary spectacle of a British naval and military force on the coast of China, a region so far removed from Europe that its existence six hundred years ago was scarcely known, and the faithful narrative of a long resident and traveller in the country received as a tissue of fables containing another El Dorado.[1]

Davis's narrative articulates this extraordinary moment. To a great extent scholars of British literature and culture have largely forgotten or ignored the importance of this event in their accounts of the early nineteenth century. But for the Chinese this war marks the beginning of their traumatic 'Century of National Humiliation' (*bǎinián guóchǐ*) that concluded in 1949 with the establishment of the People's Republic of China.[2]

This volume of historically wide-ranging essays is intended to mark this moment. It may be that in the next decade events such as the Macartney and Amherst embassies and the First and Second Opium Wars become as important to scholars of British literary culture as the impact of the American and French Revolutions and the Seven Years War and the Revolutionary and Napoleonic Wars have been to the work of literary and cultural historians of the last twenty years or so. In the field of creative writing, the Bengali novelist Amitav Ghosh has brilliantly evoked the material realities

---

[1] John Francis Davis, *Sketches of China; partly during an inland journey of four months between Peking, Nanking, and Canton; with notices and observations relative to the present war*. 2 vols (London: Charles Knight & Co., 1841), 2. 260.
[2] See William A Callahan, *China the Pessoptimist Nation* (Oxford: Oxford University Press, 2009).

of the opium trade in the lead up to the war of 1839 in his 'Ibis' trilogy of novels, completed in 2015 with *Flood of Fire*. These three novels focus on a group of Bengali, Parsee, British, and American characters caught up in the networks of the trade between Bengal and China. Ghosh's fiction shows how any binary imaginings of the relations between Britain and China are sundered by the complexities of commerce in Southeast Asia and the colonial arrangements of the East India Company.

The Amherst embassy occurred two hundred years before the publication of this volume of essays on cultural relations between Britain and China, that stretches from the early modern period to the late nineteenth century and touching the present. It is thus perhaps timely in 2016 to think again about the complex and vexed historical and cultural relations between two of the world's historic empires. The essays in this volume engage with the most recent work on British cultural representations of, and exchanges with, Qing China, extending our existing but still provisional understanding of this emerging area of study in new and exciting directions. Studies of the cultural relationship between Britain and China are still relatively few, especially when compared to those of Britain and the 'Near and Middle East' or of their encounters with the peoples and cultures of the Indian subcontinent. The reasons for this probably relate to the history of British and European colonialism more generally in the eighteenth and nineteenth centuries, a history in which India, Arabia and the Levant were both areas of occupation and of imperial rivalry between France and Britain. It may also have much to do with the continued military and economic strength of China up until around 1800, undefeated by any western power until the First Opium War and capable of resisting foreign penetration.

Gaining knowledge of Chinese languages, literature, and thought was a much harder task when Britons were forbidden to travel in the empire and had to rely on that great Jesuit missionary archival project the *Lettres édifiantes et curieuses* (1702–76) and its numerous eighteenth-century redactions for their information about China. The sheer difficulty of obtaining any competence in the Chinese script and its various spoken varieties also delayed serious direct intellectual engagement with actual Chinese texts for the British into the mid-eighteenth century. Famously, the Macartney embassy was unable to locate anyone in Britain who had a decent command of the Chinese language – the only person up to the mark, James Flint, died shortly before the embassy departed. Macartney had thus to rely on Chinese Catholic converts trained in Naples who communicated with the embassy staff via the European lingua franca of Latin.

We therefore almost entirely depend on the good faith and good-nature of the few Chinese whom we employ, and by whom we can be but imperfectly understood in the broken gibberish we talk to them. I fancy than Pan-ke-qua [Pan Youdo, a leading Canton merchant] or Mahomet Soulem would attempt doing business on the Royal Exchange to very little purpose if they appeared there in long petticoat clothes, with bonnets and turbans, and could speak nothing but Chinese or Arabic.[3]

It was not until the early nineteenth century that Britons, such as the missionary Robert Morrison and the East India Company servants George Thomas Staunton and John Francis Davis, acquired excellent levels of the Chinese script and the Mandarin and Canton spoken languages, some thirty or so years after William Jones and his fellow scholars had mastered Persian, Arabic and Sanskrit. Later in the century, as China was broken open by the Opium Wars, sinologists such as the diplomats Thomas Wade, Herbert Giles, and the missionary James Legge established themselves as major British scholars of China, and their translations of Chinese thought and literature influenced a new generation of artists and thinkers. It was in Giles's translation of the book of *Zhuangzi* that Oscar Wilde found a sympathetic and congenial thinker, as Zhang Longxi's essay in this volume demonstrates.

Thus serious study of matters Chinese was marked by a kind of belatedness for British scholarship. This separation of China from other 'eastern' cultures in the minds of the British is, to an extent, replicated in the uneasy relation between orientalism, as a discipline and discourse, and sinology. China-centred academic study has always been a more distant relation of the family of orientalist study, leading many to question whether it makes sense to regard China as involved in the same play of orientalist binary operations of self and other, however sophisticated the manner they are formulated. If sinologists may have been somewhat insulated from the dynamics of contemporary orientalist and post-colonial studies, literary scholars and cultural historians more widely have also engaged with matters Chinese in fewer numbers and in later years. True, there have been a number of important and distinguished older studies of western representations of China, but comparatively few studies have appeared in these areas since new historicist reappraisal of the literary

---

[3] J. L. Cranmer-Byng, ed., *An Embassy to China. Being the Journal kept by Lord Macartney during his embassy to the Emperor Ch'ien-lung, 1793–1794* (London: Longman, 1962), p. 210.

canon in the 1980s.[4] With the increasing presence of the PRC on the global stage, imminently, we are told, to assume the status of the world's largest economy, it might now be argued that in the second decade of the twenty-first century our critical focus should be attuned to Southeast Asia and China especially. The crucial political and cultural events, among others, that will define this scholarly enquiry will be the first two British embassies to arrive in China (Macartney, 1793 and Amherst, 1816), the end of the East India Company's monopoly of the China trade in 1833, and the outbreak of hostilities leading to the First 'Opium War' of 1839–42 and the Second Opium War of 1856–60.

The essays in this volume further the case that Ming and Qing China were important, though highly problematic, referents in the literature and culture of the Britain, and that this crucial presence has not been sufficiently addressed. China, as Eric Hayot, Haun Saussy, David Porter, Chi-ming Yang, Eugenia Zuroski-Jenkins, Elizabeth Chang, Michael Keevak, Ross G. Forman. Mingjun Lu and others have reminded us, was central to the making of modernity and the formation of the modern western self.[5] A. O. Lovejoy, for instance, many years ago, put forward

---

4 This body of work includes Jacques Gernet, *China and the Christian Impact: A Conflict of Cultures* (Cambridge: Cambridge University Press, 1985); Raymond Dawson, *The Chinese Chameleon: An Analysis of European Conceptions of Chinese Civilization* (New York: Oxford University Press, 1992); Donald F. Lach, *Asia in the Making of Europe*. 3 vols (Chicago: University of Chicago Press, 1965–93); *China in the Eyes of Europe* (Chicago: University of Chicago Press, 1968); Colin Mackerras, *Western Images of China* (Oxford: Oxford University Press, 1989); David E. Mungello, *The Great Encounter of China and the West, 1500–1800* (London: Rowman & Littlefield, 2012).

5 Eric Hayot, *The Hypothetical Mandarin: Sympathy, Modernity, and Chinese Pain* (Oxford: Oxford University Press, 2009); Eric Hayot, Haun Saussy, and Stephen G. Yao, ed., *Sinographies: Writing China* (Minneapolis, MN: University of Minnesota Press, 2008); Hain Saussy, *Great Walls of Discourse and Other Adventures in Cultural China* (Cambridge, MA: Harvard University Press, 2002); David Porter, *Ideographia: the Chinese Cipher in Early Modern Europe* (Stanford: Stanford University Press, 2001); *The Chinese Taste in Eighteenth-Century England* (Cambridge: Cambridge University Press, 2010); Chi-ming Yang, *Performing China, Virtue, Commerce and Orientalism in Eighteenth-century England 1660–1760* (Baltimore, MD: Johns Hopkins University Press, 2010); Elizabeth Hope Chang, *Britain's Chinese Eye: Literature, Empire, and Aesthetics in Nineteenth-Century Britain* (Stanford: Stanford University Press, 2013); Eugenia Zuroski-Jenkins, *A Taste for China: English Subjectivity and the Prehistory of* Orientalism (Oxford: Oxford University Press, 2013); Michael Keevak, *Becoming Yellow: A Short History of Racial Thinking* (Princeton: Princeton University Press, 2011); Peter J. Kitson, *Forging Romantic China: Sino-British Cultural Exchange, 1760–1840* (Cambridge: Cambridge

the then unconventional thesis that one of the origins of what we know of as 'Romanticism', the preference for a form of wildness and irregularity in the eighteenth-century British landscape garden, was located in a Chinese source.[6] Other scholars of British literature and culture in the long eighteenth century, most notably Robert Markley and Ros Ballaster, have addressed such issues, placing British cultural responses to China firmly in the context of a dominant sinocentric global economy, up until around 1800.[7] Such criticism has also demonstrated the sustained allure that Chinese commodities, tea, silk, porcelain, furniture, lacquer ware, and Chinese designs in gardening and interior decoration held throughout the long eighteenth century and beyond. Later scholars, notably Zhaoming Qian, have argued for the crucial importance of Chinese culture to modernist writers.[8] Indeed, recent theorizing about world literature also raises important and difficult questions about the place of China in the culture of the world.

The essays in this volume argue that the Chinese contribution to the culture of the British literature and culture generally was substantial and not simply a one-way process but, at one level, an exchange of ideas and knowledge and, at another, a part of a wider, global process that has been influentially described by Zhang Longxi as a series of 'elective affinities'.[9]

University Press, 2013); ed., 'China and the British Romantic Imagination', *European Romantic Review*, 27.i (2016); Robert Markley, ed., 'China and the Making of Global Modernity', *Eighteenth-Century Studies*, 43 (2010); Ross G. Forman, *China and the Victorian Imagination: Empires Entwined* (Cambridge: Cambridge University Press, 2013); Mingjun Lu, *The Chinese Impact upon English Renaissance Literature: A Globalization and Liberal Cosmopolitan Approach to Donne and Milton* (Aldershot: Ashgate, 2015); see also Saree Makdisi, *Making England Western: Occidentalism, Race, and Imperial Culture* (Chicago: University of Chicago Press, 2014).

[6] A. O. Lovejoy, 'The Chinese Origin of A Romanticism', in *Essays in the History of Ideas* (New York: George Braziller, 1948), pp. 99–135.

[7] Robert Markley, *The Far East and the English Imagination, 1600–1730* (Cambridge: Cambridge University Press, 2006); 'Introduction: Europe and Asia in the Eighteenth Century', in *The Eighteenth Century: Theory and Interpretation*, 45 (2004), 111–14; Ros Ballaster, *Fabulous Orients: Fictions of the East in England 1662–1785* (Oxford: Oxford University Press, 2005).

[8] Zhaoming Qian, *Orientalism and Modernism: The Legacy of China in Pound and Williams* (Durham, NC: Duke University Press, 2012); *The Modernist Response to Chinese Art: Pound, Moore, Stevens* (Charlottesville, VA: University of Virginia Press, 2003).

[9] Zhang Longxi, *Unexpected Affinities: Reading across Cultures* (Toronto: University of Toronto Press, 2007). See also his *The Tao and the Logos: Literary Hermeneutics, East and West* (Durham, NC: Duke University Press, 1992); *Allegoresis:*

We seek to enlarge the purview of such exemplary criticism to take in China and its ambivalent and complex contribution to the British domestic cultural sphere. We thus see ourselves as cognate with the larger shared project to restore Ming and Qing 'China' both as a topos and as a geographical place to its truly global presence in our understandings of the culture and literature of the late eighteenth and early nineteenth centuries, and to speculate further about the kind of cultural landscape this assertion presents and what difference it makes to our present understanding of the terrain.

Taking the cases of the Elizabethan poet Edmund Spenser's *Shepherd's Calendar* and the Ming poet Wu Cheng'en's pastoral writing, Ming Lu deploys a 'correlative comparative model' to reveal insights into the historically unrelated texts under discussion, finding that the literary register of urbanization in both Elizabethan England and late Ming China 'correlates' rather than causally connecting, thus indicating the synchronic coexistence of two distinctive modes of modernity in pre-modern times. For Lu, the lack of direct contact between the poets of Ming China and Elizabethan England does not mean that the two cultural artefacts are not comparable. Using the highly influential work of David Porter, she argues that a 'basic commensurability' in these 'two seemingly disparate contexts' rests, in part, on 'the curious alignment of their political histories' and the 'parallels in the realms of social and economic history'.[10]

The global circulation of texts is also the subject of Eun Kyung Min's essay on Thomas Percy's little-known text, *The Matrons* (1762), a collection of six short tales relating to widows culled from different periods and civilizations. That these tales share the same subject raises significant questions about how late eighteenth-century writers viewed what we now think of as 'Comparative' or 'World Literature'. One of the versions, a very popular seventeenth-century vernacular Ming tale, was complied by Feng Menglong and featured the celebrated Daoist sage, 'Master Zhuang'. Min demonstrates how Percy 'forged textual conjunctions and analogies between the Chinese texts and its western analogues', placing the tale in a 'transnational and transhistorical circuit of travelling texts' where origins are effaced, but where a dialogue between Chinese and European writing occurs.

Reading Canonical Literature East and West (Ithaca, NY: Cornell University Press, 2005) and *Mighty Opposites: From Dichotomies to Difference in the Comparative Study of China* (Stanford: Stanford University Press, 1999).

[10] David Porter, 'Sinicizing Early Modernity: The Imperatives of Historical Cosmopolitanism', *Eighteenth-Century Studies*, 43.3 (2010), 299–306.

Zhuangzi's actual philosophical writings and their late nineteenth-century reception form the subject of Zhang Longxi's essay, which instances Oscar Wilde's brief encounter with the Chinese philosopher in his little-known review of Herbert Giles's translation of the book of *Zhuangzi*. In this review, Wilde demonstrates a serious appreciation of Zhuangzi's Daoist beliefs, which clearly struck a major chord with his own aestheticism. For both thinkers, aesthetic criticism did not mark an escape from social and political reality but rather a serious engagement with it and even resistance to it. Wilde's protest against nineteenth-century British middle-class materialism and utilitarianism finds clear echoes in Zhuangzi's rejection of Confucian ethics with their social imperative to duty and action. Both writers also favoured an epigrammatic and paradoxical way of expressing their thought. Wilde found in Zhuangzi a congenial style and sympathetic outlook close to his own as Zhang, as a young man first encountering Wilde's writings and thought, appreciated how they served as a form of resistance to bureaucratic and governmental oppression in Mao's China.

The essays by Peter Kitson, Robert Markley, and Eugenia Zuroski-Jenkins are linked in their shared concerns with either the Amherst embassy or the opium trade. Kitson situates the narratives of the embassy in the global flow of commodities that was the trade with China in tea and opium. He argues that the narratives of the embassy, in their concerns with the 'kowtow' ceremonial and the ritual exchange of presents, mask the material realities of the then vastly expanding and illegal trade in East Indian opium. Deploying accounts written in 1840 by the generally sinophiliac John Francis Davis and the consistently sinophobic Thomas De Quincey, Kitson shows how opium usage and trading were crucial, if sometimes unspoken, contexts for the 'failed' embassy.

Markley's essay situates the narratives of the embassy in the context of eco-criticism. In 1815 the volcano, Mount Tambora, spectacularly erupted. The consequences of this eruption were climatologically far-reaching, leading to the year 1816 being known as 'the year without a Summer'. Few at the time were aware of the eruption and were most were perplexed by this miserable summer and its devastating crop failures around the world. Markley interrogates the accounts of the embassy, notably these by George Thomas Staunton, John Francis Davis, and the embassy's naturalist, Clarke Abel, for clues to the impact of the eruption. He argues that the embassy Britons disastrously misread the signs of this impact in China for evidence of China's economic and political stagnation during the Jiaqing reign, and he suggests that the Tambora eruption was responsible for colouring in often subtle ways those influential British understandings of China that came to view the Qing polity as 'corrupt, backward, and insufferably proud'.

Zuroski-Jenkins focuses on the subject of the opium trade in the aftermath of the Amherst embassy. She demonstrates how, while literary scholars have situated De Quincey's *Confessions of an English Opium Eater* (1821) in the context of opium and its consumption, the topos of tea is just as important if not more so; tea, not opium, may be the 'true hero' of the text. Jenkins traces this extraordinary story of the transformation of tea from foreign and addictive luxury to the national British drink in the early and mid-nineteenth century, showing how tea became a crucial commodity in the formulation of the British national self. She argues that De Quincey's text deploys tea as a frequent topos designed to represent a form of domestic normalcy, whereas it shares much in common with opium. Restoring the ambivalent and paradoxical nature of the commodity of tea to the *Confessions* leaves us with a richer, more problematic understanding of the exotic in the nineteenth century. It shows us that the familiar British topos of tea drinking remains fundamentally uncanny and strange.

If tea and opium are familiar topoi relating to China in the nineteenth century, the issue of female foot binding is also a source of sustained western interest. Elizabeth Chang's essay tackles this familiar subject again but from the fresh perspective of the representation of the practice in British periodicals of the mid-nineteenth century. Chang discusses the Victorian interest in the bound Chinese foot in periodical press writing and post-Opium War narratives. She argues that the presentation of the physical phenomenon of the deformed foot is only a part of a story involving the confrontation with imported and assimilated ideas of movement, freedom, and the power of narrative. Chang's focus here on the pre-1870 period, after which the campaign against foot binding was at its height, complicates our existing understanding of the terrain. Through reformist rhetoric, the process of unbinding Chinese feet is linked with that of the 'liberation' of Chinese international commerce, an allegedly free and easy movement.

In the final essay in this volume, Q. S. Tong refocus our attention geographically northwards to discuss orientalism and the contested territory of Tibet, which China claims to have ruled since the mid-thirteenth century. In 1720 the Kangxi Emperor expelled the Zhungar Mongols and re-established the rule of the Dalai Lama. Tong argues that from the later eighteenth century Tibet has been extensively romanticized and mythologized in the western imagination. He demonstrates how this version of a romanticized Tibet emerged in the narratives of the first Britons to visit there, George Bogle and Thomas Manning, and how it then developed into the unabashed escapism of the fantasy land of James Hilton's famous Shangri-La from his novel of 1933, *Lost Horizon*. Tong argues that this imagined Tibet was multifaceted and contradictory even from the outset, though the notion of Tibet as a form of spiritual utopia seems to have been a constant.

Bogle never got to Lhasa, the capital of Tibet, though he met and established a sympathetic relationship with the (sixth) Panchen Lama. Bogle was followed to Tibet by Samuel Turner in 1783, but it would not be until 1811 that the first Briton would visit Lhasa, when the independent scholar and later one of the interpreters for the Amherst embassy, Thomas Manning, arrived. Tong demonstrates how Enlightenment understandings of Tibet thus gave way to those that stressed a dominant spiritualism with the discovery in the later nineteenth century of 'Tibetan Buddhism'. Ultimately, Tong argues that Tibet demonstrates two forms of orientalism, an internal orientalism that continues to exist among Tibetans in exile, continuous with European imaginings, and a Han Chinese version, which others Tibetans as less 'civilized' than themselves.

The essays in this volume thus seek to extend and develop current thinking about cultural understandings of, and relationships between, Britain and China. They argue for a refocusing and recalibration of our critical endeavours to take writings about China into our purview. The time has now come for our studies to reflect and take full account of the important presence of China as both a geopolitical presence in the eighteenth and nineteenth centuries as well as an imagined topos.

Urbanization, Generic Forms, and Early Modernity: A Correlative Comparison of Wu Cheng'en and Spenser's Rural-Pastoral Poems

MINGJUN LU

New methodological trends in comparative studies that shift the ground of comparison from the Eurocentric to a broadly diffused modernity help reveal some hitherto unnoticed channels of communication in Sino-English intercourse, especially around 1600 when England began to know about China.[1] Despite their historical proximity, Elizabethan England and late Ming China are two distinctive cultures proceeding in widely separate orbits. The lack of direct contact, however, does not mean that the two cultures are not comparable. David Porter rightly argues that there does exist some 'basic commensurability' in these 'two seemingly disparate contexts', such as 'the curious alignment of their political histories' and the 'parallels in the realms of social and economic history'. But as Porter points out, 'questions of influence, coincidence, and causality may not be entirely pertinent' to account for these cross-cultural analogues that seem to go beyond a Eurocentric paradigm.[2]

This essay is an attempt to conceptualize early modern Sino-English relationship with what I would call a *correlative comparative model*, by which I mean a framework that privileges probable parallels rather than direct causal connections. Since correlation does not imply causation, I argue, a correlative model could at once provide a new ground of comparison for historically unrelated texts and bypass the limitations of comparisons premised upon 'influence, coincidence, and causality'. The variables in a correlation matrix, however, could evolve into causal ones,

---

[1] For the new methodological trends, see Haun Saussy, ed., *Comparative Literature in an Age of Globalization* (Baltimore, MD: Johns Hopkins University Press, 2006); David Porter, ed., *Comparative Early Modernities: 1100–1800* (Basingstoke: Palgrave, 2012); and Rita Felski and Susan S. Friedman, ed., *Comparison: Theories, Approaches, Uses* (Baltimore, MD: Johns Hopkins University Press, 2013).

[2] David Porter, 'Sinicizing Early Modernity: The Imperatives of Historical Cosmopolitanism', *Eighteenth-Century Studies*, 43.3 (2010), 299–306 (pp. 301–2, 303).

especially given that the two cultures involved did come into substantial contact from the middle of the seventeenth century.

Choosing genre and urbanization as two correlative variables, I examine literary responses to pre-modern urbanization through a comparative analysis of the poetic dialogues in Edmund Spenser's *The Shepheardes Calendar* (1579) and Wu Cheng'en's *The Journey to the West* [西游记] (1592).[3] Chapter Ten of *The Journey* features a debate between a Fisherman and a Woodman on the rival merits of rural versus city/court life. What marks this debate inserted in an extensive vernacular story is that each interlocutor expands on the rural ideal by composing five *ci* lyrics, one regulated poem, and a link-verse or a long poem governed by one rhyme scheme. These lyrical forms recall at once the *shanshui shi* [山水诗] (landscape poetry) pioneered by Xie Lingyun [谢灵运] (385–433), and the *tianyuan shi* [田园诗] (farmstead poetry) initiated by Tao Yuanming [陶渊明] (365–427) and perfected by Wang Wei [王维] (699–761). That two simple mountain folks compete to assert the value of rural life via sophisticated poetic forms, I will show, implies a protest against an increasingly urbanized society. A similar contest occurs in Spenser's *Calendar*, a pastoral poem comprised of twelve eclogues, each focusing on a calendric month. The point of contention here centres on the contrast between idyllic pastoral life and sober georgic realities, a theme struck home by the poet's subtle pairing of 'recreative' and 'plaintive' shepherds.[4] The October eclogue reveals a key cause of the pastoral complaints, which proves none other than the enclosure of farmlands for shepherding, a movement that ran rampant in sixteenth-century England. Spenser's pastoral poem certainly alludes to the Protestant and Catholic rivalry, but this essay focuses on its secular dimension and georgic root in the enclosure movement. The rural–urban tension is implicit in Spenser's eclogues, but Wu's poems put more emphasis on the rural–court conflict. Since courts are the places where urban problems find a most concentrated configuration, I use city/court as the counterpart of rural or georgic ideals when dealing with Wu's lyrical debate.[5]

---

[3] *Edmund Spenser: The Shorter Poems*, ed. Richard A. McCabe (London: Penguin, 1999). All quotations from Spenser are from this edition. Wu Cheng'en, *The Journey to the West*, trans. Anthony Yu. 4 vols (Chicago: University of Chicago Press, 2012), vol. 1.

[4] For the two terms 'recreative' and 'plaintive' see Michael D. Bristol, 'Structural Patterns in Two Elizabethan Pastorals', *Studies in English Literature, 1500–1900*, 10.1 (1970), 33–48 (pp. 36, 37).

[5] This essay uses rural and georgic as exchangeable equivalents.

In emphasizing the contrast between alternative modes of life, these fictional dialogues suggest an interaction between generic forms and the underlying socioeconomic forces. What is at stake in these conversations, I propose, is the contested meaning of life associated with pre-modern urbanization, by which I mean the rural–urban divide caused by pre-industrial 'agrarian capitalism' in England and 'agric–mercantile' economy of late Ming China.[6] While English urbanization received tremendous impetus from the enclosure policy, the burgeoning of cities in late Ming was precipitated by an increasingly commercialized economy. In his study of 'representations of agrarian England', Andrew McRae remarks that 'the role of literature as an 'agent in constructing a culture's sense of reality' may valuably be explored through 'attention to literary modes'. For McRae, 'the development of a literary tradition is embedded in broader social, economic and ideological movements, yet at the same time literature itself asserts a significant cultural force as it performs its distinctive labours of representation'.[7] Drawing upon McRae's insight on the enmeshing of discursive construction and its social base, this essay examines how pre-modern urbanization registers in literary genres.

Pre-modern urbanization was largely an ongoing process without clearly defined goals or agendas at both the state and social levels. Accordingly, country and city, the two key actors in this process, were in a constant flux, a condition that accounts for the fluid continuity between pastoral and georgic that are conventionally regarded as two distinct genres.[8] Louis A. Montrose considers pastoral a genre inhabited by shepherds who are 'typically occupied by singing, piping, wooing, and the other quaint indulgences of the pastoral life'.[9] While pastoral adopts such genre metaphors as 'sheep, crook, pasture, and beech tree', Alastair Fowler asserts, georgic

[6] Zhao Yifeng, 'The Historical Trend of Ming China: An Imperial Agric-mercantile Society', *Frontier History China*, 3.1 (2008), 78–100.

[7] Andrew McRae, *God Speed the Plough: The Representation of Agrarian England, 1500–1660* (Cambridge: Cambridge University Press, 1996), p. 4. For the shift from feudalism to capitalism, also see R. H. Tawney, *The Agrarian Problem in the Sixteenth Century* (London: Longman, 1912), and Eric Kerridge, *Agrarian Problems in the Sixteenth Century and After* (London: Allen & Unwin, 1969).

[8] For city versus country in pastoral, see Frank Kermode, *English Pastoral Poetry from the Beginning to Marvell* (London: Barnes & Noble, 1952), pp. 13–15; and David M. Halperin, *Before Pastoral: Theocritus and the Ancient Tradition of Bucolic Poetry* (New Haven, CT: Yale University Press, 1983), pp. 52, 55, 65.

[9] Louis A. Montrose, 'Of Gentlemen and Shepherds: The Politics of Elizabethan Pastoral Form', *English Literary History*, 50.3 (1983), 415–59 (pp. 427–8).

images usually refer to 'farmer, ox, plough, field, and fruit tree'.[10] But when viewed in light of the 'rural–urban continuum', georgic and pastoral appear in a symbiotic relationship rather than two separate forms.[11] Urbanization is a double-edged sociocultural process. While impairing and even destroying the simple georgic life, it also generates nostalgic yearnings for the lost farmstead. Despite its undoubted rawness and hardships, rural life is the fountainhead of pastoral ideals of simplicity and happiness. Just as the rural is the lost dream of the urban, the georgic is the social imaginary of the pastoral, or as Charles Kwong puts it, pastoral 'sings of those qualities in rustic life missing in the town and court'.[12]

So a more truthful account of pastoral might be anchored in its georgic roots. It is with this georgic–pastoral affinity in mind that Edward W. Taylor defines pastoral as 'the literary result of the poet's insight into the difference between rural and urban values'.[13] Likewise, Kwong argues that 'From the beginning pastoral verse is an urban myth about rural matters', and that 'the pastoral sentiment is a townsman's longing for rusticity that understands itself to be a fantasy'.[14] The pastoral's urban 'longing' for the rural is usually cast in images of nostalgia or return. Frederick Garber considers nostalgia 'the driving force that brings pastoral into being', and Peter Marinelli views 'the theme of return' as 'a central and unchanging core of meaning in the pastoral convention itself'.[15] The georgic origin of pastoral and the rural–urban dynamic are explicit in these statements.

A similar generic bond marks Chinese farmstead and landscape poetry, two lyrical forms that are intrinsically linked through a shared vision of

---

[10]   Alastair Fowler, 'The Formation of Genres in the Renaissance and After', *New Literary History*, 3.2 (2003), 185–200 (p. 192).

[11]   For the term 'rural–urban continuum', see Frederick W. Mote, 'A Millennium of Chinese Urban History: Form, Time, and Space Concepts in Soochow', *Rice University Studies*, 59.4 (1973), 35–65. I use the term differently from Mote. While Mote regards it as evidence for the lack of urbanization in imperial China, I take it as an indicator of urbanization in not only late Ming China but also early modern England.

[12]   Charles Kwong, 'The Rural World of Chinese "Farmstead Poetry" (Tianyuan Shi): How Far Is It Pastoral?', *Chinese Literature: Essays, Articles, Reviews*, 15 (1993), 57–84 (p. 75).

[13]   Edward W. Taylor, *Nature and Art in Renaissance Literature* (New York: Columbia University Press, 1964), p. 89; and Kwong, 'Rural World', p. 59.

[14]   Kwong, 'Rural World', p. 59.

[15]   Frederick Garber, 'Pastoral Spaces', *Texas Studies in Literature and Language*, 30.3 (1988), *Renaissance Culture, Literature, and Genres*, 431–60 (p. 443); and Peter Marinelli, *Pastoral* (London: Methuen, 1971), p. 13.

rural and pastoral life. For this reason, I call the farmstead–landscape poetry the Chinese counterpart of the western georgic–pastoral verse. The Chinese equivalent of the Western pastoral has been a fertile site of debate, and farmstead and landscape poetry prove two ideal candidates for a Chinese pastoral. But an effective matching seems hindered by the lack of a clear definition both of the Chinese and the western pastoral forms. J. D. Frodsham notes that Chinese critics tend to regard Tao Yuanming's verse 'as "garden poetry" and not as landscape poetry proper', but it is unclear what they mean by landscape poetry.[16] Stephen Field invents the concept of 'Chinese ruralism' to address 'poetry about the farmer'.[17] For Field, since Wang Wei's 'adoption of the role of gentleman farmer and the pose of recluse-farmer is similar to the pastoral conceit of shepherd-poet in the West', farmstead poetry 'has rightly been called pastoral by modern Chinese and Western Scholars'.[18] In contrast, Kwong contends that the rubric farmstead poetry 'certainly points to a broad, flexible tradition to which no conventional formulae applies'.[19] As farmstead and landscape poetry cover both rural and pastoral matters, there is an obvious slippage when correlating them with the western pastoral whose definition tends to ignore its georgic associations. But the farmstead–landscape compound offers a more apt parallel to western pastoral–georgic.

The thematic and generic analogues manifested in these fictional dialogues afford us a vantage point from which to reconsider the comparison of texts from historically separate contexts. I choose generic forms and urbanization as two correlates on the grounds that 'discourse at once responds to and enables shifts in social and economic practice'.[20] It is the *microcosmic correlation* between urbanization and literary genres that constitutes the ground of comparison for the *macrocosmic correlation* between the two unrelated contexts. The genre–urbanization variable serves as a meaningful ground of comparison because urbanization has been a contested ground for modernity in postmodern studies that

[16] J. D. Frodsham, 'The Origin of Chinese Nature Poetry', *Asia Major*, 8 (1960–61), 96n.

[17] Stephen Field, 'Ruralism in Chinese Poetry: Some Versions of Chinese Pastoral', *Comparative Literature Studies*, 28.1 (1991), 1–35 (p. 2).

[18] Field, 'Ruralism', p. 20. For *tianyuan shi* as Chinese equivalent of western pastoral, also see Tu Wei-ming, 'Profound Learning, Personal Knowledge, and Poetic Vision', in *The Vitality of the Lyric Voice*, ed. Shuen-fu Lin and Stephen Owen (Princeton: Princeton University Press, 1986), pp. 3–31 (p. 23).

[19] Kwong, 'Rural World', p. 57.

[20] McRae, *God Speed the Plough*, p. 7.

advocate multiple origins of modernity.[21] That both the georgic–pastoral continuum and farmstead–landscape poetic symbiosis register sociocultural changes caused by the transition from a rural to an urban society, I propose, suggests parallel modernities in pre-modern England and China.

The Correlative Comparative Model

Claims of multiple modernities have rendered provincial the conventional influence/contact comparative model based on European modernity. As Porter puts it, 'Given the degree to which received notions of modernity and, by implication, early modernity, have been founded on the presumption of radical and essential alterity, establishing not only the coevalness but the fundamental commensurability of seemingly disparate worlds must be a crucial first step.'[22] Simply stated, since the presumed ground of comparison has shifted, both synchronic and diachronic comparisons need to be reconceptualized.

A central issue that requires urgently addressing in the reconceptualization of the ground of comparison is the comparability of literary works from radically different contexts. For R. Radhakrishnan, such forced comparison, 'in enabling a new form of recognition along one axis, perpetrates dire misrecognition along another'.[23] In contrast, Zhang Longxi justifies such comparisons with the idea of 'thematic affinities', and Haun Saussy with 'the universality of human experience'.[24] In practice, the comparability of historically distinct texts has been fruitfully experimented within Sino-Hellenic studies. The unquestionable uniqueness both of ancient Greece and China is, paradoxically, reaffirmed by a postmodernism that insists on the fundamental distinctiveness of not only languages but also cultures.[25] Despite this essential incommensurability, however, Sino-Hellenic comparativists have scored an impressive achievement. As Jeremy

---

[21] For early modernities, see On Cho Ng, 'The Epochal Concept of "Early Modernity" and the Intellectual History of Late Imperial China', *Journal of World History*, 14.1 (2003), 37–61; Jack Goody, *Renaissances: The One or the Many?* (Cambridge: Cambridge University Press, 2010); and Porter, ed., *Comparative Early Modernities*.

[22] Porter, ed., *Comparative Early Modernities*, p. 9.

[23] R. Radhakrishnan, 'Why Compare?', in Felski and Friedman, ed., pp. 15–33 (p. 19).

[24] Zhang Longxi, *Unexpected Affinities: Reading across Cultures* (Toronto: University of Toronto Press, 2007), p. 6; and Saussy, 'Exquisite Cadavers Stitched from Fresh Nightmares: Of Memes, Hives, and Selfish Genes', in Saussy, ed., pp. 3–42 (p. 13).

[25] Jeremy Tanner, 'Ancient Greece, Early China: Sino-Hellenic Studies and

Tanner argues, studies such as Geoffrey Lloyd's comparison of science in ancient Greece and China and Shigehisa Kuriyama's investigation of Greek and Chinese medical imagination have enabled 'the development of much more systematic and persuasive explanations of these newly-revealed problems than would be possible on the basis of the analysis of the Greek evidence alone'.[26]

This essay engages with the same topical issue of the comparability between incommensurable texts. Referring to the synchronic comparison deployed in Sino-Hellenic studies, I propose a correlative comparative model to justify comparisons of literary works from different contexts. As a statistical concept, correlation indicates how strongly some seemingly random variables are related. Correlation does not imply causation, which means that a correlative parameter points to connections not necessarily enacted by causal principles. For instance, a country that exports does not mean that it invests much in Research and Development (R&D), but heavy investment in R&D does augment a country's comparative advantage and thereby increase its exports. So exports and R&D are correlatively but not causally connected. Thus rather than causal contact or influence, a correlative model emphasizes the relatedness of the chosen variables. This relatedness allows one to predict certain trends or patterns that could be further exploited. The strong correlation between exports and R&D should be a powerful incentive for policymakers to factor R&D into home manufacture sectors.

A correlative comparative model could avoid those limitations of comparisons based on binary oppositions and the positing of ideal archetypes typical of Eurocentric approaches. Rather than a two-dimensional linear plane, correspondences in a correlative framework are located in a three- or multiple-dimensional coordinate, depending on the numbers of variables chosen. Such a coordinate describes a relationship that could be parallel, reciprocal, complementary, or even causal. In regarding the comparative counterparts as equal vectors in a three-dimensional plane, the correlative model evades essentializing them into oppositional parts or necessarily causal actors. Jonathan Culler points out that a major problem with comparison is that 'it is likely to generate a standard, or ideal type,

Comparative Approaches to the Classical World: A Review Article', *The Journal of Hellenic Studies*, 129 (2009), 89–109 (p. 89).

26 Tanner, 'Ancient Greece, Early China', p. 93; Shigehisa Kuriyama, *The Expressiveness of the Body and the Divergence of Greek and Chinese Medicine* (New York: Zone Books, 1999); and G. E. R. Lloyd, *Principles and Practices in Ancient Greek and Chinese Science* (Burlington, VT: Ashgate, 2006).

of which the texts compared come to function as variants'.[27] But when viewed through a correlative lens, no texts under comparison function as 'variants' to an 'ideal type' or a presupposed norm. Rather, all texts or comparable aspects are equal variables that correlate to one another along a variety of axes. Thus a correlative model could bypass both Eurocentric and other ethnocentric presuppositions that inform the comparative framework premised upon direct contact and mutual influence.

Enclosure and Georgic–Pastoral Poetry in Spenser's Calendar

Both pre-modern England and China witnessed profound social transformations caused by an unprecedented shift from an agrarian to a commercialized economy. In *Utopia* (1516), Thomas More gives a vivid account of the social evils caused by enclosure. For More's speaker Hythloday, the evil practice of 'stealing' is especially grievous in England owing to a policy 'peculiar to you Englishmen alone', which refers to none other than the enclosure movement. To capitalize on an expanding wool market, Hythloday remarks, enterprising entrepreneurs compete to 'compass about and enclose many thousand acres of ground together within one pale or hedge'. Forced 'out of their known and accustomed houses', multitudes of farmers are reduced to beggars and thieves.[28] As is demonstrated by McRae, by 1600 the conflict between the pressing realities of enclosure for the wool trade and the worsening social conditions triggered by depopulation had grown so acute that it required urgent legal redress. Accordingly, bills were tabled and debated in the House of Commons in 1597 and 1601. That these debates led ultimately to the enactment of two statues bespeaks the pressing urgency to protect the rural order by arresting the irresistible trend of urbanization.[29]

But on the other hand, no one could deny the substantial benefits brought about by the enclosure policy. The explosion of the English population from two to five million in the period 1500–1660 attests to the

---

[27] Jonathan Culler, 'Comparative Literature, At Last', in Saussy, ed., pp. 237–48 (p. 244).

[28] Thomas More, *Utopia*, in *Three Early Modern Utopias: Utopia, New Atlantis, and The Isle of Pines*, ed. Susan Bruce (Oxford: Oxford University Press, 1999), pp. 21–2.

[29] The two statutes refer to 'An Act against the decaying of towns and houses of husbandry' and 'The Tillage Act'. McCrae, *God Speed the Plough*, p. 8n22. For the two legal debates, see McCrae, pp. 7–12.

tangible improvement of living standards.[30] The visible increase of agricultural productivity, the financial incentive of cash crops, the regional
specialization that cultivated comparative advantage, as well as the burgeoning of rural land property market, all these socioeconomic processes
prompted by the enclosure policy secured its strong advocates. So whereas
legislators like Francis Bacon and Robert Cecil sought to protect the old
manorial economy through state intervention, innovative entrepreneurs
like Sir Walter Raleigh advocated a rural economy oriented toward a free
market and foreign trade guided by price disparities among nations. Thus
what is at stake in the state policy debate over enclosure is 'an entire socioeconomic model based around the national primacy of arable farming and
the ideal of a stable manorial structure'.[31] The rival model is the urban
economy fostered by the wool trade and commercial farming.

Flourishing precisely at a time when the rural–urban divide grew
increasingly pronounced, English pastoral could not be a pure idyllic
devoid of socioeconomic associations. The conventional sources of pastoral are Theocritus's *Idylls* and Virgil's *Eclogues*, but georgic is usually traced
to Hesiod's *Works and Days* and Virgil's *Georgics*. This reading of classical
models induces critics either to dichotomize the two genres or regard
georgic as a variation of pastoral. Anthony Low defines georgic as 'a mode
that stresses the value of intensive and persistent labor against hardships
and difficulties', a genre that 'differs from pastoral because it emphasizes
work instead of ease'.[32] For Kwong, georgic is 'a didactic version of pastoral whose main intent is to idealize simple country life, glorify labour
(not idleness) and impart practical knowledge about agriculture and other
topics...'.[33] In fact, rather than a variant and counterpart, georgic is the
root that put forth the pastoral offshoot at the historical junction when
rural life was impinged upon by city affairs.

This innate tie between georgic and pastoral that mirrors the rural–
urban tension proves a major motif of Virgil's first eclogue. As Bart van
Es observes, Theocritus also features 'the fusion of courtly and rural'
in his eclogues, but Virgil 'adds to Theocritus a dynamic relationship
between town and country'. Though the country is the setting of Virgil's

[30] E. A. Wrigley and R. S. Schofield, *The Population History of England 1541–1871:
A Reconstruction* (London: Edward Arnold, 1981), pp. 208–9.

[31] McCrae, *God Speed the Plough*, p. 9.

[32] Anthony Low, *The Georgic Revolution* (Princeton: Princeton University Press,
1985), p. 12.

[33] Kwong, 'Rural World', p. 62n19.

first eclogue, 'urban concerns intrude'.[34] The sequestration policy Rome enacted to solve the problem of disbanded soldiers constitutes a central topic of the conversation between Meliboeus and Tityrus. Whereas Meliboeus, deprived of his lands, is forced to leave his home town and make a living elsewhere, Tityrus continues piping under the beech tree because he retains his estate through the intervention of a patron in Rome. Likewise, Paul Alpers also holds that the idyllic sense of the first eclogue 'comes solely from the speeches of the exiled Meliboeus, who lavishes on Tityrus's good fortune his own intense longing for the actual cottage and fields (67–72) which have been taken from him'.[35] Thus from its very inception, pastoral is bonded with georgic, a kinship that seems to problematize rather than valorize the pastoral ideal.

The intrusion of urban affairs upon the rural community assumes a more tangible presence in early modern English literature owing to the scale of the displacement precipitated by the enclosure movement. There is also a critical tendency to pit English georgic against pastoral. For Montrose, 'The georgic figure of the ploughman or husbandman is banished from the vast majority of Elizabethan pastoral texts' to manuals on husbandry, and 'in the culture of the literate Elizabethan classes, the omnipresent realities of rural life enter formal discourse almost exclusively in *pastoral* terms'.[36] In contrast, Katherine Little identifies in Renaissance pastoral the presence of the Piers tradition represented by William Langland's *Piers Plowman*, claiming that 'the texts that herald the emergence of early modern pastoral are haunted by medieval rural laborers'.[37] On the other hand, Low argues for an independent early modern georgic discourse distinct from both the Piers and pastoral traditions.

In fact, English georgic and pastoral continues the classical symbiosis it inherits, a nexus made the more pronounced because of the rural–urban conflict intensified by enclosure. This can be seen from the works of Spenser, presumably the first important English georgic and pastoral poet. Low locates Spenser's georgic imagination mainly in *The Faerie Queene* (1590, 1596), but the rural theme also figures prominently in his other works.[38]

---

[34] Bart van Es, 'Spenserian Pastoral', in *Early Modern English Poetry: A Critical Companion*, ed. Patrick Cheney, Andrew Hadfield, and Garrett A. Sullivan, Jr (New York: Oxford University Press, 2007), pp. 79–89 (pp. 81, 82).

[35] Paul Alpers, *What is Pastoral?* (Chicago: Chicago University Press, 1997), p. 68.

[36] Montrose, 'Of Gentlemen and Shepherds', p. 424.

[37] Katherine Little, 'The "Other" Past of Pastoral: Langland's *Piers Plowman* and Spenser's *Shepheardes Calender*', *Exemplaria*, 21.2 (2009), 160–78 (p. 161).

[38] Low, *Georgic Revolution*, p. 67.

For instance, the enclosure message is evident in *Mother Hubberds Tale* (1591). Here we see the Husbandman urging Ape to become a farmer 'To plough, to plant, to reap, to rake, to sowe, / To hedge, to ditch, to thrash, to thetch, to mowe' (263–4). Despising rural work, Ape chooses to be a shepherd, and with the Fox's help, devours the flock of sheep placed under his care. One moral of the fable is that, rather than an innocent idyllic figure, the shepherd has transformed into a greedy and ruthless agrarian capitalist. The georgic–pastoral bond is also shadowed forth in most woodcuts of the *Calendar*, in which pastoral leisure asserts itself against a background that features husbandmen laboring in the fields with axes and hoes. In effect, not only the woodcuts but also the poem itself concerns the georgic reality complicated by enclosure. The 'reciprocal pairing' identified by Michael D. Bristol shows not only structurally but also thematically in the coupling of recreative and plaintive shepherds: Palinode–Piers (May), Hobbinol–Colin (June), Morrell–Thomalin (July), Hobbinol–Diggon (September), and Cuddie–Piers (October).[39] This contrastive pairing aptly captures the rural–urban tension that triggered the legal debates in the House of Commons at the turn of the seventeenth century. Whereas the recreative or idealist shepherds tend to harp on the sundry pleasures of the pastoral life, the plaintive or practical ones seize every chance to deplore the genre's incapacity either to address social realities or afford spiritual solace.

The metamorphosis of the shepherds alluded to in *Hubberds Tale* finds a more explicit articulation in the *Calendar* through the figure of the wolf under the cover of shepherd, a key device used by the plaintive pastoralists to probe into the georgic implications of the pastoral life. To support Bacon's 1597 anti-enclosure bill, an anonymous speaker stood up to declare that,

> it is strange that men can be so unnaturall as to shake off the poore as if they were not parte of the bodye, and because we live not in a savage land, where wolfes can devoure sheepe, therefore we shalbe knowne to live in a more brutishe land, where shepe shall devoure men.[40]

The dire consequences of enclosure resonate resoundingly in the 'more brutishe land, where shepe shall devoure men', and this barbarian land is reproduced with graphic vividness in the *Calendar*. In the May eclogue,

---

[39] Bristol, 'Structural Patterns', pp. 36, 37.
[40] J. E. Neale, *Elizabeth I and Her Parliament 1584–1601* (London: Jonathan Cape, 1957), p. 340.

Piers expressly identifies the wolves 'vnder colour of shepeheards' with those 'Louers of Lordship and troublers of states', who 'crept in' as 'Wolues, ful of fraude and guile' and 'often deuoured their owne sheepe' (123–9). In the September eclogue, the 'brutishe land' appears in the guise of the 'forrein costes' (28) recently visited by Diggon Davies. As Diggon deplores:

> I thought the soyle would haue made me rich:
> But nowe I wote, it is nothing sich.
> For eyther the shepeheards bene ydle and still,
> And ledde of theyr sheepe, what way they wyll:
> Or they bene false, and full of couetise,
> And casten to compasse many wrong emprise. (78–83)

Rather than real 'forrein costes', the land here most likely refers to other parts of England where enclosure was proceeding under full swing. The verb 'thought' is crucial to bearing out the disappointment at the enclosure policy, which turns out to impoverish rather than enrich the simple country folks. As a result of the 'wrong' encompassing that leaves little field for tillage, rural life is reduced to a desolate scene, with 'Fewe chymneis reeking' and 'The fatte Oxe, that wont ligge in the stal' 'nowe fast stalled in her crumenall' (117–19) The 'false' shepherds certainly mean those 'rauenous Wolues' (148) bent on devouring sheep entrusted to them. Hobbinol wonders why such wolves could roam at large when 'Well is knowne that sith the Saxon king, / Neuer was Woolfe seene many nor some, / Nor in all Kent, nor in Christendome' (151–3). This is because, Diggon replies, 'they gang in more secrete wise, / And with sheepes clothing doen hem disguise' (156–7).

This cannibalistic episode thrust into a seemingly idyllic scene raises grave doubts about the conception of pastoral as a generic utopia sheltering recreative shepherds from the assaults of realities. But for Spenser, this is an illusion, and he invents the figure of those discontented pastoralists precisely to undercut such false images by disintegrating the genre from within. The wedge proves none other than the georgic message associated with the enclosure movement. According to David R. Shore, though the September eclogue tests the limit of pastoral to 'enter into the contemporary urban world as an instrument of reform, it does nevertheless remain a pastoral eclogue in a pastoral poem', because 'Hobbinol's ideal of contentment' is the same 'to which Cuddie, Palinode, and Morrell owe allegiance'.[41] But this 'ideal of contentment' is ruthlessly undermined

---

[41] David R. Shore, *Spenser and the Poetics of Pastoral: A Study of the World of Colin Clout* (Montreal: McGill-Queen's University Press, 1985), pp. 54, 53.

by Diggon's perception that pastoral life is constantly threatened by the dread of 'rauenous Wolves' (148). As he sharply points out: 'For thy with shepheard sittes not playe, / Or sleepe, as some doen, all the long day: / But euer liggen in watch and ward, / From soddein force theyr flocks for to gard' (232–5). Diggon's insight is apparently shared, though to varying degrees, by other plaintive shepherds such as Piers and Thomalin.

Spenser seeks not only to deconstruct the pastoral genre with his 'georgic vision' but also propose alternative ways to transcend its limitations.[42] But rather than the generic progression figured in the Virgilian paradigm of *pastoral–georgic–epic*, it is in the return to a georgic reshaped by urbanization that Spenser tends to locate the possible solution. I would cast Spenser's generic model as *georgic–pastoral–epic–georgic*, since Book VI of his epic poem *The Faerie Queene* seems to entertain, as Low forcefully demonstrates, a georgic perspective. A reorientation towards a georgic reality transformed by enclosure also marks the *Calendar*. When Diggon complains that 'all this long tale' (242) cannot cure his 'piteous plight' (244), Hobbinol's remedy is to ask him 'to my cottage thou wilt resort' (254). The October eclogue suggests a similar remedy. Urging Cuddie not to leave idle his pastoral art, Piers remarks that 'Soone as thou gynst to sette thy notes in frame, / O how the rurall routes to thee doe cleaue' (25–6). The 'rurall routes' here symbolize the way that leads those recreative pastoralists out of the illusive Arcadia and into the realistic world. The rural might not offer the ultimate solution, but it does serve to open the eyes of those utopian pastoralists to the sober realities graphically figured in the merciless devouring of sheep by those avaricious wolves. Like the cover of shepherds used by wolves, pastoral proves a deceptive shell that masks deep-seated georgic realities.

Urbanization and Rural–Pastoral Poetry in *The Journey*

Concurrent with English enclosure movement, the same rural–urban transition went on in Ming China, which witnessed 'a progressive and unstoppable expansion of commerce from the late fourteenth to the mid-seventeenth century'.[43] It is the abundance brought about by the rural-based economic policy instituted by the Ming founder Emperor Hongwu (1368–1398) that gave rise to the 'unprecedented prosperity

---

[42] For the term 'georgic vision', see Low, *Georgic Revolution*, p. 39.
[43] Timothy Brook, *The Confusions of Pleasure: Commerce and Culture in Ming China* (Berkeley: University of California Press, 1999), p. 11.

of market-orientated economy' in the late Ming.[44] That the population increased from 60 to 100 million from the founding of the Ming until the rule of Emperor Wanli (1572–1620) attests to the success of this rural policy. The circulation of agricultural surplus led to the flourishing of towns and regional markets, commercial centers that gradually converged to form a unified state market system. In response, cities mushroomed almost overnight. In the late Ming, Siyen Fei observes, urbanization is 'an automatic by-product of commercialization', and the city is 'the site in which many of the silver-driven social and cultural developments materialized with higher frequency and greater density'. In addition, Fei argues, this urbanizing tendency was also augmented by taxation reform.[45] As rurally orientated fiscal policy became inadequate to address an increasingly commercialized society, Emperor Wanli put in place the 'One-Whip' policy to convert corvée labour and other taxes into silver payments. This 'silverization' of taxation greatly enhanced social mobility and the intercourse between city and country life.

Like its English counterpart, what is at stake in the rural–urban shift in the late Ming is the moral basis of society rooted in the traditional agrarian order. The fuzzy boundary between rural and urban life proved a rich source of anxiety over the corrupting influence of cities. As Timothy Brook puts it,

> The proliferation of both domestic and maritime trade was troubling to the scholastic Confucian commitment to social hierarchy resting on settled village life. Commentators of the mid-Ming remark on the decreasing distance between the urban world of markets and traders and the rural world of agricultural production, worrying about the invasive expansion of the former and the corruption of the latter.[46]

Fei also observes that '[t]he social energy unleashed by economic development profoundly challenged the prescribed social norms for an agrarian community', and this 'erosion of cultural norms stirred deep anxieties' and caused 'grave concerns over corrupted social customs'.[47]

These concerns expressed over the contamination of rural by urban values prove the implicit assumption underlying the poetic debate between

---

[44] Zhao Yifeng, 'Historical Trend of Ming China', p. 89.

[45] Siyen Fei, *Negotiating Urban Space: Urbanization and Late Ming Nanjing* (Cambridge, MA: Harvard University Asia Center, 2009), p. 9.

[46] Brook, *Confusions of Pleasure*, p. 124.

[47] Fei, *Negotiating Urban Space*, pp. 5–6.

the Fisherman and Woodman in Wu's *The Journey*, a vernacular fiction based on the real story of Tripitaka Xuan Zang's [玄奘] quest for Buddhist scripture during the reign of Tang Taizong [唐太宗] (626–649). Wu recasts the historical story by creating a vast gallery of allegorical figures as either helpers or impediments to Tripitaka's spiritual pilgrimage. The Fisherman and Woodman are just two minor secular figures showing up but once in the novel. The debate is cast as a three-round contest. The first requires each interlocutor to compose lyrics to five *ci* tunes. The second round centres on one regulated poem, and the third on a linking-verse. The dialogue appears between the miserable life story of Tripitaka and the killing of the River Dragon by Prime Minister Wei Zheng. This poetic insertion is not unique, since the novel 'abounds with verse of far greater variety', a feature also characterizing other late Ming novels.[48] What distinguishes this cluster of poems, however, is the sophistication of the poetic forms it employs and its passionate defence of rural against city/court life. The purpose of the debate, the Fisherman declares, is to assert the superiority of 'our carefree existence' in 'blue mountains and fair waters' over those bent on chasing after 'fame', 'fortune', 'titles', and 'official favors'. As 'mountain folks who knew how to read', the two lyrical poets are, unlike the Western pastoralists, georgic laborers happily engaged in their rural occupations. Accordingly, their pastoral vision is organically meshed with a georgic horizon.[49]

At first glance, the fourteen idyllic poems celebrating the rural life of the Tang dynasty appear the least likely candidates for a discussion of late Ming urbanization. But what function does this vignette of lyrical contest serve here? Why assert a rural ideal amid tales about grand state figures and events, and in an allegorical story about the search of spiritual faith? Is it a mere critique of contemporary society by alluding to real historical events? The import of this simple idyllic runs deeper: rural values seem to hold the key to the spiritual quest. It turns out that the two rustics' casual talk about a famous fortuneteller is overheard by the retinues of the River Dragon, an accident that sets off a chain of events that ultimately lead to Tripitaka's pilgrimage.

---

[48] Anthony C. Yu, 'Heroic Verse and Heroic Mission: Dimensions of the Epic in the *His-yu chi*', *The Journal of Asia Studies*, 31.4 (1972), 879–97 (p. 884). Yu traces the practice of inserting poems into prose writings to the *bianwen* [变文] texts discovered in the caves of *dunhuan* [敦煌石窟] in 1899. Most of these texts dated from the eighth and ninth century and focus on Buddhist saints. Yu, p. 882.
[49] Unless specially noted, all the fourteen lyrics are quoted from *The Journey*, vol. 1, pp. 232–7.

Lyrical verse proves a most effective means to bring out the appeal of rural life, as both farmstead and landscape poetry originated from a rural–urban complex. Like Western georgic–pastoral, Chinese farmstead–landscape poetry arose from a nostalgic obsession with rural life, which explains the preeminence of the two motifs of nature and return in such poems. On the one hand, farmstead poetry incorporates landscape images from its very inception. In his celebrated 'Five Poems on Return to Farmstead: I' [归园田居其一], Tao Yuanming writes,

> In youth I declined to follow trends,
> By nature I love mountains and hills.
> By mistake I fell into the dust world,
> Far gone into its net for three decades.
>
> Fettered birds yearn for old woods,
> Trapped fish longs for former waters.
> Clearing up a field from south wilds,
> Rural-bound I return to my farmstead.[50]

So by *tianyuan*, Tao refers not merely to 'farmstead' but also 'mountains and hills', 'woods', and 'waters', that is, nature itself. On the other hand, farmstead images also abound in landscape lyrics. The oft-quoted couplet in Xie lingyun's 'Mounting a Pond Tower' [登池上楼], that is, 'The pond breeds spring grass, garden willows raise singing birds' [池塘生春草, 园柳变鸣禽], depicts none other than lively farmstead scenes. Two features, however, distinguish Chinese from Western pastoral. First, farmstead–landscape poetry tends to give a rationale for return, which is usually grounded in the rural–urban contrast. Tao concludes his poem by comparing city/court life to curbing 'cages': 'Long detained in confining cages, I return freely to embrace Nature' [久在樊笼里, 复返得自然]. Similarly, the reason Xie gives for his return to mountains and waters also involves a negotiation between country and city/court life. As he states in 'A Pond Tower': 'My mind is inapt for cultivating illustrious virtues, and my body too weak for the plough. For salary's sake I return to the seaside, lying sick to an empty woods' [进德智所拙, 退耕力不任, 徇禄返穷海, 卧屙对空林].[51] Second, unlike the Western pastoral utopia, Chinese return describes both a symbolic and factual state. Most

50 Tao Yuanming, 'Five Poems on Return to Farmstead', in *Selections from Chinese Ancient Literature*, ed. Yanjin Zhang (Beijing: Social Sciences Press, 2010), p. 254; my own translations.
51 Xie Lingyun, 'Mounting a Pond Tower', in *Poems Selections from Hanwei*

exemplary figures in the Chinese pastoral tradition seem to straddle the two worlds of country and city. Tao returned from court to become a real farmer, and Wang Wei supervised a farm estate in his official capacity.

The fusion of farmstead and landscape poetry marks almost every one of the fourteen lyrics composed by the Fisherman and Woodman in *The Journey*. In the two linking-verse poems, the Fisherman declares that 'My boat rests on the green water's mist and wave. / My home's deep in mountains and open plains'. In reply, the Woodman claims that he is 'A rustic who feigns to be romantic; / An oldie taking pride in streams and lakes'. Whereas the Fisherman 'love[s] the streams and bridges as spring tide swells', the Woodman 'befriend[s] with ardor both pines and plums'. What these remarks conjure up is a seamless merging of farmstead and landscape scenes. That the two poets are rustic folks who range freely over the whole gamut of rural landscape renders them an ideal medium via which farmstead and landscape imagery come to interact and converge.

The sheer number (ten) of *ci* lyrics employed in the conversation attests to the importance of this form in expressing pastoral ideals and sentiments. The *ci* lyrics that flourished in the Song dynasty (960–1279) saw a revival in the seventeenth century under the championship of Zhu Yizun [朱彝尊, 1629–1709] and Wang Shizhen [王士禎, 1634–1711]. The continued relevance of *ci* lyrics at a time when vernacular fiction dominated the literary scene consists in their adaptive flexibility. According to Grace S. Fong, 'the *ci* is one of a few genres that offers the potential for fictionality in poetic discourse with its more diverse use of roles, masks, and relatively conventionalized figures of representation'.[52] Further, the lack of uniform semantic rhythms typical of *shi* poetry also contributes to the form's expressive scope. It is this expansive symbolic range that enables the two poets to claim superiority over those 'Vassals in cold nights tending court'. In his lyric composed to the tune of 'Butterflies Enamored of Flowers', the Fisherman depicts himself leaning against 'a single sail' amid misty waves, counting soaring seagulls. In response, the Woodman chants the marvelous ease and freedom with which he traverses through 'all four climes'. In his poem written to the tune of 'The Heavenly Immortal', the

Liuchao, ed. Guanying Yu (Beijing: Zhonghua shuju, 2012), p. 276; my translation.

52   Grace S. Fong, 'Inscribing Desire: Zhu Yizun's Love Lyrics in Jingzhiju qinqu', *Harvard Journal of Asiatic Studies*, 54.2 (1994), 437–60 (pp. 459–60); also see Stephen Owen, *Traditional Chinese Poetry and Poetics: Omen of the World* (Madison, WI: University of Wisconsin Press, 1985); and Pauline Yu, *The Reading of Imagery in the Chinese Poetic Tradition* (Princeton: Princeton University Press, 1987).

Fisherman appears as a careless pedlar, bartering fish 'for wine I drink till drunk'. To match up this envious autonomy, the Woodman portrays himself lying 'in the pine shade' and 'Sodden with wine'. Rather than recluses, the two rustic poets live in a rural community where they could freely 'make' and 'break' rules.

If the expressive amplitude of the *ci* lyrics allows the pair to bring out the rich plenitude and variations of the rural life, the strict formal feature of regulated verse or *lushi* [律诗] enables them to stage a cogent critique of city/court life by harnessing the narrative impulse and tightening the leisured pace of the *ci* form. Critics seem to concur that compared with the *ci* lyrics, Chinese *shi* poetry, in emphasizing 'an empirical world mediated by the personal experience of the poet', appears incapable of fictional flights.[53] With a fixed length of eight lines and its 'complex, interlocked sets of rules for word choice, syntax, structure, and tonal patterning', regulated verse looks like a more restricted form.[54] But it is precisely these seemingly inflexible rules that allow the two rustic poets to achieve their intended goal: to strike home the supremacy of rural over city/court life. Take the Fisherman's poem as an instance:

> Freely watching white cranes flying in the sky,
> I left my boat idle at riverside and my door ajar.
> Teaching my son to knit fishing yarns by the awning,
> Joining my wife to dry nets on retiring from sailing.
> My tranquil mind truly captures the receding tides,
> My calm self naturally feels the ebbing winds.
> Dressed in green coir and bamboo hat at will,
> My state beats those robed in purple sash.

> 闲看天边白鹤飞，
> 停舟溪畔掩苍扉。
> 倚篷教子搓钓线，
> 罢棹同妻晒网围。
> 性定果然知浪静，
> 身安自是觉风微。
> 绿蓑青笠随时著，
> 胜挂朝中紫绶衣.[55]

---

53 Fong, 'Inscribing Desire', pp. 459–60.

54 Zongqi Cai, 'Recent-Style *Shi* Poetry: Pentasyllabic Regulated-Verse', in Cai, ed., *How to Read Chinese Poetry* (New York: Columbia University Press, 2008), pp. 161–80 (p. 161).

55 Wu Cheng'en, *Xi You Ji* [西游记], commentary by Li Zhuowu (Nanjing: Phoenix Publisher, 2010), p. 58; my translation.

Here the beginning couplet states the pastoral setting and theme of the poem, through such graphic images as white crane and idle boat. The second couplet continues the theme of rural leisure and pleasure by offering a pair of concrete family activities – teaching his son to 'knit fishing yarns' and joining his wife to 'dry nets'. The third couplet introduces a shift from the external to the inner world, with an emphasis on the natural harmony between the two realms. The tidy parallelism in the two middle couplets serves to deepen the theme set out in the first two – this simple rural life is not imposed upon but accords with inner wishes and is thereby freely chosen. The serene autonomy enjoyed by the Fisherman vividly registers in such words as 'calm', 'tranquil', 'receding', and 'ebbing', adjectives that recall the Daoist ideal of living at peace with Nature. The final couplet presents a closure through a comparative vision: the author pits typical rural objects 'green coir and bamboo hat' against the hallmark symbol of city/court life, that is, robes in purple sash. The color images of 'green' and 'purple' that reverberate the 'white' in the first line effectively join the opening and final couplets into a coherent whole. Though devoid of the rich allusiveness marking those grand Tang poems, the spontaneous immediacy gathered within the compact poetic form and conveyed by those direct and explicit images evoked more compellingly an unmediated pastoral life. This life, the rustic poet resolutely announces, 'beats those robed in purple sash'. The Woodman's response verse follows the same formal and thematic patterns.

The two long link-verse poems rehearse these various images and activities, though in greater detail. What is revealing here is the conclusion reached, especially in comparison with the solutions suggested in Spenser's *Calendar*. Whereas Spenser's remedy is doubtfully alluded to, the Chinese close-up portrayal conveys an undoubted reaffirmation of the pastoral ideal. The Fisherman concludes by styling himself a free and unconcerned 'fool'. The Woodman declares that 'Content, I seek not the Three Dukes' seats', because 'Cities, though tall, must resist a siege; / Dukes, though of high rank, must the summon heed'. After the long debate, both poets agree to the superiority of 'blue mountains and fair waters', and they thank 'heaven, Earth, and the gods' for their good luck to enjoy such a life. Compared with the uncertain tone of the Western pastoralists, the Chinese counterparts sound happy with both their simple lots and the capacity of the lyrical forms to articulate their feelings.

Urbanization, Generic Forms and Early Modernity

The correlative comparative model reveals two insights into the two historically unrelated texts under discussion. First, the correlation between urbanization and generic forms allows us to see the interaction between literary discourse and its socioeconomic basis. Second, the literary register of urbanization in Elizabethan England and late Ming China correlates rather than causally connects, thus indicating the synchronic coexistence of two distinctive modes of modernity in pre-modern times.

Max Weber's famous pronouncement that western modernity consists in its unique urban societies and that pre-modern China lacks such an entity has precipitated a vigorous debate over the origin of Chinese urbanization and modernity.[56] Building on Weber's theory, Frederic Mote proposes the idea of 'rural–urban continuum', arguing that the elite in imperial China was 'psychologically oriented toward as many rural ties as urban ones'.[57] In Mote's view, Fei comments,

> despite the continuous urbanization of late imperial China, the 'urban' still failed to register in the political, social, and, above all, cultural realms … the urban-continuum prevailed in the Chinese psyche and prevented the development of a distinct urban tradition in imperial China.[58]

Both Weber and his critics tend to entertain a restricted view of the historical phenomenon of 'rural–urban continuum'. In fact, the 'rural–urban continuum' is a socioeconomic process characterizing not only late Ming China but also early modern England, a process that inevitably spilled into imaginative literature. Despite the urban and courtly focus of its literary elites, early modern England was largely an agrarian society. As Montrose states:

> Nine out of ten people in Elizabethan England were rural dwellers, and sheep outnumbered people, perhaps by as many as three to one. This was a society dependent upon unreliable sources of agrarian production for its physical survival, and dependent upon sheep for food and fertilizer as well as for wool, the raw material of England's basic industry.[59]

---

56 For Weber's theory of Chinese cities and economics, see Weber, *The Religion of China: Confucianism and Taoism*, trans. Hans Gerth (Glencoe, IL: Free Press, 1951); and *Economy and Society: An Outline of Interpretive Sociology*, ed. Guenther Roth and Claus Wittich. 2 vols (Berkeley: University of California Press, 1978).

57 Mote, 'A Millennium', p. 54.

58 Fei, *Negotiating Urban Space*, p. 14.

59 Montrose, 'Of Gentlemen and Shepherds', p. 421.

The georgic–pastoral dynamic testifies to the unmistaken impact of the rural–urban continuum upon literary discourse. As Montrose puts it, the response to 'the controversy about this agrarian transformation' has given rise to a literature in which 'the fundamentally opposed interests of Commons and Gentlemen were metamorphorized in the opposition of Ploughman and Shepherd; that is, in terms of the single issue that repeatedly catalyzed agrarian discontent throughout the century'.[60] As I have shown above, both the metamorphosis and complaints occasioned by early modern agrarian capitalism are vividly reproduced in Spenser's *Calendar*.

Similarly on the Chinese side, Weber's Eurocentric thesis has initiated a plethora of scholarly attempts to reclaim Chinese modernity in urban studies.[61] Most of these studies trace the emergence of Chinese urbanization to the late Ming. As Richard von Glahn writes,

> Historians seeking the stirrings of urban social and political consciousness in China usually have turned to the convulsive century between 1550 and 1650, when the rapid pace of commercial growth and urbanization began to generate new economic tensions fraught with political implications.[62]

As a result of these sweeping commercializing waves, '[f]ew studies of intellectuals, the arts, literature, and popular culture in this period fail to include a prefatory invocation of the social consequences of the growth of the market economy'.[63] For Fei, an informed study of the late Ming should take into account how urbanization is 'registered in Chinese culture and society'.[64] The dramatization of the rural ideal through a poetic contest in *The Journey* bespeaks the literary register of late Ming commercialization and urbanization, albeit in an indirect and allusive way.

---

[60] Montrose, 'Of Gentlemen and Shepherds', p. 425.

[61] For a typical critique of Weber, see Mark Elvin, 'Why China Failed to Create an Endogenous Industrial Capitalism: A Critique of Max Weber's Explanation', *Theory and Society*, Special Issue on China, 13.3 (1984), 379–91 (p. 388).

[62] Richard von Glahn, 'Municipal Reform and Urban Social Conflict in Late Ming Jiangnan', *Journal of Asian Studies*, 50.2 (1991), 280–307 (p. 280).

[63] Richard von Glahn, *Fountain of Fortune, Money and Monetary Policy in China, 1000–1700* (Los Angeles: University of California Press, 1996), pp. 2–3.

[64] Fei, *Negotiating Urban Space*, p. 269n24.

Master Zhuang's Wife:
Translating the Ephesian Matron in Thomas Percy's The Matrons (1762)

EUN KYUNG MIN

> Before you die, they all profess wifely love;
> After you're gone, they all rush to fan the graves.
> You may draw dragons and tigers –
> But how do you draw their bones?
> You may know people's faces –
> But how do you know their hearts?[1]

The recent surge of interest in Thomas Percy as the first European 'translator' of a full-length Chinese novel, *Hau Kiou Choaan; or, The Pleasing History* (1761), has underscored important links between his early sinology and his achievements as a literary editor and historian. As critics have pointed out, before establishing literary fame as the editor of *Reliques of Ancient English Poetry* (1765), the ballad collection that has been described as 'the seminal, epoch-making work of English Romanticism', Percy published two multi-volume books on Chinese culture: *Hau Kiou Choaan* (1761) and *Miscellaneous Pieces Relating to the Chinese* (1762).[2] When examined together with *Reliques*, these books show that Percy's interest in China played a formative role in his 'production of eighteenth-century British aesthetic culture', recovery of 'Gothic genius', 'theorization of a non-classical, alternative English antiquity', and forging of 'a nascent British Romantic sinology'.[3] This essay will not attempt to retrace these

---

[1] 'Zhuang Zhou Drums on a Bowl and Attains the Great Dao', in *Stories to Caution the World*, vol. 2 of *A Ming Dynasty Collection*, trans. Shuhui Yang and Yunqin Yang (Seattle: University of Washington Press, 2005), p. 25.

[2] Nick Groom, *The Making of Percy's* Reliques (Oxford: Clarendon Press, 1999), p. 3. *Hau Kiou Choaan* was published in 4 vols by Robert and James Dodsley; *Miscellaneous Pieces* was published in 2 vols, also by the Dodsley brothers.

[3] James Watt, 'Thomas Percy, China, and the Gothic', *The Eighteenth Century*, 48 (2007), 95; David Porter, *The Chinese Taste in Eighteenth-Century England* (Cambridge: Cambridge University Press, 2010), p. 155; Eun Kyung Min, 'Thomas Percy's Chinese Miscellanies and the *Reliques of Ancient English Poetry* (1765)',

arguments. Instead, it will take up a text that has received very little attention until now: Percy's book *The Matrons* (1762), a collection of six short
tales about widows drawn from various historical periods and civilizations
around the world.

It is not difficult to guess why *The Matrons* 'sank without a trace' when
it was published, as Nick Groom puts it, or why it has failed to attract
critical scrutiny to this day.[4] The six 'matrons' in question – 'The Ephesian Matron', 'The Chinese Matron', 'The French Matron', 'The British
Matron', 'The Turkish Matron', and 'The Roman Matron', in this order
– are collected together in a highly haphazard way. Percy's justification of
his collection is deliberately, but not always convincingly, casual. 'Having
met with half a dozen pleasant stories on the same subject,' he writes, 'the
Editor has here thrown them together – with the primary intention of
enlivening a dull or vacant hour.' As Percy himself is acutely aware, the
logic of his collection is deeply problematic. By implicitly arguing that
widows all over the world, and from all ages of history, share a common
'levity or wantonness', Percy's *The Matrons* appears to advance a thesis that
is both sweepingly universalistic and shamelessly misogynistic.[5] Further-
more, not only does Percy skirt the question of whether or not it is fair
to generalize about wanton widows worldwide on the basis of fictional
tales, he elides the difference between the different kinds of literary texts
he has collected, which include a first-century Roman novella, a medieval romance, a seventeenth-century Chinese vernacular tale, and several
eighteenth-century British scandal chronicles. Here his editorial strategy
is very much at odds with that which he shows us in *Hau Kiou Choaan*.
There, he asserted his editorial presence whenever possible, in the form
of voluminous, intrusive footnotes in which he cross-referenced the cultural content of the novel with existing European literature on China in
order to defend his questionable authority as translator and editor. In
The Matrons, however, Percy remains remarkably silent as an editor. Percy
began *Hau Kiou Choaan* with a bibliography of books he had consulted
in order to footnote his Chinese novel. In *The Matrons*, however, he does
not reveal his sources. What information he does provide about his source
material is sketchy and reluctant at best. Thus, while he tells the readers on

Eighteenth-Century Studies, 43 (2010), 308; Peter J. Kitson, *Forging Romantic
China: Sino-British Cultural Exchange, 1760–1840* (Cambridge: Cambridge
University Press, 2013), p. 27.

4 Groom, *Making*, p. 211.

5 Thomas Percy, *The Matrons* (London: prtd for R. and J. Dodsley, 1762), pp.
ii–v.

the contents page that 'The Ephesian Matron' and 'The Chinese Matron' are 'new translations', he does not say which Latin/English versions of Petronius's *Satyricon* he used, nor in what ways he improved on the existing English translations of the story of the Chinese widow taken from Jean-Baptiste Du Halde. He claims the 'The Turkish Matron' comes from 'a MS. copy' without supplying any more details about the provenance of this manuscript, and all we learn about the copy of *The Seven Wise Masters of Rome* from which he took 'The Roman Matron' or the medieval English version of the Ephesian Tale is that it was 'an ancient copy in black letter'.[6]

Judging by a listing of Percy's boyhood library that survives in manuscript form in the Bodleian Library, Percy's biographer Bertram H. Davis has conjectured that Percy used his boyhood black-letter copy of *The Seven Wise Masters of Rome* for the text of 'The Roman Matron'.[7] It would indeed seem that *The Matrons* is representative of the eclectic range of Percy's personal reading history that began in his boyhood and is evinced in his Chinese books. I would like to suggest, however, that *The Matrons* demands to be read as something more than a self-indulgent record of haphazard connections the bibliophile Percy made in the course of a lifetime of reading. Given that Percy had been doing a great deal of research on China for *Hau Kiou Choaan* and was actively working on *Miscellaneous Pieces* at the same time that he prepared *The Matrons* for publication, it is likely that the main idea for *The Matrons* originated from his reading of the tale of the Chinese matron in Du Halde's 1735 *Description géographique, historique, chronologique, politique, et physique de l'empire de la Chine et de la Tartarie Chinoise*. Du Halde's book, which contains the first printed European translation of the Chinese tale, was rapidly translated into English: Richard Brookes's *The General History of China* was published by John Watts in four volumes octavo (London, 1736); Green and Guthrie's *A Description of the Empire of China* was published by Edward Cave (London, 1738–41) as a lavish two-volume folio edition.[8] Percy, who relied heavily on Du Halde in his editorial comments in *Hau*

6   *The Matrons*, pp. 189, 225.

7   Bertram H. Davis, *Thomas Percy: A Scholar-Cleric in the Age of Johnson* (Philadelphia: University of Pennsylvania Press, 1989), p. 94. Davis references Bodl. MS. Percy c. 9, ff. 33–42. See *Thomas Percy*, p. 11.

8   In the bibliography that prefaces *Hau Kiou Choaan*, Percy acknowledges that his references are 'chiefly made to' the two-volume folio edition by Cave, although 'recourse was occasionally had to the grand Paris edition of the original'. See *Hau Kiou Choaan, or The Pleasing History. A Translation from the Chinese Language*. 4 vols (London: prtd for R. and J. Dodsley, 1761), p. xxix. Du Halde's book appeared in 4 vols and was published in Paris in 1735.

Kiou Choaan, included both the first French edition and the Cave edition in the bibliography appended to *Hau Kiou Choaan.*

Today we are able to trace the tale of the Chinese matron to a seventeenth-century Ming story collection called *Stories to Caution the World* (*Jingshi tongyan,* 警世通言). This collection of vernacular stories, which was compiled by Feng Menglong (馮夢龍, 1574–1646), is the second of a series of three books collectively known as *Three Words* (*Sanyan*) and frequently compared to *A Thousand and One Nights* and Boccaccio's *Decameron.*[9] The story was originally titled 'Zhuang Zhou Drums on a Bowl and Attains the Great Dao' (*Zhuang Zixiu gupen cheng dadao*) and features an apocryphal story involving Master Zhuang, the Daoist sage featured in the great Chinese classic, *Zhuangzi* or *Master Zhuang* (c. 300 BCE). In Feng Menglong's tale, Master Zhuang comes across a young woman fanning a fresh grave with a white silk fan. Struck by this spectacle, he approaches her to ask what she is doing; she explains to him that prior to his death her husband gave her permission to remarry as soon as the earth on his grave had dried. Master Zhuang smiles when he hears this frank admission of her haste to remarry. 'Your arms are too soft and delicate' for 'this fanning job', he says, and proceeds to fan the grave himself. Using his magical powers, he manages to dry it almost instantly. As a token of her gratitude, the widow presents him with the fan. At home, he begins to recite despondent verses about the fleetingness of love while looking at the fan. When his wife Tian-shi demands to know what he is lamenting, he shows her the fan and tells her about the widow. Tian-shi bursts into 'righteous indignation' and denounces the widow. She becomes even more irate when Master Zhuang continues to versify and provoke her with such lines as 'After you've gone, they all rush to

---

[9] I have consulted the most recent modern English translation of this text in *Stories to Caution the World.* See note 1 above. For a general introduction to Feng Menglong and the *Sanyan* stories, see Shuhui Yang's introduction to this volume. See also Tina Lu, 'The Literary Culture of the Late Ming (1573–1644)', in *The Cambridge History of Chinese Literature.* 2 vols, ed. Kang-i Sun Chang (Cambridge: Cambridge University Press, 2010), 2. 63–151 (especially pp. 121–7). Wilt L. Idema, who has collected vernacular texts that feature Master Zhuang and his wife in *The Resurrected Skeleton,* notes that 'Although Feng Meng-long provides us with the earliest text, the story must have circulated earlier, since we encounter an allusion to it in the *Gu mingjia saju* edition (ca. 1588) of Guan Hanqing's (ca. 1231–ca. 1310) *Dou E Yuan*'. Idema cites Lan Liming, ed., *Huijiao xiangzhu Guan Hanqing ji* (Beijing: Zhonghua shuju, 2006), p. 1054. See Idema, *The Resurrected Skeleton: From Zhuangzi to Lu Xun* (New York: Columbia University Press, 2014), p. 56n103.

fan the graves' (see epigraph above). Tian-shi accuses Master Zhuang of condemning all women on the basis of one egregious example. 'How can you so lightly dismiss all women as being alike? Aren't you being unfair to good women just because of some bad ones?,' she demands. She then snatches the fan from Master Zhuang and tears it to pieces.

Soon thereafter, Master Zhuang falls ill and dies. Initially, the narrator tells us, 'Memories of Zhuang's love so overwhelmed her that she lost all desire for food and sleep.' However, when a young bachelor turns up with an old servant to pay respects to him, Tian-shi promptly begins to lust after the young man. She enlists the services of the old servant as a go-between and, although the servant proves more of an obstacle than anything else, she manages finally to make the young man agree to marry her. On their wedding night, however, her new husband falls down in a seizure, and she learns that he can only be resuscitated by eating a decoction of fresh human brains cooked in wine. Without hesitation, she proceeds to Master Zhuang's coffin to avail herself of his brains. As soon as Tian-shi breaks open his coffin, however, Master Zhuang rises up to chastise her. It turns out that he had used his supernatural powers to play a cruel joke on her; in fact, he had faked his own death and impersonated both the bachelor and his old servant. When Tian-shi learns the truth, she ends up committing suicide out of shame. The tale ends with a scene that is found in *Zhuangzi*: Master Zhuang nonchalantly beating on a bowl after his wife's death and singing a song.[10]

In Cave's 1738–41 folio edition of *A Description of the Empire of China*, the tale of the Chinese matron appears in the second volume, under the title '*Another* NOVEL. Chwang tse, *after burying his Wife in an whimsical Manner, wholly addicts himself to his beloved Philosophy, and becomes famous among the Sect of* Tau'.[11] In the original four-volume French edition, it appears in the third volume, as one of several 'little Histories' (*petites histoires*) or 'Novels' included by Du Halde as examples of 'the *Chinese* taste'. Du Halde notes that the tale was originally 'translated from the *Chinese* by P. *Dentrecolles*' or François Xavier Dentrecolles (1664–1741), a French Jesuit best known for his letters in the Jesuit *Recueil des lettres édifiantes et curieuses écrites des missions étrangères* (28 vols, 1702–58) about the making

---

10 *Stories to Caution the World*, pp. 21–32 (esp. pp. 24–6).

11 J. B. Du Halde, *A Description of the Empire of China and Chinese-Tartary, Together with the Kingdoms of Korea and Tibet: Containing the Geography and History (Natural as well as Civil) of Those Countries*, trans. John Green and William Guthrie. 2 vols (London: prtd for Edward Cave, 1738–41), 2. 167–74.

of Chinese porcelain.[12] It is not known precisely how the story of the Chinese matron came to the attention of Dentrecolles, who arrived in Canton in 1698 and established a church in Jingdezhen, the great center of porcelain manufacture in the province of Jiangxi in southeastern China, eventually presiding over the French missionary residence in Beijing until 1732. While in Beijing, Dentrecolles translated Chinese texts on medicine, currency, government administration, and reported on how the Chinese raised silkworms, made artificial flowers in silk and paper, manufactured synthetic pearls, inoculated the population against smallpox, and cultivated such curiosities as tea, ginseng, and bamboo.[13] Given the popularity of the story of the Chinese matron in the seventeenth century and its energetic afterlife in the form of adaptations in multiple genres over the next several centuries in China, however, it is not surprising that he would have come across it during his long sojourn in China. Isabelle Landry-Deron suggests that Dentrecolles found the story in *Marvels New and Old* (*Jingu qiguan*, 今古奇觀), a popular anthology published in the 1630s that culled stories from Feng Menglong's *Sanyan* books as well as the story collections of his contemporary Ling Mengchu (1580–1644), on the basis of its inclusion in Étienne Fourmont's catalogue of Chinese books in the Bibliothèque du roi.[14] As Wilt Idema has noted, from the seventeenth century onward the story of the Chinese matron was the most popular story about Master Zhuang, the central figure in *Zhuangzi*, even though it had no clear source in that Chinese classic.[15] Along with the story of Master Zhuang's encounter with a skull, it inspired numerous adaptations, in particular dramatic adaptations including operas such as Xie Guo's seventeenth-century *The Butterfly Dream* (*Hudie meng*),[16] as

---

[12] Du Halde, *Description of the Empire of China*, 2. 147.

[13] Robert Finlay, *The Pilgrim Art: Cultures of Porcelain in World History* (Berkeley: University of California Press, 2010), p. 17.

[14] Isabella Landry-Deron, *La preuve par la Chine: La «Description» de J.-B. Du Halde, jésuite* (Paris: L'École des hautes études en sciences sociales, 2002), p. 332.

[15] Idema, *Resurrected Skeleton*, p. 1.

[16] Jin Jiang, '*The Butterfly Dream* – Narrating Women, Sex, and Morality in Chinese Theater', *Chinese Historical Review*, 16 (2009), 125–46 (pp. 127–8); Idema, *Resurrected Skeleton*, p. 36. Jiang notes that the story of Master Zhuang and his wife was also popularized in the 1930s and 1940s in China in the form of opera plays with titles such as *Young Widow Fanning the Grave* (*Xiao guafu shanfen*), *Zhuang Zhou Tests His Wife* (*Zhuang Zhou shi qi*), and *Break Open the Coffin* (*Da piguan*). See Jiang, 'Butterfly Dream', p. 130. Jiang's essay interestingly discusses a 2001 feminist Yue opera production produced in Shanghai that portrayed Master Zhuang's wife Tian Xu in a sympathetic manner. The twentieth century has seen

well as youth books or bannermen tales (*zidishu*) designed for prosimetric storytelling such as the Manchu Chunshuzhai's version of *The Butterfly Dream*.[17]

Percy, who would not have known anything about the complex historical and literary context of Feng Menglong's tale, was not the first to bring the Chinese story to the attention of English readers. His friend Oliver Goldsmith had already published a version of the tale in the 15 March 1760 issue of the *Public Ledger* as one of a series of apocryphal letters written by a Chinese philosopher traveling in London. However, Goldsmith changed the location of the story to Korea and handled the Chinese original with great freedom, comically heightening its eroticism and giving it a happy ending. He renamed 'Chwang tse' and 'Tyen' in the English translation as 'Choang' and 'Hansi', characterized them as a 'pattern of conjugal bliss' ('their mouths were forever joined, and to speak in the language of anatomy, it was with them one perpetual anastomosis'), omitted the fact that the story concerned Master Zhuang's third wife, and ended the story with him marrying 'the widow with the large fan' after his wife's suicide.[18]

Percy's contribution, then, had to do not so much with introducing the Chinese tale to an English audience but with forging textual conjunctions and analogies between the Chinese text and its western analogues. Here too, however, he could not claim real precedence. Dentrecolles, the first translator of the Chinese tale, had already noted the similarity between Master Zhuang's wife and the Ephesian matron. In a handwritten note scribbled on the translation manuscript, he had written 'This wife is another matron of Ephesus but she is duped by her husband who is supposed to be dead' (*Cette femme est une autre matrone d'Ephèse mais elle reste dupe du mari prétendu mort*).[19] Du Halde did not include Dentrecolles's comment that the Chinese wife was 'another matron of Ephesus' in his

---

the appearance of film versions that testify to the enduring popular appeal of this tale. *Zhuang Zhou Tests His Wife* was turned into a feature film in Hong Kong in 1913, a historical drama in Taiwan in 1969, and a Huangmei opera television drama in 1989.

[17] Idema, *Resurrected Skeleton*, pp. 35–6.

[18] These letters were later published in 1762 under the title *The Citizen of the World; or Letters from a Chinese Philosopher Residing in London, to his Friends in the East*. See *The Citizen of the World*, in Oliver Goldsmith, *Collected Works of Oliver Goldsmith*, ed. Arthur Friedman. 5 vols (Oxford: Clarendon Press, 1966), 2. 76–80.

[19] My translation. See Landry-Peron, *La preuve par la Chine*, p. 334. I am grateful to Wilt Idema for pointing out this passage to me.

editorial introduction to the Chinese *histoires* in the *Description,* perhaps because the connection was clear to him. The resemblance seems to have been obvious enough to his readers who mined it both for their own creative and critical purposes. For instance, Voltaire, who included his own version of the Chinese tale in the second chapter of *Zadig, ou la Destinée, histoire orientale* (1747), explicitly noted the similarity between the Roman and the Chinese tales in a 1774 letter to 'M. du M***' (probably Charles Du Molard-Bert) published in *Mélanges littéraires.*[20] Voltaire went so far as to suggest that Petronius had taken the story from the Greeks, who had taken it from the Arabs, who in turn had taken it from the Chinese.[21] Like Pierre Daniel Huet, who opined in his *Traité de l'origine des romans* (1670) that romances 'deriv'd from the *Eastern* Nations' or 'the *AEgyptians, Arabians, Persians,* and *Syrians*', Voltaire assumes that a transnational and transhistorical genealogy of literary texts can be constructed backwards by tracing each text to its historical antecedent.[22] What he playfully adds to Huet's thesis, however, is the idea that the literature of the Near East ultimately can be traced to yet more antique sources in China and India. By linking the ancient Roman tale of the Ephesian matron to its Greek and Chinese versions, he effectively places the tale within a transnational and transhistorical circuit of traveling texts in which it becomes radically unclear just when and where the tale originated.

Clearly, the appearance of a Chinese story that echoed Petronius so closely posed a problem to literary critics. The question of just what to make of the resemblance between the Chinese story and Petronius's Ephesian matron was taken up more seriously in an essay by Bon-Joseph Dacier published in the 1780 issue of *Histoire de l'Académie des inscriptions et belles-lettres.* In this essay entitled 'Examination of the history of the

[20] For a discussion of French adaptations of the Ephesian matron tale, see Peter Ure, 'The Widow of Ephesus: Some Reflections on an International Comic Theme', in *Elizabethan and Jacobean Drama: Critical Essays by Peter Ure,* ed. J. C. Maxwell (Liverpool: Liverpool University Press, 1974), pp. 223–9.

[21] '*La Matrone d'Ephèse,* par exemple, a été mise en vers par la Fontaine, en France, et auparavant en Italie. On la retrouve dans Pétrone, et Pétrone l'avait prise des Grecs. Mais où les Grecs l'avaient-ils prise? des contes arabes. Et de qui les conteurs arabes la tenaient-ils? de la Chine. Vous la verrez dans des contes chinois, traduits par le père Dentrecolles, et recueillis par le père Duhalde; et, ce qui mérite bien vos réflexions, c'est que cette histoire est bien plus morale chez les Chinois que chez nos traducteurs.' I am indebted to Wilt Idema for this reference also.

[22] Huet's book was translated into English by Stephen Lewis and published under the title *The History of Romances* (London: prtd for J. Hooke and T. Caldecott, 1715). I cite this edition, p. 13.

matron of Ephesus and the different imitations which it has produced',
Dacier exclaims,

> What are we to think of a story (*histoire*), so similar both in its sub-
> stance and moral message, that is found among the pieces of Chinese
> literature that Father Du Halde has published in his *Description of
> China*! Should we regard it as an imitation of the story by Petronius?
> But then by what route did Petronius manage to penetrate China?[23]

Dacier's solution was different from Voltaire's. He declared that he
preferred to believe (*j'aime donc mieux croire*) that a Chinese novelist or
storyteller (*Romancier chinois*) had invented or imagined the tale inde-
pendently of Petronius, inspired perhaps by some event in his 'canton' or
by his opinion of the women of his 'nation'. Nonetheless, he noted that
in order to solve this difficulty one would need to know whether or not
the tale (*Conte*) existed in ancient China and if it was known before the
arrival of the first missionaries. Du Halde, he added, had not clarified the
issue at all.[24]

Voltaire's theory that Petronius derived his tale from earlier, eastern
sources was revived in the nineteenth century by orientalists such as
Theodor Benfey and Eduard Grisebach who proposed an Indian origin,
but this theory has been largely put to rest.[25] Today it is generally recognized that Petronius's tale has two other ancient Greek analogues.
Another version can be found in the works of his rough contemporary
Phaedrus (c. 18 BCE–c. 54 CE), a Greek freedman who retold the Greek
Aesopic fables in Latin verse,[26] and scholars have speculated about a possible Greek source for both Phaedrus and Petronius in 'the lost Milesian

---

[23] Bon-Joseph Dacier, 'Examen de l'histoire de la matrone d'Éphèse, et des
différentes imitations qu'elle a produites', in *Histoire de l'Académie des inscriptions
et belles-lettres*. 51 vols (Paris: Imprimerie Royale, 1780), 41. 523–45. Dacier read
the essay to the Académie Royale on 20 June 1773. All translations of this essay
are mine.

[24] Dacier, 'Examen de l'histoire', p. 530. Dacier's essay ends with reprints of
several Latin and French versions of the tale, including a fourteenth-century
French manuscript version of *The Seven Wise Masters of Rome*. See Dacier, 'Examen
de l'histoire ', pp. 533–45.

[25] William Hansen, *Ariadne's Thread: A Guide to International Tales Found in
Classical Literature* (Ithaca, NY: Cornell University Press, 2002), p. 277.

[26] Hansen, *Ariadne's Thread*, pp. 272–3; Lawrence Kim, 'Orality, Folktales and the
Cross-Cultural Transmission of Narrative', in *The Romance between Greece and the
East*, ed. Tim Whitmarsh and Stuart Thomson (Cambridge: Cambridge University
Press, 2013), p. 308; Edward Wheatley, 'Rereading the Story of the Widow of

tales of Aristides'.[27] William Hansen, who agrees that the 'Greek color' in Petronius's narrative as well as its setting in the Greek city of Ephesus suggest that it was originally transmitted from Greece, nonetheless points out that, since Aristides's tales have never been found, these views about the Greek origins of Petronius's tale 'rest upon nothing more solid than conjecture'.[28] Noting that Petronius's story has its basis in a recognizable type of folktale found all over the world, ranging from China to Russia and North Africa, Hansen instead has proposed that the story of the Ephesian matron has multiple oral, as well as written, origins.[29]

Although Percy's *Matrons* does not intervene in the debate about possible oriental sources for Petronius's story, it appears to anticipate Dacier's query about just how the story circulated and how it is that it can be found in so many places all over the world. By collecting the Roman, Chinese, and medieval English versions together, *The Matrons* displaces the question about literary foundations, and opens up the possibility that the Roman tale of the Ephesian Matron in fact may be an oriental tale. Indeed, we could say that Percy's collection implicitly questions the very idea of an ancient, classical, European tradition of literature defined in contradistinction to a non-European one. In this sense, Percy's *Matrons* could be read as an instance of 'Enlightenment Orientalism' – which, as Srinivas Aravamudan has recently theorized, offers 'a transcultural conjectural history located within identifiable geographies, where experimental antifoundationalism allowed multiple epistemologies and metanarratives'.[30]

However, this is not the approach that *The Matrons* explicitly invites. Although Percy clearly had ambitions to become an anthologist of world literature, his criticism of French sinophilia makes it unlikely that he would have agreed with Voltaire about the eastern sources for Petronius's tale.[31] Committed to rescuing the English romance tradition from the

Ephesus in the Middle Ages and the Renaissance', *Comparative Literature Studies*, 51 (2014), 627–43 (p. 630).

[27] Ure, 'Widow of Ephesus', p. 222.

[28] Hansen, *Ariadne's Thread*, pp. 274, 277.

[29] Hansen, *Ariadne's Thread*, p. 272. See A. Aarne, *The Types of the Folk Tale*, trans. and enlarged by S. Thompson (Helsinki, 1928). Cited in Ure, 'Widow of Ephesus', p. 221. See also Hansen, *Ariadne's Thread*, pp. 266–7; Kim, 'Orality, Folktales', p. 308.

[30] Srinivas Aravamudan, *Enlightenment Orientalism: Resisting the Rise of the Novel* (Chicago: University of Chicago Press, 2012), p. 8.

[31] Percy proposed to write a book entitled *Specimens of the ancient Poetry of different Nations*, including Hebrew, East Indian, Peruvian, Lapland, Greenland,

Gauls and Arabs alike, Percy would go on to redefine it in *Reliques* as a Gothic, Saxon, and northern European inheritance. Percy shows little interest in probing what it means precisely that a Chinese analogue exists for the story of the Ephesian matron. Neither is he interested in asking whether or not there might have been earlier Greek sources for the Ephesian matron. He shows no awareness of Aristides or Phaedrus. There is nothing in *The Matrons* that suggests that he was aware of, or would have accepted, multiple folkloric sources for the Ephesian matron and its many historical analogues. Percy accepts Petronius as the literary source for the Ephesian Matron, and assumes that the medieval English version in *The Seven Wise Masters of Rome* is taken from him. He writes, the 'outlines of the picture are evidently taken from Petronius, though the finishing is done by a much coarser and less skillful hand' of 'one of our rude unpolished ancestors'.[32] However, when we consider that the story cycle in *The Seven Wise Masters* or *The Seven Sages of Rome*, found in almost every European language after the Middle Ages, in fact derives from the *Sindbād-nāma* or *Book of Sindbad* that originated in the Near East, it is clear that what we are dealing with in *The Matrons* is a much more vertiginous mix of eastern and western literary traditions.[33] Percy's collection implicitly points to this vortex but refrains from theorizing about it.

By beginning his collection with 'The Ephesian Matron from the Latin of Petronius', Percy confidently signals the centrality of this first-century text to a long European tradition of adaptations and commentaries. In England alone, examples include John of Salisbury's twelfth-century *Policraticus*; the medieval story cycle entitled *The Seven Wise Masters of Rome*; George Chapman's satiric comedy *The Widow's Tears* (performed 1605/6; published 1612); Jeremy Taylor's commentary in *The Rule and Exercises of Holy Dying* (1651); and Walter Charleton's neo-Epicurean treatise *The Ephesian Matron* (1659).[34] Although Percy shows his familiarity

and Saxon poetry, to Evan Evans in the summer of 1762. See Davis, *Thomas Percy*, pp. 92–3, and E. K. A. Mackenzie, 'Thomas Percy's Great Schemes', *Modern Language Review*, 43 (1948), 34–8 (p. 35).

[32] Percy, *The Matrons*, pp. 225–7.

[33] See Ben Perry, 'The Origins of the Book of Sindbad', *Fabula*, 3 (1960), 1–94; Stephen Belcher, 'The Diffusion of the Book of Sindbād', *Fabula*, 28 (1987), 34–58; John A. Boyle, 'Literary Cross-Fertilization between East and West', *British Society for Middle Eastern Studies Bulletin*, 4.i (1977), 32–6.

[34] See Ure, 'Widow of Ephesus', pp. 223–5. For discussions of Chapman, see Wheatley, 'Rereading', pp. 636–9; for Charleton, see Helen Thompson, 'Plotting Materialism: W. Charleton's *The Ephesian Matron*, E. Haywood's *Fantomina*, and Feminine Consistency', *Eighteenth-Century Studies*, 35 (2002), 195–214. Dacier

with John of Salisbury's *Policraticus*, he makes no reference to Chapman, Taylor, or Charleton. Instead, he curiously includes stories that are not directly related to Petronius's Ephesian matron but merely feature treacherous widows: George Etherege's story of his encounter with a French widow taken from a 1689 letter to the Duke of Buckingham; a story entitled 'The British Matron'; and an oriental tale titled 'The Turkish Matron'. Peter Ure, who is the only critic I have found who discusses Percy's *Matrons* at any length, notes that Percy's book is 'second only to Charleton as a curiosity of the subject'.[35] Although Ure leaves the last two stories unidentified, 'The British Matron' is not difficult to trace, since Percy notes that it is taken 'From a Narrative, intitled The Widow of the Wood, 1755'.[36] It is in fact a slightly modified version of Benjamin Victor's 1755 scandal chronicle *Widow of the Wood*, which recounts the real-life machinations of a young widow Ann Whitby who seduced her wealthy neighbor William Wolesley, then ran away with another lover, John Robins, resulting in a lengthy and well-publicized trial.[37] As to 'The Turkish Matron', using the powerful search engine in the ECCO database, I have been able to trace it to George Lyttelton's oriental satire, *The Court Secret: A Melancholy Truth* (1741).[38]

Alda Milner-Barry has suggested that 'the three [texts] first sold to Dodsley were the Ephesian, Chinese, and Roman, and that the other three

mentions coming across a Latin translation of Charleton's epicurean treatise in his essay and dismisses it as a 'boring book' that does not deserve much circulation. 'Examination', p. 531.

[35] Ure, 'Widow of Ephesus', p. 229.

[36] Percy, *The Matrons*, p. 113.

[37] See Ana C. Vogrinčič, 'A Novel between Gossip and a Court Testimony: The Peculiar Case of Benjamin Victor's *Widow of the Wood* (1755)', *The AnaChronisT*, 15 (2010), 60–72.

[38] George Lyttelton, *The Court-Secret: A Melancholy Truth. Now Translated from the Original Arabic* (London: prtd for T. Cooper, 1741). Although this text claims to be a translation from Arabic, it is in fact a satire on the affair between Richard Lumley, second Earl of Scarborough, and the Duchess of Manchester. See Sarah Searight, *The British in the Middle East*, 2nd ed. (London: East-West Publications, 1979), p. 92. Jerry C. Beasley notes that 'The Newberry Library copy of *The Court Secret* contains anonymous marginal notes identifying Achmet as the Earl of Scarborough, an ally of the administration who possibly began to frequent Patriot assemblies before taking his life in 1734.' See 'Portraits of a Monster: Robert Walpole and Early English Prose Fiction', *Eighteenth-Century Studies*, 14 (1981), 406–31 (p. 424n35). Lyttelton's authorship of this text has recently been challenged by Sandro Jung, who writes that David Mallet and Chesterfield are 'equally likely' as Lyttelton to be the authors. See *David Mallet, Anglo-Scot: Poetry, Patronage, and Politics in the Age of Union* (Newark, DE: Delaware University Press, 2011), p. 39.

were makeweights added to make the book a reasonable size'.[39] Davis also
notes that when Percy recorded in his diary the five contracts he signed
with Dodsley in May 1761, he referred to his collection as '3 Matrons'.[40]
It is possible that when Percy brought the '3 Matrons' to Dodsley, the
publisher felt that they would make a flimsy volume with little popular
appeal. The addition of Etherege's gossipy letter, Victor's scandal chronicle, and Lyttelton's satire was no doubt a calculated market ploy to arouse
a very different kind of literary curiosity than that which originally drove
Percy's project. Assuming, then, that the Ephesian, Chinese, and Roman
matrons were indeed the '3 Matrons' that Dodsley initially contracted for,
we need to ask how Percy's book conceptualizes – or fails to conceptualize
– the literary field it maps out. In what sense do these three stories in
particular form a collection or a collective? And what are we to make of
the organizing principle behind the collection?

When we consider that both Lyttelton and Victor were close allies of
Dodsley, and that Dodsley's career was built on skirmishes with Walpole
and his ministry, it is likely that it was Dodsley rather than the politic
Percy who decided to print the scandalous as well as potentially libel-
ous stories about misbehaving English aristocrats with the '3 Matrons'.[41]
These stories belong to the genre of the 'secret history' that publishes
well-known but politically repressed truths about public dealings under
the guise of amatory romance or oriental narrative. William Wolesley, the
duped husband of a machinating, double-dealing widow in *Widow of a
Wood*, was Victor's close friend. In addition, we may note, Lyttelton's *The
Court Secret*, which portrays Walpole as a Behemoth-like 'Monster of a
Vizier', was possibly 'the most serious reflection upon Walpole to be found
in all the fictions written against him'.[42] It is possible, then, that Dodsley
hijacked Percy's project for his own political purposes, using Percy's three
matron stories as a useful cover for political satire on 'the scandals of
people in high places'.[43]

---

[39] Alda Milner-Barry, 'A Note on the Early Literary Relations of Oliver Goldsmith and Thomas Percy', *Review of English Studies*, 2.v (1926), 51–61 (p. 58).

[40] Davis, *Thomas Percy*, pp. 76–7. The contracts were for *Song of Solomon*, *Five
Pieces of Runic Poetry*, *Reliques of Ancient English Poetry*, *Miscellaneous Pieces*, and
The Matrons. Percy's first contract with Dodsley, dated 8 March 1759, was for *Hau
Kiou Choaan*.

[41] For a discussion of Robert Dodsley's career and his associates, see Harry M.
Solomon, *The Rise of Robert Dodsley: Creating the New Age of Print* (Carbondale,
IL: Southern Illinois University Press, 1996).

[42] Lyttelton, *Court Secret*, p. 3; Beasley, 'Portraits of a Monster', p. 424.

[43] Michael McKeon, *The Secret History of Domesticity: Public, Private, and the*

The chief interpretive problem for Percy seems to have been not how to account for the similarities between the three matrons, but what to do with their misogynistic content. According to Ure, a new kind of 'half-ironic nervousness about the anti-feminist implications of the story' of the Ephesian matron begins to appear in the eighteenth century, and Percy is a case in point.[44] Percy was clearly troubled enough by the antifeminist content of his tales to mount both a direct and an indirect defense. In the dedication to *The Matrons*, Percy pointedly addresses himself to 'The Matrons of Great Britain and Ireland' and warns them against reading his collections as a 'rude commonplace invective' against the female sex. Although his 'pleasant stories' all deal with 'the levity of wantonness of those Widows, whose weeds are only a cloak for immodesty, or a lure for solicitation', he argues, his 'miscellany is in effect a real panegyric'. He was after all 'obliged to ransack the mouldy volumes of Antiquity, and to take a voyage as far as China' to find such non-paragons of female virtue. However, in a contradictory move, Percy also defends the didactic nature of his collection by arguing that it aims at the readers' amusement, 'but not without the further moral view of deterring the Fair Reader from falling into that misconduct, which is here so pleasantly exposed to ridicule'. This second, satirical and moralistic purpose of the collection, however, potentially undermines his argument that his stories are simply entertaining fictions, since the value of the collection depends precisely on the reader's recognition of the representative exorbitance of female sexual desire that Percy denies in the first instance.

Percy appears to have sought a solution to this problem in John of Salisbury's discussion of the Petronian tale. Although it is difficult to know precisely where Percy's contribution ended and Dodsley's began in *The Matrons*, given the importance of *Policraticus* to the dissemination of Petronius in the European middle ages, it seems quite likely that Percy was responsible for including John of Salisbury's comments.[45] By inserting two quotes from the original Latin text of John's *Policraticus*, and using them as bookends to open and close *The Matrons*, I believe, Percy intended to provide a secret key to his collection for the witty and learned reader. In the first quote, we see John introducing the story of the Ephesian matron as false (*falso*) but nonetheless instructive fiction:

Division of Knowledge (Baltimore, MD: Johns Hopkins University Press, 2005), pp. 472, 470–1.

[44] Ure, 'Widow of Epesus', pp. 228, 230.

[45] On the role of *Policraticus* in the dissemination of Petronius's tale, see Dacier, 'Examination', p. 526.

'some fictions are morally edifying and therefore suitable for philosophical contexts', he says, even though they are far from the truth (*nihil tamen impedit ridentem dicere verum & fabulosis narrationibus, quas philosophia non rejicit, exprimere quid obese possit in moribus*). After retelling the story, however, John changes his tone and claims that the story is historical, on the authority of a certain 'Flavianus': 'You may call what Petronius narrates in these words history or fiction' (*Tu historiam aut fabulam, quod refert PETRONIUS, pro libitu appelabis*), 'but Flavianus is authority that this actually happened at Ephesus' (*Ita tamen ex facto accidisse EPHESI, & FLAVIANUS auctor est*).[46] However, in the absence of any information about Flavianus, his authority is highly dubious at best.[47]

Janet Martin has argued that John's reason for making these contradictory claims was to throw doubt on both of them rather than to espouse either the historical veracity or the value of the story as a moral exemplum. There is in fact nothing in Petronius's tale that supports either claim. As Martin notes, 'Petronius's text at times implies that the episode is merely a *fabula* and elsewhere that it actually happened'.[48] Indeed, the whole point of Petronius's text, in Victoria Rimell's words, seems to have been 'to fuzz the conventional distinction between the literary and the everyday', between history (*historia*) and fiction (*fabula*).[49] It is likely, then, that John of Salisbury was playing with an ambiguity built into Petronius's own text in order to signal his distance from its apparently misogynistic content. With his remarks, in other words, he was pointing to the inherent humor of Petronius's tale and cautioning against the impulse to use it as a true exemplum against the female sex.[50] By pointing

[46] I cite Janet Martin's translations of these passages, in 'Uses of Tradition: Gellius, Petronius, and John of Salisbury', *Viator*, 10 (1979), 57–76 (p. 73).

[47] 'Faute de savoir qui étoit ce Flavien, & en quel temps il vivoit, on ne sauroit fixer le degré d'autorité que doit avoir son témoignage'. Dacier, 'Examination', p. 524.

[48] Martin, 'Uses of Tradition', p. 73.

[49] Victoria Rimell, *Petronius and the Anatomy of Fiction* (Cambridge: Cambridge University Press, 2002), p. 126.

[50] Cary J. Nederman and N. Elaine Lawson suggest that the antifeminist satire in *Policraticus* needs to be read in political terms as a rhetorical attack not so much on women as on an effeminate court. 'The Frivolities of Courtiers Follow the Footprints of Women: Public Women and the crisis of Virility in John of Salisbury', in *Ambiguous Realities: Women in the Middle Ages and Renaissance*, ed. Carole Levin and Jeanie Watson (Detroit, MI: Wayne State University Press, 1987), pp. 82–96, esp. pp. 92–3. Martin has suggested that 'one of the important uses of the classical tradition for John and his circle may have been the reinforcement of their sense of being a small group, an elite'. See Martin, 'Uses of Tradition', p. 68.

to John of Salisbury as a critical guide to his '3 Matrons', then, Percy was wittily and learnedly warning his readers against taking his tales as serious indictments of feminine vice.

As many critics have noted, in Petronius's version the larger narrative frame helps to accommodate the seemingly anti-feminist content of the tale and strongly suggests that an anti-feminist response is only a misreading. The context is a 'postprandial conversation' on board a ship; the story is told by one Eumolpus who, 'to save our jollity from falling dumb for want of good stories' (*sine fabulis*), recounts the story of 'an affair which happened in his lifetime' (*rem sua memoria factam*). In Eumolpus's story, the Ephesian matron does not go so far as to facilitate cannibalism or mutilate her husband's coffin, as in the Chinese case. She mourns in her husband's sepulchre, refusing to eat, until she is eventually seduced by a young soldier who is stationed as a guard for the corpses of several robbers crucified nearby; when one of the corpses disappears, she advises her new lover to nail her dead husband's body on the cross instead. At the end of Eumolpus's recital, the members of his audience show a comically diverse array of responses: the sailors laugh; a woman named Tryphaena blushes; and Lichas, whose wife had recently left him for another man, angrily says, 'If the governor of the province had been a just man, he would have put the dead husband back in the tomb, and hung the woman on the cross.' His outburst, however, is soon lost in the general merrymaking. As Edward Wheatley points out, the larger narrative provides a biographical context for Lichas's misogynistic outburst and also subjects his desire for narrative closure to ridicule.[51] As Rimell puts it, Lichas's 'misogynistic outburst is all part of the joke'.[52] Lichas's fault is not simply that he is a cuckold; he is also a bad reader who has been so 'seduced by the supposed historical veracity of the text' that he is tempted to rewrite it in real life.[53]

Percy's 'Roman Matron', which redacts a medieval English version of the Ephesian Matron, follows the plot of Petronius's story quite closely, but then departs dramatically from it by giving it precisely the kind of violent closure demanded by Lichas. Whereas both tales end with the failure of womanly ruse, Petronius's version of the tale ends literally with a question mark, with the Ephesian populace wondering just 'how the

---

[51] I am here relying on Wheatley's summary of Petronius's story. 'Rereading', pp. 628–9. Wheatley cites the edition of *Satyricon* in *Petronius and Seneca: Apocolocyntosis*, trans. Michael Heseltine and W. H. D. Rouse (Loeb Classical Library; Cambridge, MA: Harvard University Press, 1969), pp. 268, 269.

[52] Rimell, *Petronius*, p. 128.

[53] Wheatley, 'Rereading', pp. 628–30.

corpse of the gentleman deceased could find its way up to the top of the gibbet'.[54] In contrast, the macabre medieval version brings back the theme of justice, so wittily postponed in Petronius, with a vengeance, ending the tale with a veritable orgy of blood. Like the Ephesian matron, the Roman matron moves from an excess of mourning to an excess of matrimonial eagerness, and is given the challenge of rescuing her new would-be husband from the threat of death. However, she has the much more difficult task of replacing a corpse that is heavily mutilated. In Percy's version, the dead thief is missing two teeth, two ears, as well as two thumbs. When her new lover, a knight who was formerly a friend of her husband, falters at her suggestion that he cut off the same parts from her husband's body, the Roman matron scoffs at his squeamishness. 'I never saw man soe fearfulle,' she declares, as she performs the deeds he dares not to. Her new lover is so horrified by these acts of bodily mutilation, however, that in a sudden surge of manliness he draws his sword and cuts off her head 'with one stroke'.[55]

What did Percy make of the sensational content of this 'Gothic' story? What caused this transformation of 'one of the most gay and pleasant tales of antiquity to a downright bloody and tragical narrative'? Turning this medieval English author into a kind of gloomy Eumolpus figure, Percy surmises that 'one of our rude unpolished ancestors' had 'fallen in with the melancholy turn of his countrymen, and humoured their propensity for dismal stories'.[56] Percy does not go any farther than this joking pun about British black humor to explain the endurance of the Ephesian matron in English cultural memory. We should note, however, that this medieval English tale differs from the Petronian original in its insistent obsession with the impotent and castrated male body. The joke in 'The Roman Matron' is equally on her first husband, who swoons away and dies when he first 'sawe his wife bleede', as on her second would-be husband whose inability to act is impatiently answered by her 'manlye stroke' on the dead man's body. The medieval tale rewrites female sexual aberrancy, in other words, as conditioned by the multiple failures of virile agency. In a footnote, Percy noted that he had supplied the word 'thumbs' in the story since the original word 'was unfortunately every where erased'.[57] A quick

---

[54] Percy, *The Matrons*, p. 16. For a reading of the tale as an ironic inversion of and pagan response to Christ's story, see Helen Deutsch, *Loving Dr. Johnson* (Chicago: University of Chicago Press, 2005), pp. 159–60.

[55] Percy, *The Matrons*, pp. 239, 241.

[56] Percy, *The Matrons*, p. 227.

[57] Percy, *The Matrons*, pp. 228, 238, 239.

comparison with the Bodleian copy of the 1682 edition of *The History of the Seven Wise Masters of Rome* in the Early English Books Online database reveals that the supposedly erased word was 'stones'. In this edition, when the Roman matron tells the knight to cut off her dead husband's stones, he replies in horror, 'That I may not do in any wise, and therefore I pray you spare me, for you know what a man is without his stones.'[58] Percy's halfhearted attempt to cover up this central violation comically mimics the erasure effected in the plot, translating it into a literal erasure of the text. The proliferation of phallic symbols of course easily gives the secret away.

What Percy made of the tale of the Chinese matron and its relationship to the Ephesian and Roman tales is a tantalizing question. It is unfortunate that Percy declined to comment on the very question that Dacier asked so pointedly in his 1773 essay – namely, what are we to think of the similarities between the Ephesian, the Chinese, and the Roman matrons? Dacier, for one, believed that the story of the Chinese matron was 'infinitely more complicated than that of Petronius'. He noted that the tale of Master Zhuang's wife was preceded by a lengthy and complicated introduction including the famous story of his butterfly dream; that it contained a supernatural element as evidenced in Master Zhuang's use of magic to impersonate all the male characters of the story, including the new bachelor husband and even the servant; and he also noted that the Chinese version contained not one but two Ephesian matrons, since the widow with the large fan was 'no less deserving of recognition than the Ephesian matron'.[59] The Chinese matron is, in fact, much more similar to the Roman than the Ephesian matron insofar as she comes to a tragic end. Although Bakhtin reads Petronius's tale as 'an uninterrupted series of victories of life over death' culminating in the triumph of life (food, drink, sex) over death (and longing for death), we would have to concede that this carnivalesque affirmation of 'the material bodily lower

---

[58] *The History of the Seven Wise Masters of Rome* (London: prtd for J. Wright, 1682), n. pag.

[59] Dacier, 'Examination', pp. 530–1. In the original Chinese text, Master Zhuang's magic is clearly explained by the narrator who notes 'there was no young man of Chu or his old servant'; 'It was Zhuang Zhou who had assumed their forms, using his magic of self-replication and body concealment'. See *Stories to Caution the World*, p. 31. This line, however, does not appear either in the French or English translation. The supernatural ruse seems to have been equally evident to Pierre-René Lemmonier who based his comedy *La matrone chinoise* (1765) on Du Halde's version of the tale. See Lemmonier, *La matrone chinoise; ou, l'épreuve ridicule*, ed. Ling-Ling Sheu (Exeter: University of Exeter Press, 2003).

stratum', as Daniel McGlathery puts it, dramatically fails to take place in either 'The Roman Matron' or 'The Chinese Matron'.[60] In the English *Seven Wise Masters of Rome* version, which is graphically obsessed with blood and bodily mutilation, in particular male castration, what we see is a persistent fascination with this 'material bodily lower stratum', but it is a repressed fascination marked as much by fear of female sexuality as male impotence. The savaging of the male body bespeaks an anxiety about male performance, both in and out of the marital bed. In 'The Chinese Matron', the mutilation of the male body is planned but never successfully effected, and the various male characters are magically revealed to be the same. In this sense, 'The Chinese Matron', we could say, reveals the structural secret common to the tales of the Ephesian and the Roman Matrons: the men in the stories are in fact one and the same figure; the dead husband and his would-be replacement represent different incarnations of a single male character whose fate is to be indifferently substituted in the face of female desire. Analogously, we might note, the widow with the fan is Tian-shi's own secret double.

In another important sense, though, the Chinese tale is very similar to Petronius's tale in its attentiveness to the effects of literary performance and the subtlety with which it hints at its characters' inner motivations. The reason why the Chinese matron is punished may have to do as much with her failures of literary interpretation as her infidelity. On the one hand, Tian-shi is an acute reader of signs. Surely she has good reason to be suspicious when her husband returns from his travels with a lady's fan! When Master Zhuang brazenly proceeds to lecture her on *female* infidelity when, from her perspective, she has basically caught him *in flagranti*, she angrily points out that he is himself hardly 'a perfect pattern of fidelity'. 'Your first wife dies; soon after you take a second; this again you divorce; I in short am the third,' she remonstrates. 'As for us women who are married to philosophers [...] we are much less at liberty to marry again: if we should do it, we should become just objects of derision.'[61] Her point that Chinese culture imposes different moral standards on men and women is well put. Her cynicism about philosophers also has a mean bite. Even though she comes to a bad end, we feel that she has been unfairly

[60] See M. M. Bakhtin, *The Dialogic Imagination: Four Essays*, ed. Michael Holquist, trans. Caryl Emerson and Michael Holquist (Austin, TX: University of Texas Press, 1981), pp. 221–4; Daniel McGlathery, 'Petronius' Tale of the Widow of Ephesus and Bakhtin's Material Bodily Lower Stratum', *Arethusa*, 31 (1998), 331–6.

[61] Percy, *The Matrons*, pp. 48–9.

tricked by her philosopher husband, master of metempsychosis and trans-migratory tricks. While it would be difficult to call Feng Menglong's tale a feminist text, his portrait of Master Zhuang's wife as a spirited woman who sees right through her sage husband boldly turns the joke on Master Zhuang as well. One reason why she is so thoroughly defeated despite these virtues is that, like Lichas, she is basically humourless. Obsessed with her own fears and desires, she takes everything personally. She cannot appreciate a joke; she even hangs herself over one. Master Zhuang, who had a hard time hiding his laughter before the hapless confession of the naïve widow with the fan, literally has the last laugh as he puts Tian-shi's dead body in the coffin that was meant for him. He who laughs last laughs best, as they say.

One important effect of Percy's collection is that, by being placed in the company of her Ephesian and Roman counterparts, Master Zhuang's wife comes into a new prominence. Of Percy's '3 Matrons', she is the only one with a name. She may have no magic powers, but she is a forceful and determined character, in no wise subservient to Master Zhuang.[62] The Chinese tale stages a comic battle of the sexes and creates havoc out of the Ming ideals of chaste widowhood and widow suicide, both of which played an important part of literati ethics.[63] Though the overriding message of the tale is moralistic, there is a clear comic undertow. The con-ventional reading of the tale would emphasize Tian-shi's hypocrisy, infidel-ity, and sexual insatiability. These womanly vices are what supply 'the final impulse for her husband to retire to the mountains and pursue religion'.[64] From a feminocentric viewpoint, however, both Tian-shi and 'the woman fanning the grave' are 'eminently practical'.[65] They are variations on the popular character of the shrew in seventeenth- and eighteenth-century Chinese vernacular fiction – a figure who is punished for deviating from 'the ancestor-worshipping, kin-oriented family' but who also reveals the rifts in Ming and Qing attitudes toward women. As Keith McMahon

[62] At one point she even spits into her husband's face – a detail that is missing in both the French and English translations. Compare *Stories to Caution the World*, p. 25; *Description*, 3. 329; Percy, *The Matrons*, p. 46.

[63] There is a great deal of critical literature on this topic. A useful place to start is Janet M. Theiss, *Disgraceful Matters: The Politics of Chastity in Eighteenth-Century China* (Berkeley: University of California Press, 2004).

[64] Idema, *Resurrected Skeleton*, p. 34.

[65] Keith McMahon, *Misers, Shrews, and Polygamists: Sexuality and Male–Female Relations in Eighteenth-Century Chinese Fiction* (Durham, NC: Duke University Press, 1995), p. 61.

says, a subversive 'shrew's reading' of the tale of Master Zhuang's wife
would say that

> the woman who is not allowed financial independence before or during
> widowhood should be able to hurry on to a new husband once the old
> one is dead; or that the deceased husband may have been one she was
> forced to marry and that she can at least choose her next husband.

The point is that there is no reason why men should not be just as replace-
able as women, and that 'Ming and Qing propaganda against widow
remarriage' is inherently problematic.[66]

In the context of Percy's collection, 'The Chinese Matron' reads humor-
ously, sometimes even like an English Restoration play. The following
scene where Tian-shi snatches the widow's fan out of her husband's hand
is particularly well-rendered by Percy:

> Then of a sudden seizing the fan, which her husband held in his hand,
> she snatched it from him, and out of mere spite tore it in pieces.
> Compose yourself, said Chuang-tse, your quick resentment gives me
> pleasure; I am overjoyed to see you take fire on such an occasion.[67]

Percy's fluent translation of this passage brings out both the wit and
sexual charge of this marital squabble, highlighting the expressiveness of
her gestures and the almost rakish language with which Master Zhuang
attempts to appease his all too perceptive wife. As with his 'translation' in
Hau Kiou Choaan, Percy's priority in his 'new translation' of 'The Chinese
Matron' is legibility and readability. He subdivides the Chinese tale into
'The Chinese Author's Preface' and 'History', separating out the commentary from the tale proper; dispenses with many of the verses that are
preserved in Du Halde to speed up the narrative; and generally opts for
a more direct and accessible language than that in the more ponderous
Cave edition.[68] Sometimes, as in the scene just analyzed, he comes up
with particularly felicitous renditions.

---

66 McMahon, *Misers*, pp. 56, 61.
67 Percy, *The Matrons*, pp. 49–50.
68 Kai-chong Cheung remarks that, in his translation of *Hau Kiou Choaan*, Percy
tends to omit verses that distract from the narrative flow and 'condenses much
of the prose in the interest of brevity and a smooth and polished style'. James
St André points out that Percy is interested in retaining local flavor whenever
possible. See Kai-chong Cheung, 'The *Haoqiu zhuan*, the First Chinese Novel

As many critics have already noted, Percy's own role in the encounter between Chinese and European literature was strictly not that of the native informant or the eye-witness traveler, but that of the translator several times removed from the geographical or textual source. All the knowledge that Percy had of China was borrowed from books and mediated by other translations from the Chinese language. The fact that Percy could still pose as a 'translator' of the Chinese tale – he placed the Chinese tale directly after Petronius's Ephesian Matron in *The Matrons*, and claimed that he had provided 'new translations' of both tales – signals the highly flexible meaning of translation in his time. Translation in Percy's collection is not just about translating from the classical languages into the vernacular, but also from non-European languages into European languages; it involves first-hand but also second-hand translations via intermediary languages, as we can see from the case of 'The Chinese Matron', which was translated from Chinese into English via French. Translation refers to the domestication of foreign texts, but also to the deliberate 'foreignizing' of domestic content, as in the case of the English secret histories disguised as oriental narratives.[69] In all these different kinds of translation at work in Percy's collection, we see a striking indifference to authors, origins, and sources, and a much greater interest in the mobility of narrative across temporal, geographic, and even generic boundaries.

In this sense, we could say that Percy's collection participates in the widespread interest in fiction's mobility that is so strongly evidenced by translation practice in the eighteenth century. As Mary Helen McMurran notes in *The Spread of Novels*, literary histories written after Huet's *Traité sur l'origine des romans* commonly shared the 'single unifying idea' that 'fiction is by nature transmissible, and thus its history cannot be told except as a kind of travel narrative in which fiction moved from one country and language to another'. As McMurran shows, however, this conceptualization of fiction's mobility in universalist terms was soon

Translated in Europe: With Special Reference to Percy's and Davis's Renditions', and James St André, 'Modern Translation Theory and Past Translation Practice: European Translations of the *Haoqiu zhuan*'. Both essays are collected in *One into Many: Translation and the Dissemination of Classical Chinese Literature*, ed. Leo Tak-hung Chan (Amsterdam: Rodopi, 2003), pp. 29–37 (esp. p. 35) and pp. 39–65.

[69] I have found Peter Burke's discussion of the cultures of translation very helpful for my summary of the multiple dimensions of Percy's translations. 'Cultures of Translation in Early Modern Europe', in *Cultural Translation in Early Modern Europe*, ed. Peter Burke and R. Po-Chia Hsia (Cambridge: Cambridge University Press, 2007), pp. 7–38, esp. pp. 21–38.

challenged as these 'paths of mobility' were soon 'subordinated to the
relation between fiction and culture', so that fictions became stories
people would 'tell about themselves and their nation'. On the one hand,
eighteenth-century prose fiction was 'a mixed form and culturally hybrid-
ized through translation and transmission'; on the other hand, it began to
be identified as a nation-specific form, especially in the modern form of
the novel.[70] This latter approach is precisely that which Percy takes as the
translator of *Hau Kiou Choaan*, where he reads the novel for its cultural
rather than literary content. In *The Matrons*, however, it is the older ideal
of fiction as transmission that rules.

Unfortunately, since *The Matrons* lacks a theoretical apparatus, unlike
Hau Kiou Choaan or *Reliques of Ancient English Poetry*, we can only guess
what Percy meant to achieve with his collection. When Percy introduced
or rather reintroduced Master Zhuang's wife into the vernacular canon of
storytelling in Europe, it is unlikely that his interest in fiction's mobility
had anything to do with a desire to orientalize a beloved Roman classic,
even though his collection was clearly influenced by the eighteenth-
century trend of questioning the 'prevailing orthodoxy that considers the
genealogy of the European literary tradition to be, almost exclusively,
Latin and Greek'.[71] The pseudo-oriental narrative of 'The Turkish Matron'
suggests that, by Percy's time, the 'interface between Romance and Arabic
languages and literatures' had become a cultural cliché almost before it
could be taken seriously.[72] *The Matrons* does not theorize a similar interface between Chinese and western literatures. However, it does participate
in the eighteenth-century building of that interface. Indeed, one important effect of Percy's collection is that, even in the absence of a coherent
literary theory or literary history, it marks the entry of Chinese literature
into a vernacular European canon of storytelling in a much more effective manner than Du Halde's ponderous compilation. Percy may not have
been the first to notice the resemblance between 'The Chinese Matron'
and 'The Ephesian Matron', but he made the connection obvious and

[70] Mary Helen McMurran, *The Spread of Novels: Translation and Prose Fiction in
the Eighteenth Century* (Princeton: Princeton University Press, 2010), pp. 37, 41,
7.

[71] Madeleine Dobie, 'Translation in the Contact Zone: Antoine Galland's *Mille et
une nuits: contes arabes*, in The Arabian Nights *in Historical Context: Between East
and West*, ed. Saree Makdisi and Felicity Nussbaum (Oxford: Oxford University
Press, 2008), p. 28.

[72] Dobie argues that this interface between Christian and Muslim cultures has
nonetheless been a 'blind' one, marking 'a border that is at once highly permeable
and rigidly impenetrable'. See Dobie, 'Translation in the Contact Zone', p. 29.

accessible in print for a popular readership. Indeed, with *The Matrons*, Percy arguably made Chinese literature portable and legible in a new way by placing it in conversation with a very ancient strand in European literature. At the same time, he identified the popularity of the story of the Ephesian matron, which has been called 'one of the world's most popular novelle', as truly global in scope.[73] For this reason, it would be a mistake to overlook the role of *The Matrons* in what Patricia Sieber has called the 'transcultural archive' of Chinese literature that began to be popularly disseminated in the eighteenth century.[74] This essay is a very preliminary effort at repositioning Percy's richly allusive, as well as confoundingly elusive, book in this archive, about which much still remains to be learned.

---

[73] Hansen, *Ariadne's Thread*, p. 267.
[74] Patricia Sieber, 'The Imprint of the Imprints: Sojourners, *Xiaoshuo* Translations, and the Transcultural Canon of Early Chinese Fiction in Europe, 1697–1826', *East Asian Publishing and Society*, 3 (2013), 31–70.

The Dark Gift: Opium, John Francis Davis, Thomas De Quincey and the Amherst Embassy to China of 1816

PETER J. KITSON

There has been a great deal of historical and cultural criticism relating to the first British embassy to arrive in China, led by Viscount Macartney, of 1792–94, including three substantial historical accounts, but comparatively little has been written about its successor, either from the British or the Chinese viewpoints, which has tended to be largely viewed, when it is noted at all, as a farcical repetition of, or postscript to, its more famous predecessor.[1] This is unfair. The embassy, along with the two earlier British attempts to take possession of the Portuguese enclave of Macao in 1802 and 1808, urgently demand the serious attention of both historians and critics of the cultural relations between China and Britain in the nineteenth century. This essay, along with that of Robert Markley, argues for the importance of the embassy as well as its crucial significance to British understandings of China and the accounts to which it gave rise. They make a case for the significance of the still largely unexplored accounts produced by the embassy and the extensive knowledge they contained.[2]

---

[1] For the details of the embassy, see the Introduction to this volume. H. B. Morse, *The Chronicles of the East India Company trading to China, 1634–1833*. 5 vols (Oxford: Clarendon, 1926), 3. 256–306; Hao Gao, 'The Amherst Embassy and British Discoveries in China', *History*, 99 (2014), 568–87; Eun Kyung Min, 'Narrating the Far East: Commerce, Civility and Ceremony in the Amherst Embassy to China 1816–1817', in *Interpreting Colonialism*, ed. Bryan R. Wells and Philip Stewart (Oxford: Voltaire Foundation, 2004), pp. 160–80; Alain Peyrefitte, *The Collision of Two Civilisations: The British Expedition to China 1792–94* (London: HarperCollins, 1993), pp. 504–11; James L. Hevia, *Cherishing Men from Afar: Qing Guest Ritual and the Macartney Embassy* (Durham, NC: Duke University Press, 1995), pp. 210–18.

[2] Henry Ellis, *Journal of the Proceedings of the Late Embassy to China* (London: John Murray, 1817); George Thomas Staunton, *Notes of Proceedings and Occurrences during the British Embassy to Pekin in 1816*, ed. Patrick J. Tuck, *Volume 10, Britain and the China Trade 1635–1842* (London: Routledge, 2000); *Miscellaneous Notices Relating to China, and our Commercial Intercourse with that Country* (London, 1822); Robert Morrison, *A Memoir of the Principal Occurrences during an Embassy from the*

With the publication in 2014 of Wensheng Wang's major reappraisal of the reforming reign of the Jiaqing Emperor (1796–1820), we are now presented with a more complex and nuanced account of this crucial period in Chinese history.[3] Whereas H. B. Morse referred to 'the degenerate and corrupt court' of 1816, Wang instead describes a frugal, thoughtful, self-critical and reforming monarch, keenly aware of the British attempts to take over Macao and nervous about their power.[4] The Jiaqing Emperor emerges not as a ruler imprisoned in an ossified ritualistic ceremonialism but one capable of reacting pragmatically to the complex and challenging political events that faced him.

Contemporary responses to the earlier Macartney embassy were certainly mixed. Macartney and his admirers regarded his embassy as, on the whole, something of a success. He purred about how his mission had 'laid a foundation of amity, good offices, and immediate intercourse with the Imperial Court'.[5] Contemporary views of the Amherst embassy generally viewed it as a failure; John Crawfurd, reviewing Henry Ellis's *Journal of the Proceedings of the late Embassy to China* for the *Edinburgh Review*, commented: 'everybody who knew anything of the matter, we believe, was prepared for that catastrophe of this new Chinese mission, which actually ensued'.[6] Historian Patrick Tuck has claimed that the embassy 'was not merely a failure, it was a fiasco'.[7] Eun Kyung Min, in her ground-breaking

---

British Government to the Court of China in the year 1816 (London, 1820); Clarke Abel, *Narrative of a Journey in the Interior of China in the years 1816–1817* (London, 1818); John Macleod, *Narrative of a Voyage in His Majesty's Late Ship Alceste to the Yellow Sea, along the Coast of Corea [...] to the island of Lewchew* (London, 1817); Basil Hall, *Narrative of a Voyage to Java, China and the Great Loo-Choo Island* (London, 1840); John Francis Davis, *Sketches of China; partly during an inland journey of four months between Peking, Nanking, and Canton; with notices and observations relative to the present war.* 2 vols (London: Charles Knight & Co., 1841); 'Henry Hayne Diary 1816–1817', *China Through Western Eyes: Manuscript Records of Traders, Travellers, Missionaries and Diplomats, 1792–1842.* 4 vols (London: Adam Matthew Microfilm Publications, 1996); William Fanshawe Martin, 'Journal of Sir William Fanshawe Martin as 1st Class Volunteer on board H. M. S. "Alceste" during her voyage with Lord Amherst's abortive mission to China; 3 Feb. 1816–17 Aug. 1817'. Martin Papers, vol. 111. British Library Add. MS. 41456.

[3] Wensheng Wang, *White Lotus Rebels and South China Pirates Crisis and Reform in the Qing Empire* (Cambridge, MA: Harvard University Press, 2014).

[4] Morse, *Chronicles*, 3. 258.

[5] Cited by E. H. Pritchard, *Anglo-Chinese Relations during the Seventeenth and Eighteenth Centuries* (Urbana, IL: University of Illinois Press, 1929), p. 375.

[6] *Edinburgh Review*, 29 (1818), 436–7 (p. 433).

[7] Staunton, *Notes*, p. viii.

essay, argued that the various narratives of the embassy took on 'the added burden of interpreting the history of their failed mission to open up trade with China [...] by attempting to sort out the convolutions of commerce, civility, and ceremony'.[8] Yet at least two of the embassy's participants, John Francis Davis and George Thomas Staunton, viewed it as leading to a distinct improvement in trading conditions, and thus paradoxically a success because it was a failure.[9] More recently Lo-shu Fu has rightly pointed to the new and important knowledge that the embassy gained of the northern Chinese coast and especially of Korea, surveyed by the embassy's ships while Amherst journeyed overland to and from the Qing court and disseminated in John Macleod (M'Leod) and Basil Hall's narratives.[10] Gao Hao stresses the importance of the embassy's discoveries in China after the official proceedings were concluded.[11] The embassy was granted unprecedented and unexpected freedom of movement during its four-month journey from Beijing to Guangzhou (Canton), taking a different route from that of Macartney's 1793 return, one that had not previously been taken by a Briton. Macartney's mission travelled to the southern end of the Grand Canal, whereas Amherst's party transferred from Guazhou to the Yangtze River. They sailed 285 miles along the Yangtze to Poyang Lake and from there on smaller inland waterways to Guangzhou.

Britons thus visited parts of the lower Yangtze delta, hitherto unexplored by any European. As Amherst wrote to Canning, the embassy enjoyed 'a greater degree of liberty than has been granted to any former embassy'.[12] The members of the embassy were also able to communicate more fully with the Chinese government and its peoples than they had hitherto under the jealously guarded Macartney embassy, rambling in the countryside, visiting cities and towns, purchasing souvenirs and even playing the first recorded game of cricket in China. At times more like tourists than guests, the embassy garnered valuable first-hand knowledge of China, and, as Hao argues, such 'important perceptions laid the

8   Min, 'Narrating the Far East', p. 162.
9   John Francis Davis, *The Chinese: A General Description of the Empire of China and Its Inhabitants*. 2 vols (London: Charles Knight, 1836), 1. 81; George Thomas Staunton, *Memoirs of the Chief Incidents of the Public Life of Sir George Thomas Staunton, BART* (London: L. Booth, 1856), pp. 67–8.
10 Lo-Shu Fu, ed., *A Documentary Chronicle of Sino-Western Relations, 1644–1820* (Tucson, AZ: University of Arizona Press, 1956), p. 403.
11 Hao, 'Amherst Embassy', p. 571.
12 Letter from Amherst to George Canning, 8 March 1817. British Library, London: India Office Records (hereafter IOR), G/12/197. f. 281.

foundation for future changes in Sino-British relations and led, indirectly, to the outbreak of the first Opium War in 1839'.[13] The strategic and formal mission of the embassy was not accomplished, yet it was of major importance in changing British views of China in the lead-up to the First Opium War, and, arguably, marked the first major event taken in that process.

The Macartney embassy to China had left Britain shortly before the outbreak of hostilities with revolutionary France and while in China was shocked to receive the news of Louis XVI's execution.[14] Despite its impeccable Enlightenment credentials and its brash promotion of British science and technology in the form of the gifts for the emperor, that embassy still had more than a whiff of the *ancien régime* about it, led by a former ambassador to the court of Catherine the Great of Russia.[15] The Amherst embassy left Britain twenty-three years later in the wake of the defeat of Napoleonic France from which the nation emerged as the century's single superpower. Its attitudes were formed by this historical moment as well as by the increased knowledge that Britons had gleaned since Macartney. It was John Barrow who proposed to the government 'a Mission to the Court of Pekin, in order to announce the restoration of a general peace in this quarter of the World; and of congratulating the Emperor upon his recent escape from assassination [in 1813]'.[16] The emperor was probably not that delighted to be reminded of his recent danger, nor as anxious to receive news of the British victory over the French as Barrow supposed. Whereas the Macartney embassy notoriously could not find any British person who understood written or spoken Chinese to act as interpreter, relying instead on the linguistics skills of Italian Chinese Catholic converts with whom they communicated in Latin, the Amherst embassy included the most accomplished Chinese experts of the day. The missionary Robert Morrison, was the embassy's official interpreter and George Thomas Staunton its deputy commissioner. Both were expert China scholars. The embassy also included a youthful John Francis Davis, who would emerge

---

13 Hao, 'Amherst Embassy', p. 587.

14 'A Journal of his Majesty's ship Lion'; 1 Oct. 1792–7 Sept. 1794; kept by Sir Erasmus Gower during his voyage to China, when he conveyed there the British Ambassador, Lord Macartney; illustrated with maps and sketches'. British Museum Add. MS. 21,106, f.93.

15 See Peter J. Kitson, *Forging Romantic China: Sino-British Cultural Exchange, 1760–1840* (Cambridge: Cambridge University Press, 2013), pp. 126–52.

16 'Minute of Secret Court of the Directors held on Wednesday the 22nd February 1815'. IOR/G12/196, f. 44.

as Britain's major sinologist of the mid-century. It also had the services of the somewhat eccentric 'independent' China scholar and friend of Charles Lamb, Thomas Manning, as well as the surgeon Alexander Pearson and Francis Hastings Toone, both skilled linguists. Amherst, though inexperienced in Chinese matters, was a former Governor of Bengal. The embassy included a naturalist, Clarke Abel, and a gardener, to botanize, as well as a 'draughtsman', the artist William Havell.

Opium, Tea, and China

In the eighteenth and early nineteenth centuries, tea was not the quintessentially British commodity we regard it as today; it was often seen as a foreign, addictive, and exotic drink associated with China and imbricated in extremely complex ways with the prestige of Chinese culture, as Eugenia Zuroski-Jenkins shows in her essay in this volume. Tea slowly became naturalized and domesticated by the early nineteenth century, as the much-sought-after China teas were gradually displaced by the new varieties of tea grown in British India (chiefly the recently acquired province of Assam).[17] It shared with the general discourse of China a tendency to be viewed in terms of opposed extremes and paradoxical ambiguities, alternately considered as a universal panacea, an exotic and effeminizing addiction, or a botanical enigma resistant to transplantation elsewhere.[18]

All the world's tea exports came from China. It was not until 1839 that the very first Indian tea was sold on the British market.[19] For many the China trade was 'the most important in the world'.[20] It was during

[17] See Julie E. Fromer, '"Deeply Indebted to the Tea-Plant": Representations of English National Identity in Victorian Histories of Tea', *Victorian Literature and Culture*, 36 (2008), 531–47; *A Necessary Luxury: Tea in Victorian Britain* (Athens, OH: Ohio University Press, 2008).

[18] Kitson, *Forging Romantic China*, pp. 76–80; 120–5.

[19] William Harrison Ukers, *All About Tea*. 2 vols (New York: Tea and Coffee Trade Journals, 1935), 1. 130. For Canton and the EIC, see Morse, *Chronicles*, especially volume 2; Pritchard, *Anglo-Chinese*; Michael Greenberg, *British Trade and the Opening of China, 1800–42* (Cambridge: Cambridge University Press, 1951); C. H. Phillips, *The East India Company, 1784–1834* (Manchester: Manchester University Press, 1940); Paul A. Van Dyke, *The Canton Trade: Life and Enterprise on the China Coast, 1700–1845* (Hong Kong: Hong Kong University Press, 2007); John E. Wills Jr, ed., *China and Maritime Europe 1500–1800: Trade, Settlement, Diplomacy and Missions* (Cambridge: Cambridge University Press, 2011); William T. Rowe, *China's Last Empire* (Cambridge, MA: Belknap Press, 2009), pp. 120–48.

[20] Frederic Wakeman Jr, 'The Canton Trade and the Opium War', in *The Cambridge History of China. Volume 10: Late Chi'ing, 1800–1911*. Part 1 (Cambridge:

this crucial period that tea began its long and extraordinary process of naturalization from a potentially invasive and enfeebling oriental luxury to the robust and quintessentially British drink of the Victorian period.[21] Yet for most of the eighteenth century, as Zuroski-Jenkins points out, tea was different and a signifier of luxury.[22] The problem for the East India Company was that the Chinese would not import British goods in anything like the volumes required to offset the massive payment of silver bullion required for these huge volumes of tea. In the early nineteenth century the disruptions caused by Latin American emancipation movements drastically reduced the supplies of silver and gold, causing a global depression in the world economy.[23] It was thus even more important for the Company to pay for Chinese imports with other currencies than with this increasingly scarce specie. It is well known that the British solution to this imbalance was for the Company, after 1799, to indirectly export larger volumes of its opium grown at Bombay and at Patna in Bengal to China. The opium was auctioned off to private, or 'country traders' who shipped the drug to China thus allowing the Company to deny its participation in the illegal trade.[24] As both poison and medicine, opium is paradoxical.

Cambridge University Press, 1978), pp. 163–212 (p. 173); J. L. Cranmer-Byng and John E. Wills Jr, 'Trade and Diplomacy with Maritime Europe, 1644–c.1800', in *China and Maritime Europe 1500–1800*, ed. John E. Wills Jr (Cambridge: Cambridge University Press, 2011), p. 183. The literature on the tea trade is substantial. The following are especially important: Morse, *Chronicles*; Ukers, *All About Tea*; K. N. Chaudhuri, *The Trading World of Asia and the East India Company* (Cambridge: Cambridge University Press, 1978); Hoh-Cheung Mui and Lorna H. Mui, *The Management of Monopoly: A Study of the East India Company's Conduct of its Tea Trade, 1784–1833* (Vancouver, 1984); Robert Gardella, *Harvesting the Mountains: Fujian and the China Tea Trade, 1757–1937* (Berkeley: University of California Press, 1994); Markman Ellis, Richard Coulton, Ben Dew, and Matthew Mauger, eds, *Tea and the Tea-Table in Eighteenth-Century England*. 4 vols (London: Pickering and Chatto, 2010).

21 Ukers, *All About Tea*, 2. 179.

22 Ukers, *All About Tea*, 1. ix; Ellis et al., *Tea and the Tea-Table*, 2. vii.

23 See Lin Man-houng, *China Upside Down: Currency, Society and Ideologies, 1808–1856* (Cambridge, MA: Harvard University Press, 2006).

24 For the opium trade, see Wakeman, 'The Canton Trade', pp. 163–212; Chang Hsin-pao, *Commissioner Lin and the Opium War* (New York: W. W. Norton, 1960), pp. 1–84; Barry Milligan, *Pleasures and Pains: Opium and the Orient in 19th-Century British Culture* (Charlottesville, VA: University of Virginia Press, 1995), pp. 3–30; Cranmer-Byng and Wills Jr, 'Trade and Diplomacy', pp. 183–254; Carl A. Trocki, *Opium, Empire and the Global Political Economy: A Study of the Asian Opium Trade 1750–1950* (London: Routledge, 1999); Van Dyke, *The Canton Trade*, pp. 120–41; and Julia Lovell, *The Opium War: Drugs, Dreams and the Making of China*

On the one hand, in the form of laudanum, opium was commonplace in nineteenth-century Britain, a popular, legal, and highly effective analgesic, one of the few medicinal compounds that worked to relieve pain and treat dysentery.[25] Yet, on the other, it was addictive, destructive, and a source of great anguish. The extreme cases of the Romantic writers Coleridge and De Quincey are well known, though their opium would have been largely sourced from Smyrna in Turkey, not India. In China, opium was used for many years, but in the early eighteenth century it was increasingly combined with tobacco and smoked for pleasure.[26]

While the opium trade was legal in Britain and most parts of Southeast Asia, importation of the drug into China was formally, though ineffectually, prohibited by imperial decree in 1729 (reaffirmed in 1796) but only something like 200 chests per annum were imported by Europeans at this time. This steadily rose to around 1,000 chests in 1760, 1,300 chests in 1780, and about 3,159 by 1805. The Chinese merchants paid for their contraband Bengal opium with European silver. By the 1830s the imbalance in silver bullion export between Britain and China had been drastically reversed, with a surplus in the Company's favour of around £38 million and something like 40,000 chests of opium per annum exported into China by the end of that decade. It was a hugely profitable, contraband trade making it 'the world's most valuable single commodity trade of the nineteenth century'.[27] Opium was thus firmly enmeshed in British commercial and colonial policy: the profits from the trade funded the British in India. The British traders simply claimed they were only satisfying an existing demand not creating a new one, and that the trade was illegal in name only as its open conduct required Chinese corruption on a massive scale with the co-operation of conniving Qing government officials. As Julia Lovell shrewdly sums up,

---

(London: Picador, 2011), pp. 17–38. The impact of the flow of silver bullion on China is discussed by Lin, *China Upside Down*. For opium and Chinese culture, see Zheng Yangwen, *The Social Life of Opium in China* (Cambridge: Cambridge University Press, 2005).

[25] Alethea Hayter's *Opium and the Romantic Imagination* (London: Faber and Faber, 1968) remains the classic, if rather dated, account. See also Martin Booth, *Opium: A History* (New York: St Martins Press, 1996); Victoria Berridge and Griffith Edwards, *Opium and the People: Opiate Use in Nineteenth-Century England* (London: Allen Lane, 1987); Milligan, *Pleasures and Pains*, pp. 3–30; Thomas Dormandy, *Opium Reality's Dark Dream* (New Haven, CT: Yale University Press, 2012).

[26] See Zheng, *Social Use of Opium*, pp. 41–70.

[27] Wakeman, 'Canton Trade', p. 172.

although by no means a blemish-free ethical choice, the move into opium by British traders was not, as claimed by contemporary historians in the People's Republic, a deliberate conspiracy to make narcotic slaves of the Chinese empire; it was a greedy, pragmatic response to a decline in sales of other British imports, (clocks, watches, furs).[28]

The scale of the trade by the late 1830s was so immense and its effects so debilitating that the Qing government, in the person of Commissioner Lin Zexu, took those extreme steps to eradicate it that led to the conflict between Britain and China known as the 'Opium War'. Whatever the complexities of the debate, however, the opium trade had devastating economic and social effects for Qing China.

The British position on the opium trade was conflicted. Macartney's embassy in 1793 had noted that opium smoking was then almost entirely an elite practice. George Leonard Staunton, Macartney's deputy, commented on how the mandarins indulged themselves in 'the habits of luxury', employing 'part of their intervals of leisure in smoking tobacco mixed with odorous substances, and sometimes a little opium, or in chewing the areca nut'.[29] Macartney noted the importance of China as 'a market for cotton and opium' and as a provider of the 'indispensable luxury, or rather and absolute necessary of life: tea'. He estimated the 'illegal and contraband trade of opium' to consist in 1792 of 'around 2,500 chests'. At this time the balance of trade was very much in China's favour, but even then he speculated that should the British trade with China continue to improve and 'the value of exports and imports between England and China should become nearly equal, and the balance between China and India remain still in favour of the latter, may not the Chinese take alarm at so much silver being sent out of their country in discharge of the balance?' Macartney believed that the 'opium of Bengal' had become a necessity in China, 'having grown into general demand through all the southern provinces'.[30] In his *Travels in China* of 1805 John Barrow directly accused the Chinese elite of hypocrisy and corruption when it came to opium, a claim to be repeated many times by the British in justification of the trade. He writes of how the governor of Canton

---

[28] Lovell, *Opium War*, p. 25.

[29] George Leonard Staunton, *An Authentic Account of an Embassy from the King of Great Britain to the Emperor of China* (London: G. Nichol, 1797), 2. 70; 174.

[30] J. L. Cranmer-Byng, ed., *An Embassy to China. Being the journal kept by Lord Macartney during his embassy to the Emperor Ch'ien-lung, 1793–1794* (London: Longman, 1962), pp. 212, 260–1, 275.

[...] after describing in one of his late proclamations on the subject the pernicious and fatal effects arising from the use of opium, observes, 'Thus it is that foreigners by the means of a vile excrementitious substance derive from this empire the most solid profits and advantages; but that out countrymen should blindly pursue this destructive and ensnaring vice, even till death is the consequence, without being undeceived, is indeed a fact odious and deplorable in the highest degree.' Yet the governor of Canton very composedly takes his daily dose of opium.[31]

Yet the Qing court was beginning to take alarm, and in 1797 the Jiaqing Emperor issued an edict confirming the illegality of the trade. The habit of opium smoking, as even Macartney noticed, was moving spatially beyond the coastal regions into the interior of China with the increase in the British supply from India. More worryingly for the emperor, it seemed to be used extensively by the military. Although Macartney openly discussed commodities such as tea, silk, woollens, and porcelain with Chinese officials, there seems to be no record of the subject of the opium trade being openly broached in this way by members of the embassy.

Amherst and the Opium Trade

The Amherst embassy thus takes place at a crucial period in the developing opium trade now governed by established practices and procedures. Smoking opium in China was in the process of transforming itself from an elite, sophisticated cultural practice into a more popular pastime, and the British were noticing the impact of this developing trade and the substantially increasing supply: Chinese exports of tea doubled between 1813 and 1833, and imports of opium quadrupled.[32] In 1799, the Jiaqing Emperor introduced serious measures to curtail the trade, making it difficult for Company ships to carry the commodity, which was henceforth auctioned off in Calcutta and Bombay to licensed British, Parsee, and American merchants. Later, in 1813, he instructed his ministers to draft codes of punishment for those who smoked the drug.[33] When he learned of the substantial networks for opium smuggling located around the Portuguese enclave of Macao in 1814 he took further initiatives to suppress

---

[31] John Barrow, *Travels in China* (London, 1804), p. 153.
[32] Peyrefitte, *Collison of Two Civilisations*, p. 519.
[33] Peyrefitte, *Collison of Two Civilisations*, pp. 58–9.

the contraband trade in the region.[34] On the very eve of the embassy in 1815, additional measures were taken to prohibit the trade, the emperor declaring, 'Opium spreads its poison intensively' and claiming that it 'is usually smuggled in by barbarian ships'.[35] It seems clear that the Jiaqing Emperor regarded the British as the most troublesome and dangerous of the westerners, possessed of an insatiable appetite for trading, especially in opium, and his response to Amhert's embassy should be considered in the light of this, not simply as a recourse to ossified ritualism. It was a period of much uncertainty and anxiety for both empires; as Wang puts it, 'British policy toward China, aiming to find out how the vast empire might be pressured, was tentative and experimental and could have gone in different directions.'[36]

When Macartney visited China in 1793 it was nearing the end of the prosperous Qianlong era. When Amherst arrived, the empire was in a more troubled state, subject to overpopulation, land shortages, frequent rebellions, attacks by pirates, and serious financial problems. The empire was also experiencing a currency crisis owing to the shortage of silver.[37] To add to the emperor's woes, during this period opium consumption in China was becoming more popular, largely driven by the increasing supply of the drug from British-controlled Bengal.[38] In this process, the Company accrued a staggering profit during the period 1805 and 1813 of between 500 and 900 per cent, and the amount of opium entering Canton increased tenfold. With the abolition of the Company's monopoly over all but the China trade in 1833, Indian commerce was opened up to all, instituting a lucrative 'opium rush'.[39] It was at this time that Chinese farmers seeking profit began to harvest the poppy for themselves.[40]

Wang presents us with the picture of the Jiaqing Emperor as a capable and reforming monarch who did much to stabilize his realm. In his dealings with the British over the attempted invasions of Macao in 1802 and 1808 he acted shrewdly and highly successfully, forcing climb-downs on both occasions. Wang claims that he was a flexible and adaptable ruler who

---

[34] Van Dyke, *Canton Trade*, pp. 131–2.

[35] Fu, *Documentary History*, pp. 399–400.

[36] Wang, *White Lotus Rebels*, pp. 250, 233–51.

[37] James M. Polachek, *The Inner Opium War* (Cambridge, MA: Harvard University Press, 1992).

[38] Zeng, *Social Uses of Opium*, pp. 59, 63–4.

[39] Zeng, *Social Uses of Opium*, p. 70.

[40] Zeng, *Social Uses of Opium*, p. 65.

toned down the much celebrated rhetoric of tributary superiority, which had long dominated Chinese thinking about their relationship with the outside world [...] emphasizing the relatively new norms of formal equality, territorial right, reciprocity, and non-intervention, which would appeal much more to Western sensibilities by exposing their 'organized hypocrisy'.[41]

Following the two failed Macao invasions, he argues, Britain turned now away from its failed policy of an early form of gunboat diplomacy to a more successful one of intensified commercial imperialism spearheaded by the opium trade, which would 'eventually led to the first Sino-British War'.[42] While this may overestimate the coherence and direction of British policy, it is clear that the Jiaqing Emperor understood something of the threat the British might pose. His defence of Macao and the subsequent British withdrawals of 1802 and 1808 were, like his father, Qianlong's conduct of the reception of the Macartney embassy, notable Qing foreign policy successes against the formidable power of the British. Again it is rather in this context, not one of simple dynastic decline, that the emperor's insistence on the ceremonial *koutou* during the Amherst embassy should be viewed.

Given the importance of the opium trade in funding the Company's trade in tea with China and the substantial structural changes that were occurring with regard to the trade in the middle of the Jiaqing period when the embassy arrives in Beijing, it is surprising to note that there is no obvious mention of the trade and British participation within it, in any of the documents, published or otherwise, relating to the embassy, at least that I have yet located. Whereas pressing issues such as trading privileges, recent skirmishes with American vessels in Chinese waters, and British involvement in the kingdom of Nepal are extensively detailed in both government and Company secret instructions and advice to Amherst, I have discovered no discussion of the opium trade itself in this correspondence. Henry Ellis's *Journal of the Proceedings of the Late Embassy to China* (1817), which became the de facto official account of the embassy, does not mention the subject at all. The naturalist Clarke Abel's *Narrative of a Journey into the Interior of China* contains one brief mention of the practice of opium smoking and its deleterious effects:

No opium is exposed for sale in the shops, probably because it is a contraband article, but it is used with tobacco in all parts of the empire.

[41] Wang, *White Lotus Rebels*, p. 244.
[42] Wang, *White Lotus Rebels*, p. 247.

The Chinese indeed consider the smoking of opium as one of the greatest luxuries; and if they are temperate in drinking, they are often excessive in the use of this drug. They have more than one method of smoking it: sometimes they envelope a piece of the solid gum in tobacco, and smoke it from a pipe with a very small bowl; and sometimes they steep fine tobacco in a strong solution in the same way. The smokers of opium have a very peculiar, sottish, and sleepy physiognomy, in consequence of whole visage being turgid with blood.[43]

Abel notes that the substance is a 'contraband article' and a 'luxury', but does not discuss the place of the drug in the Company's network of trading with China. Robert Morrison's *Memoir* of the embassy comments on the drug and its use by Mandarin 'Chang' who accompanied the embassy. Morrison described him as 'rather old, tall, thin, and emaciated, it is to be apprehended by the use of opium'. Morrison, a later opponent of the trade, here typifies an upper-class Chinese as the drug user. Yet subsequently he records how one of the local governors enquired of the gentlemen of the embassy if they possessed any of the drug, adding that it was now being used by the people of his 'poor district'. This is a further confirmation that the increasing supply of the drug was lowering its price and encouraging its consumption by the less well off. [44] Sadly, Morrison provides no information about any British consumption or lack of it.

More interesting, however, in this regard is the most substantial and richest published account of the Amherst embassy, *Sketches of China*, penned by John Francis Davis about his experiences but not published until 1842 and written in part from perspective of the still uncertain ongoing cusp of military conflict with China in the First Opium War. Davis presents his recollection of the events of the embassy twenty-four years before, over two substantial volumes, describing the diplomatic events of the embassy as well as the returning journey overland. He argues that

> whatever may be the ultimate result of our armed measures towards the government of that country – whether one of renewed and more intimate intercourse, or of exclusive and lasting hostility – this account of the internal features, physical and moral of the empire, may in either case be useful.[45]

43 Abel, *Narrative*, p. 215.
44 Morrison, *Memoir*, pp. 12, 77.
45 Davis, *Sketches*, 1. i. Further references to this edition will be cited by volume and page number in parenthesis in the text.

Although Davis hoped for an exercise of the pliancy the Chinese government occasionally showed and a 'peaceful termination of our existing difficulties', he remained pessimistic. In the second volume of *Sketches* he wrote that:

> the year 1840 was destined to present the extraordinary spectacle of a British naval and military force on the coast of China, a region so far removed from Europe that its existence six hundred years ago was scarcely known, and the faithful narrative of a long resident and traveller in the country received as a tissue of fables containing another El Dorado. (2. 260)

He defends the publication of his long, rambling narrative because, 'as we are now at war with the empire, every part of the military system of that country becomes in some measure interesting' (2. 136).

Throughout, Davis records the events of the embassy as a recollection of the past from the perspective of the present, developing an apologia for armed conflict in the intransigency of the Jiaqing and Daoguang courts, which he links with the 'outrageous exploits of Commissioner Lin at Canton', the 'implacable enemy of the British name', who famously destroyed the merchants' opium stock at Canton in 1839, igniting the conflict (2. 263). In Davis's mind the Amherst embassy thus inaugurated a new phase in Sino-British relations that has led to the 'pending hostilities' from which there is 'no saying what may result [...] as regards a repetition of our hitherto fruitless visits to their shores' (2. 19, 135, 138). Davis frequently notes areas of Chinese vulnerability as well as what he views as the theatricality of their military arrangements; notably he speculates that the 'great object of an invading army would be to arrest' the progress of the grain junks northwards up the Yangtse, cutting off northern China from its supply of grain. This was, of course, the successful tactic actually employed at the time the publication of the *Sketches* by Sir Henry Pottinger (2. 14–15, 80–1) that brought the military conflict to a swift conclusion. Davis believes that the embassy's 'little guard of picked men, from the marines of the frigate, could have marched through Tien-tsin with great ease, and in spite of the opposition it might have met with from all the troops we saw there' (2. 89). His final and considered judgement is that 'the best peace-maker with them [the government] is an overwhelming force, and as few words as possible' (2. 295).

Davis's *Sketches* is sensitized to the frequent evidence he is presented of what he calls 'the difficult subject of the opium trade', a subject about which he was notably conflicted (2. 316).[46] He noted that its presence was still largely coastal, 'the only article of trade on the coasts to the eastward of Canton', and blames this on the 'unconquerable passion for opium, which leads the people to use it until the emaciation consequent thereon make them resemble, "a paddy-bird in figure, and a pigeon in the face", to use their own expression'. He translates the Chinese maxim that 'he who has a yellow face and white teeth is an opium smoker' (2. 100), and records that of a reinforcement of a thousand men sent from the neighbourhood of Canton to Lien-chow in 1832 to quell an uprising, 'two hundred of these were sent back, as being quite unfitted for service by the use of *opium*' (2. 138). Yet he acknowledges that the opium trade is necessary to finance the British in Bengal. Notably, at one stage he speculates that if the engineering science of a Brunel were allowed to operate on the Yellow River and Grand Canal, 'a benefit might be conferred that would more than compensate for *all the evil that we have inflicted with our opium and our guns*' (my italics, 1. 270). His own solution to the problem is to induce the Chinese to legalize the trade (2. 316).

Davis's references to the opium trade and its effects, particularly on the Chinese military, are by far the most explicit in all of the accounts of the embassy. They indicate that the subject was present in the mind and observations of at least one of the members of the embassy, both at the time and subsequently. Yet the issue of the ceremonial of the *koutou* and the failed exchange of presents seems to occupy the embassy to a much greater extent than the opium trade.

Gifts for an Emperor

The remainder of this essay will focus on the ritual of gift exchange that lay at the heart of the British embassies to China. It argues that concerns about the presents for the emperor, like the formal issue of the *koutou*, were fetishized or overdetermined in the British imagination as a compensatory mechanism disguising Britain's growing involvement in the opium trade. The subject of the gifts of the Macartney embassy for the Qianlong Emperor, presented in September 1793, has already been extensively discussed in a series of powerful critiques.[47] Macartney's gifts included the

---

46 Kitson, *Forging Romantic China*, pp. 120–5.

47 J. L. Cranmer-Byng and Trevor H. Levere, 'A Case Study in Cultural Collision: Scientific Apparatus in the Macartney Embassy to China, 1793', *Annals of Science*, 38 (1981), 503–25; Hevia, *Cherishing Men From Afar*; Kitson, *Forging Romantic China*, pp. 126–52; Maxine Berg, 'Britain, Industry and Perceptions of China:

famous planetarium or '*Weltmaschine*', an orrery, a coach, a diving bell, several scientific lens, various clocks and singsongs, and numerous examples of British manufactured goods. They were intended to reflect British progress and superiority in the arts and sciences, and to inspire both awe and admiration. As Simon Schaffer puts it, these apparently utilitarian scientific instruments had to be both 'distinctively British yet universally meaningful and had to be seductively and theatrically impressive while displaying the principles of civility and utilitarian commerce'.[48]

As is well known, the Qing court accepted the gifts but affected a studious indifference to them, apparently viewing them as inappropriate tribute in that they did not completely represent the produce of the giving nation. The '*Weltmaschine*' was actually of German not British origin and was regarded as a 'boastful' item. Much of the narrative of the embassy was given over to discussion of the presents, and the scene certainly captured the public imagination, as can be seen here in James Gillray's imagined depiction of the reception of the Macartney embassy (Fig. 1) and George Cruikshank's parallel depiction of Lord Amherst receiving his instructions from the Prince Regent (Fig. 2). In the latter, a despotic and corrupt regent, hungry to consume expensive and exotic chinoiserie items, requests Amherst to get him 'fresh patterns of Chinese deformities to finish the decoration of ye Pavilion'. The embassy's gifts are now not the infant's toys of Gillray's scene, but more adult items, signifying the Regent's voluptuousness, vanity, greed, and lust. In an open chest labelled 'Presents for the Emperor of China' can be seen two portraits of the regent most helpfully described as 'Front & back view of myself'. The actual portraits of the Regent and Princess Caroline taken to China by Amherst would feature most significantly in the diplomatic business of the embassy. Next to these are large volumes inscribed 'Fanny Hill' and 'Pretty books', presumably indicative of the Regent's taste for pornography and need for sensual stimulation, which he assumes his brother monarch will share.

Behind Gillray's and Cruikshank's satires is the notion of the appropriateness of the gift and what it symbolizes.[49] Numerous scholars have

Matthew Boulton, "Useful Knowledge" and the Macartney Embassy to China', *Journal of Global History*, 1.ii (2006), 269–88.

[48] Simon Schaffer, 'Instruments as Cargo in the China Trade', *History of Science*, 44 (2006), 217–46.

[49] The classic account of how gifts function in mediating social relationships is Marcel Mauss, *The Gift: The Form and Reason for Exchange in Archaic Societies*, trans. W. D. Hall (London: Routledge, 1990 [1922]).

Figure 1: James Gillray, *The Reception of the Diplomatique & his Suite at the court of Pekin* (1792)

addressed the British understanding of civility and the function of the gift exchange in constituting the semiotics of international trade and diplomacy. Eun Kyung Min has argued that in the narratives of the embassy the 'languages of state, the merchant and the court' merged 'on the assumption of their perfect coherence: the ceremonious, courtly encounter between representatives of two nations can open up international commerce conducted along the lines of mutual civility'. The problem for both the embassies, Min argues, was that they needed to 'procure honour for British commerce through "the pomp of majesty" that ran contrary notions of individual civility, refinement and politeness popularized in the eighteenth century'.[50] Cynthia Klekar has persuasively argued that the language of gift exchange, reciprocity, and obligation featured heavily in Macartney's understanding of his embassy. The notion of a gift

---

[50] Min, 'Narrating the Far East', pp. 162–3, 167–8.

Figure 2 and Cover illustration: George Cruikshank, *The Court at Brighton à la Chinese!!* (1816)

'as an equal exchange between reciprocally respectful nations – becomes problematic: what the English viewed as civility the Chinese interpreted as ritual subjection'.[51] Robert Markley has also shown how such ceremonies were crucial in establishing extremely complex relationships of obligation, deference, and duty. In the process of the Macartney gift exchange, the Qianlong Emperor reciprocated by presenting his embassy with various examples of traditional Chinese arts and crafts, including jade sculptures, silk purses, and vases.[52] In Qing guest ritual, as James Hevia, has shown, the appropriate gift should explicitly be linked to the 'lesser lord's domain'

---

[51] Cynthia Klekar, '"Prisoners in Silken Bonds': Obligation, Trade, and Diplomacy in English Voyages to Japan and China', *Journal of Early Modern Cultural Studies*, 2 (2006), 84–105 (pp. 84–6). See also Klekar, 'Sweetness and Courtesie: Benevolence, Civility, and China in the Making of European Modernity', *Eighteenth-Century Studies*, 43 (2010), 357–69.

[52] Robert Markley, 'Anson at Canton, 1743: Obligation, Exchange, and Ritual Passage in Edward Page's "Secret History"', in *The Culture of the Gift in Eighteenth-Century England*, ed. Linda Zionkowski and Cynthis Klekar (New York: Palgrave Macmillan, 2009), pp. 215–34.

and consist in 'things that are differentiable from other things of other domains'.[53]

David Simpson has more generally considered the crucial significance of the gift exchange in his account of encounters with the stranger in the Romantic period. He argues for the importance of studying the Romantic reception of the stranger/guest rituals, and regards the foundational cultural dialectic of the hospitality or rejection of the stranger as crucial in an age of developing mercantile and colonial expansion. The key trope is that of the *pharmakon*, which, like the alien or stranger, may either cure or poison the host culture, or, in the mode of *pharmakós*, act as a scapegoat whose ritual exclusion or sacrifice is imagined as securing the integrity of the community. The formulation of a hospitality that 'enunciates the common linguistic positing and synthesis of host and guest, hospitality and enmity, welcome and unwelcome stranger' is thus central to Romantic period understandings of such encounters. Simpson claims that earlier, more utopian, eighteenth-century discourses of polite and sociable cosmopolitanism gave way to encounters with truly strange strangers in Romantic accounts. What is new is the element of the 'undecidable' or 'uneconomizable', fuelling a 'distinct ramping up of the depth and scope of the stranger syndrome'. Such encounters are thus calibrated on a scale between a form of 'unconditional hospitality and absolute aversion'. Ideas of universalism and cosmopolitanism thus conflict with nascent, emerging Romantic understandings of the organic nation state and fears of the foreign invader.[54]

Simpson, though he discusses a number of crusader narratives, is less concerned with the reception of Britons abroad than their treatment of foreigners at home and the cases of the Macartney and Amherst embassies with their acceptance/rejection scenarios complicate his reading further. His thesis nevertheless provides a fruitful and enabling paradigm within which to situate those events. Notably gift exchange features prominently in his account, as does the problematic *pharmakon*, opium: the exemplary cure and poison. The complex and unspoken (unspeakable?) relationship between opium and the gifts is a crucial though denied one; opium is the doppelganger of the formal British present; it is the dark gift in the real exchange of commerce. In particular, we see the movement from the cosmopolitan discourse of open and enlightened and rational civility that underpinned the embassy of Macartney to the more troubled, anxious,

---

[53] Hevia, *Cherishing Men From Afar*, pp. 127, 128–9.
[54] David Simpson, *Romanticism and the Question of the Stranger* (Chicago: University of Chicago Press, 2014), pp. 5–10.

emergent discourse of organic nationalism, emerging in Britain post-1815 in the run-up to the First Opium War, and which infiltrated the discourse of the Amherst embassy.

Informed by the perceived failure of the Macartney gifts to impress the Chinese, in preparing for the Amherst embassy, the British took a different tack. They confined the embassy gifts mainly to useful or decorative manufactured products, again not quite understanding the process they were entering into, but attempting to fathom the ritual in a more sensitive and nuanced manner. This embassy would, unlike Macartney's, impress the court not with grandstanding spectacular scientific gifts but with its informed and improved expertise in dealing with Chinese procedures and cultural prejudices, exemplified in its quite exceptional cadre of China experts: Morrison, Staunton, Manning, and Davis. Its new political understanding combined with the outstanding linguistic resources of its interpreters would be key. Ironically, this embassy fared less well than that of Macartney.

The selection of the presents for the emperor was a complex process. Barrow, who had served as comptroller for the Macartney embassy, established himself as the government's most prominent 'China expert', and became second secretary at the Admiralty in 1804. He was a driving force behind the initiative to send a second embassy to China, and had first proposed to do this the year following his appointment. Though angry at the Qing's dismissive attitude to the Macartney gifts, he seems subsequently to have absorbed the key desideratum of Qing guest ritual that the gifts must be local produce and should not be 'boastful'. In a 'Minute of Conference between the Chair of the East India Company and John Barrow', Barrow correctly laid 'it down as a general principle that the Chinese Court *prefer articles* of *intrinsic value*, to those of mere shew or curiousity, though the latter are not to be wholly omitted'. He suggested that for the emperor such items as a golden cup, several silver vessels, fine broadcloths ('the softer and finer the better'), velvets, ermine, mirrors, porcelain, portraits ('the Prince in a Gold Box set with Diamonds), ornamental clocks, perfumes, and liquers, all these might be appropriate. He itemized other presents for the ministers and mandarins. Among those presents he suggests including: 'Paintings, chiefly of the Buildings, Flowers and Animals'; 'Coloured Prints &c – Plan of London – views on the Thames – of St Paul's'; 'Prints of distinguished Persons [...] Maps – Russia; England, Scotland, Ireland [...] Charts of the Navigation from Europe to China, Panoramic Views; cutlery, razors, penknives, telescopes, pocket books, locks', 'fire engines'; and the 'Model of a Ship of War'. All were products of the British Isles and some were manufactured goods that the Chinese might take up. Barrow also advised against sending any horses or dogs ('the value of the best species of these not understood by the Chinese'), carriages ('impossible to make them to suit the Chinese taste'), maps of either India or China (which would create jealousy in that people'), botanical drawings ('they excel us in this branch'), and no military weapons, as the 'Chinese disliked what they saw of these with Lord Macartney'.[55] Barrow's suggestions seem to have been largely followed when the actual gifts were chosen. The Secret Committee of the Company wrote to Amherst in January 1816 that the gifts were 'magnificent both as to their Value and their Workmanship', but 'consist more of Articles of intrinsic worth, composed of precious Metals and Stones, than of things of mere fancy, being thus intended to suit the supposed taste of the Chinese'. Importantly they were 'all of the manufactures of this Country, and exquisite specimens of the high degree of refinement to which the useful and elegant Arts are advanced here'.[56] The Committee was especially concerned about the cloths sent with the embassy 'as it appears probable that these very fine Cloths may attract the attention of the Chinese, and may also open a Mart for the introduction of these articles into general use, among the superior Mandarins and principal Officers of the Chinese Government'. The total cost of the presents was £22,005.13s.7p.[57] Among the presents finally selected were:

> A very handsome large chased Gold Box, enriched in the Centre of the Cover with a fine Enamel of the Prince Regent, set round with large and fine sapphires & a cluster of brilliant ruby rays outside intended to contain the Letter from His Royal Highness the Prince Regent to the Emperor of China £1570.
> A fine Gold enamel picture of the Prince Regent £55
> ***
> Maps on Springs in Mahogany Cases. England, Scotland, Ireland & Russia.
>
> £42[58]

[55] 'Minute of Conference between the Chairs, & Mr Barrow respecting Presents for China', IOR/G/196, ff. 44–7 (f. 47).
[56] Letter from Secret Commercial Committee of the EIC to Amherst, 17 January 1816, IOR/G12/196, f. 105.
[57] 'An Account of Presents sent with the Ambassador to be made to the Emperor of China in the name of His Royal Highness the Prince Regent; also of Presents to be distributed among the Chief Ministers & Mandarins of the Imperial Court', IOR/G/196, ff. 144–54.
[58] Ibid., ff. 146–7.

As the embassy never received an audience, the gifts were never formally presented. The emperor, however, after he became aware of his courtiers' mishandling of the embassy, proposed a limited exchange of gifts, ostensibly out of respect for the sincerity of the Regent's motives.

In his account of the 'bulky and numerous' gifts, Davis generally adopts a rather utilitarian and materialistic approach to the exchange, presenting the emperor as shrewd and pecuniary, acting without regard to the monarch's understandings of his nation's cultural value. Noting the presents conferred on the embassy in Beijing, Davis remarks 'they looked very well when arranged in order at the hall of reception' but consisted simply of paper wrapped in silk. As with Macartney, there is little understanding of the Qing symbolism of the gift. When describing the golden box encrusted with precious stones that contained the letter of the Regent that the legates were allowed to see, Davis comments:

> though this was a magnificent thing of its kind, and valued at fifteen hundred pounds, they expressed little or no admiration at the sight of it. Infinitely greater was the veneration with which they regarded a yellow silk purse, which had been given by the late emperor, Kienlong, to the second commissioner [Staunton], and which he produced to them on this occasion. (2. 84)

The *Account* of Macartney's embassy by Staunton's father records how the young Staunton's 'modest countenance or manner' was so 'pleasing' to the Qianlong Emperor that he presented the boy with a purse from his person: 'Purses are the ribands of the Chinese monarch [...] but his own purse was deemed a mark of personal favour, according to the Eastern nations, among whom anything worn by the person of the sovereign is prized beyond all other gifts.'[59]

The Macartney embassy experience, and the emperor's gift to Staunton as a 12-year-old boy, is imbricated with that of Amherst. The fact that Staunton has the gift still on his person in China suggests some unacknowledged personal sentimental veneration for this unique memento irrespective of its material form, unexpressed but perhaps not as different from the reverence of the Chinese. Notably Davis may highly value the gold- and diamond-encrusted box the most, but Thomas De Quincey

---

[59] Staunton, *Authentic Account*, 2. 234–35. In his accounts Staunton does not mention his possession this gift from the Qianlong Emperor, *Notes*, pp. 133–5; *Memoirs*, pp. 11–16. The incident is not mentioned either by Ellis, Amherst, or Morrison in their respective accounts.

would scorn the appropriateness of such ubiquitous golden boxes as diplomatic gifts to eastern potentates in his mordant retelling.

Of the presents received by his embassy, Davis records 'a *joo-y*, or scepter of good fortune, made from large piece of jade, called by the Chinese *Yu*; a dozen of the purses which the emperor wears at his side; and some necklaces of large Chaou-choo or "court bead"'. Again, not understanding the symbolic function of the gifts, Davis assesses them as 'paltry enough with reference to their intrinsic value, but fully equal to the presents of the last embassy' (2. 159–60). Macartney back in 1793, ccommenting on the emperor's gift to him of a sceptre (*ruyi*), symbolizing peace and prosperity, noted more precisely that his gift was 'a whitish, agate-looking stone about a foot and a half long, curiously carved and highly prized by the Chinese', but not appearing 'in itself to be of any great value' (Cranmer-Byng, Embassy, p. 122). Macartney, more balanced here than Davis, is aware both of the economic value of the gift in itself shorn of its cultural capital, but he also appreciates that the gift is genuinely and sincerely 'highly prized' by the Chinese, whereas Davis assumes that both parties are fully aware of the relative economic values of the exchange and the Chinese are condescending and insolent. What is at stake in both embassies here are differing and conflicting notions of value, a symbolic versus a utilitarian exchange, metonymic of the larger cultural encounter.

In return for its gifts, the court accepted from Amherst's embassy, 'the pictures of their majesties; four large maps, three of which were the United Kingdoms; and the books of engravings'. The reason the emperor gave for accepting these gifts in an edict of 8 October (in Davis's translation) was that given the 'sincere and entire devotedness' of the British nation, he could not 'bear to reject altogether their expressions of veneration and obedience'. He thus requires 'that the most trifling articles of tribute should be presented, and the kindness of receiving them conferred'. The emperor claims that in conferring the 'joo-y of white jade, sapphire court beads, and purses' he is 'giving much and taking little'. Davis adds in a note 'setting the insolence of this document aside, there was good taste in selecting those among the intended presents which were not of the greatest intrinsic value' (2. 9, 9n). The emperor claims to select the presents on the basis of their trifling value (in symbolic terms) to offset the serious cultural value of his own presents, but Davis interprets this as simply as a sham with the most valuable among the gifts chosen.

We do not have the benefit of the emperor's reasoning here, but the possibility that the expensive gifts were selected and described as 'trifling' may have been a comment on British values and their inflated estimations of their gifts. Wang has shown how the Jiaqing Emperor was generally of a reforming and very frugal disposition and, unlike his father, actively discouraged excessive tribute.[60] It is very unlikely that any notion of greed, as Davis would understand it, had motivated his choice. The gifts he selected ('the geographical atlas, the landscape paintings and your portraits') also have an intrinsic connection to the territory of Britain and were thus most appropriate. In his edict of 30 August, the emperor acknowledged that the embassy was 'presenting native products' and thus appropriate gifts as specified in Qing guest ritual.[61] The selection of the maps is also significant. The Qing's fascination with cartography and the determination of borders was well known.

Davis interprets the exchange as a 'peace-offering on their part' whereas the Chinese legates gave as the reason 'their emperor's wish that our king might not be *very angry* with us on our return'. By this time the Jiaqing Emperor had publicly accused those responsible for the reception of the embassy as deficient in not informing him of its very late arrival and the state of Amherst's condition. The symbolic status of this moment is also not investigated by the Amherst himself, who commented that these presents were to him 'matters of no moment, and as the emperor desired to have them they might go to Peking'. Amherst's response, however, is belied by his next actions. When the portraits of the Regent and Princess Caroline are inspected, the ambassador insists on the clearing of the hall as 'the Chinese attach such sanctity of the image of their own sovereign, it would not be right to subject these more lively representations to the vulgar gaze'. As a parting shot, when the images are displayed, the party 'made precisely the same obeisance with which they had consented to honour the yellow curtain of the Chinese emperor on the occasion of the late feast at Tien-tsin' (2. 170). Davis reports with satisfaction that he noticed the mandarin Kwong, looking as 'black as thunder, so completely had this ceremony discomposed his established notions of the universal supremacy of the great emperor'. Returning the narrative frame to 1840, Davis adopts the pedagogic metaphor that would become a cliché in subsequent nineteenth-century British discourses of China, commenting that 'it might be well for Chinese assumption if lessons of this kind were more frequently taught it'.[62] He adds that 'increasing means of direct communication from the west' are 'calculated to multiply the opportunities' (2. 170). Ultimately, Davis predicts the long decline and fall of the Qing

---

[60] Wang, *White Lotus Rebels*, pp. 188–90, 228.
[61] Fu, *Documentary History*, pp. 404, 405.
[62] See James L. Hevia, *English Lessons: The Pedagogy of Imperialism in Nineteenth-Century China* (Durham, NC and London: Duke University Press, 2004).

or 'Tartar' dynasty, commenting 'it remains to be seen whether internal insurrection or foreign invasion is to overthrow a government that has already existed in profound peace for nearly two hundred years' (2. 247).

In Davis's *Sketches*, then, we can trace the crucial movement that Simpson has claimed differentiates a Romantic from an eighteenth-century attitude to the foreign and strange. In this intercultural encounter, not only does the full ritual and symbolic gift exchange no longer occur, but the partial exchange of presents is depicted entirely as a mean-spirited and hypocritical sham, cloaking the mercenary greed of a decaying despotism, brought to the point of military defeat some twenty-three years later. In framing the encounter this way, Davis ultimately privileges war and armed conflict as a means of settling accounts with China.

De Quincey, Gifts, and the Amherst Embassy

In most respects Davis, who was to become the mid-century's leading sinologist and foremost translator of Chinese literature, is a polar opposite from the century's British arch-sinophobe, Thomas De Quincey. De Quincey never visited China, he never learnt a Chinese written or spoken language, and he developed an intense phobia for all, or nearly all, things Asiatic. Yet in some ways, his writings on China may be placed on the same spectrum as, though far apart from, Davis's more sympathetic *Sketches*. Both De Quincey's much-discussed essay 'Opium and the China Question' (published in 1840 in *Blackwood's Magazine*) and Davis's *Sketches* were composed at roughly the same time during the beginning of the First Opium War. They belong to what I propose as a genre of Opium War writing that is deserving of critical attention in its entirety. Notably, both regard the Amherst embassy, rather than its more celebrated predecessor, as the touchstone of the modern British attitude to China, the moment that defines the relationship for the coming century.

De Quincey's essay is more extreme in its attitude to the Chinese and much less sympathetic than that of Davis, who genuinely appreciated Chinese culture and expressed sympathy with its peoples, if not always its emperors and courtiers. Throughout his essay De Quincey employs the informing, underlying master trope of the national, organic state to describe England. The Chinese empire is by contrast inorganic, 'torpid', and 'stagnant'. I have elsewhere discussed how De Quincey's writings on China extensively employ a new form of 'Romantic' anatomical and biological racism by locating the moral, ethic, and governmental characteristics of a culture in the ground of biological determinism. Zuroski-Jenkins's essay in this volume also surveys the substantial criticism relating De Quincey's psychology to contemporary pressures of empire more generally.[63] For instance, De Quincey states that a 'war for money, a war for indemnities, cannot be a hopeful war against a lazy, torpid body, without colonies, ships, commerce, and consequently without any great maritime depots'.[64]

In employing such somatic metaphors to explain what he sees as the dysfunction of Qing China, De Quincey is, once and for all, rejecting the eighteenth-century discourses of relativist cosmopolitanism and enlightened, civil rationality that informed the ideology of Macartney's embassy. He marshals a series of arguments, political, diplomatic, economic, legal, and racial, to justify the necessity, indeed inevitability, of armed conflict with China. He attacks Qing pretensions to universal overlordship as represented by the emperor and the ceremonial of the *koutou*. Significantly, writing in 1840, he picks out neither events from the Macartney embassy nor the from the reigning Daoguang Emperor's rule for his chief exemplars of this tendency but returns to 1816, the Amherst embassy and the reign of the Jiaqing Emperor:

> A sovereign who affects to make a footstool of the terraqueous globe, and to view all foreigners as barbarians, could not be approached with advantage by a body of manly Englishmen. In their character of merchants they were already contemptible in Oriental eyes; and the language of respectful homage, when coupled with the tone of self-respect, was viewed with indignation. Such a prince could be propitiated only by the Eastern style of servile prostration; and, were this style even steadily adopted, under the infinite caprices of absolute despots, it would but the more certainly court the vilest outrages. Some of our anti-national scribblers at home – as of course in vast capitals every variety of human nature will be developed – insisted upon it, that our English ambassador ought to have performed the *koutou*; that it was a mere form; and that the Pekin court usage was the law for those who had occasion to visit Pekin. Had Lord Amherst submitted to such

---

[63] Peter J. Kitson, *Romantic Literature, Race and Colonial Encounter* (New York: Palgrave, 2007), pp. 11–50; see also John Barrell, *The Infection of Thomas De Quincey: A Psychopathology of Imperialism* (New Haven, CT: Yale University Press, 1991); Nigel Leask, *British Romantic Writers and the East: Anxieties of Empire* (Cambridge: Cambridge University Press, 1992); Milligan, *Pleasure and Pains*, pp. 31–45.

[64] Thomas De Quincey, 'Opium and the China Question' and 'Postscript on the China and the Opium Question', *The Works of Thomas De Quincey, Volume 11: Articles from* Tait's Magazine *and* Blackwoods Magazine, ed. Julian North (London: Pickering and Chatto, 2003): 11. 532–72 (p. 546). Further references to this work will be cited by page number in parenthesis in the text.

degradation, the next thing would have been the requisition from the
English factory of beautiful English women, according to fixed description as annual presents for the Emperor. (548)

Here De Quincey moves from the imagined alterity of a despotic Jiaqing
Emperor to the paranoid image of the sexual sacrifice of English beauty
to what would later be described in numerous nineteenth- and twentieth-
century racist fictions as the 'yellow peril', apparently oblivious to the facts
that the Chinese did not allow European women to be present in Canton
and that the emperor had nowhere shown any such proclivities in this
area. De Quincey here imagines that so degraded have the merchants at
Canton become and so unmanly, that they might have actually acceded
to such a demand. Behind this comment is the trope of the infection of
'evil influences' of the east that De Quincey explored so vividly in his
Confessions of an English Opium Eater (1821). In this essay the Chinese are
immoral, wicked, bestial, degenerate, stupid, and even demonic.

So too De Quincey focuses upon the gift exchange. However, he cas-
tigates the British for their folly in selecting presents that meant nothing
to the Chinese and were illegible as signs to them. He reverses the chain
of signification fabricated by both embassies and exemplified in Davis's
account. Whereas I have argued that the discourse of the presents in both
embassies, but especially that of Amherst, serves to disguise the new, brutal
realities of British economic and commercial power, in effect, the burgeoning opium trade that they disavow through evasion or condemnation, De
Quincey argues that the British should not disguise their real message to
China: 'what we want with Oriental powers like China, incapably savage
in the moral sense, is a full explanation of our meaning under an adequate
demonstration of our power' (554). However conflicted and slippery De
Quincey may have been about his personal relationship to opium and
empire, he certainly was not shy of naming, establishing, and detailing in
full measure the facts of the trade. Rather the embassies had 'ruinously'
selected presents that they thought might appeal to the Chinese simply
because they appealed to themselves, including the ubiquitous diplomatic
gold and diamond snuff boxes. Focusing on the Amherst embassy De
Quincey writes that:

> As respected China the matter was worse. Amongst the presents
> assorted for the Celestial Emperor was actually a complex apparatus
> (suited to the bedchamber of an invalid), which cannot be mentioned
> with decorum. Oriental princes will not believe that the sovereign,
> who is nominally the presenter of such offerings, has not a personal

cognizance of the affront [...] And besides not to have cognizance of what concerned a brother potentate, is already an affront. (555)

The item that De Quincey comically or mischievously mentions here, presumably a commode of some description, does not feature in the inventory of either embassies. His point, however, is that the language of the gift exchange is arbitrary and simply determined by the customs of the giving nation, the British seem to want to give the standard overpriced gold and diamond snuff boxes to all and sundry on every diplomatic occasion. Power, for De Quincey, must be made visible and the language of diplomatic exchange rendered transparent as realpolitik: 'we must no longer allow our ambassadors to be called tribute-bearers, as were Lords Macartney and Amherst' (558). The British should 'dazzle' the Chinese with a gift of 'a train of our field artillery, with its entire establishment of horses, &c'. A 'visible demonstration of power contrasted with our extreme forbearance in using it' (560) is recommended by De Quincey as the appropriate message that should be sent to the Chinese. In this he is close to Davis, though the latter had recommended the full deployment of overwhelming force to shock and awe the court rather than De Quincey's threat.

The Amherst embassy provides an exemplar for both Davis and De Quincey of Britain's changing relations with China in the early half of the nineteenth century. Both writers explicitly link the Amherst embassy with the opening of the First Opium War. The new discourse of China that came to dominate British thinking later in the century is apparent in both of them to differing extents. Davis, an old China hand, who would become the second governor of the new treaty port of Hong Kong, ceded to the British in 1842 in the Treat of Nanking (Nanjing), demonstrates in his *Sketches* the emergence of this new understanding, whereas for De Quincey it seems to have appeared virtually fully formed in the essay. As well as noting the similarities between these two writers, we must also appreciate the nuances and differences and not assume, as so many seem to, that De Quincey, with his formidable rhetorical power, must provide *the only* representative voice of Romantic Britain on China. There is still much to be done in this area with many significant texts needing research and many voices both Chinese as well as British awaiting recovery. The literature of the First Opium War itself largely remains unexplored, except as historical source material despite the growth of recent studies about the experience of war in literature. This essay has modestly attempted to advance this process by complicating our understandings of the terrain in focusing on the Amherst embassy and its presence in the works of two notable writers on China of the Romantic period.

The Amherst Embassy in the Shadow of Tambora: Climate and Culture, 1816

ROBERT MARKLEY

On 10 April 1815, on the Indonesian island of Sumbawa, Mount Tambora exploded in the largest volcanic eruption in modern history. The force of the blast created a plume of aerosol sulfates, covering roughly nine million square kilometers, that reached the stratosphere and cooled temperatures in the northern hemisphere by approximately three degrees Centigrade for three years. In his recent study, *Tambora: The Eruption that Changed the World*, Gillen D'Arcy Wood documents Tambora's far-ranging effects in Switzerland, North America, Ireland, India and Yunnan Province in China: unseasonable cold, anomalous precipitation patterns, crop failures, famine, and millions of deaths worldwide from starvation and disease.[1] As Wood demonstrates, Tambora created a worldwide climatological catastrophe that paradoxically went nearly unrecognized at the time; there were only a handful of first-hand reports about the eruption from British ships in the vicinity of the island, and only one eyewitness account by the Raja of Sanngar, whose kingdom on Sumbawa was buried under meters of pyroclastic lava flows and ash. Across the northern hemisphere, from Thomas Jefferson's estate in Virginia to the Swiss Alps, where Byron and the Shelleys spent a wet, cold, and miserable summer in 1816, commentators grimly noted devastatingly unseasonable cold, crop failures, and the impoverishment of peasants and small farmers who found themselves starving, even as grain prices soared. Yet without eyewitness reports of the eruption and without a modern scientific understanding of volcanology, writers across Eurasia and North America interpreted the Year without a Summer in *moral* terms: the cascading effects of Tambora were seen, at once, as political failures of regimes in power; as proof of the moral and socioeconomic corruption of entire societies; and as evidence of divine or heavenly retribution. Tambora emerged as a *climatological* phenomenon only with the development in the late twentieth century of tree ring and ice core analyses and sophisticated computer modeling. Therefore, as

---

[1] Gillen D'Arcy Wood, *Tambora: The Eruption that Changed the World* (Princeton: Princeton University Press, 2014).

Wood suggests, the significance of this massive eruption for nineteenth-century global history – and for our understanding of 'future impacts of multidecadal climate change' – only recently has begun to reshape how scientists and now humanists can study the wide-ranging ecological effects of the Year without a Summer.[2]

In this essay, I want to resist the tendency to explore the litanies of horrors visited on unsuspecting populations by Tambora in order to examine how the aftermath of the eruption helped to color, in often subtle ways, the accounts of the failed Amherst embassy to Beijing in the summer of 1816. Although Amherst's abrupt dismissal before his audience with the Jiaqing Emperor solidified British perceptions of China as corrupt, backward, and insufferably proud, this spectacular failure was exacerbated, if not precipitated, by the unrecognized effects of Tambora. Assuming that the unseasonably hot and dry weather they encountered in August and September was normal, the British were put off by the difficulties they experienced in finding suitable accommodations, securing provisions, and adjusting to demands that they conduct negotiations with their hosts early in the morning before the heat soared. In an era when the state of a nation's agriculture still served, across Eurasia, as a barometer of its political and moral stability, these inconveniences – tied to unflattering observations about Chinese agro-political culture – helped to reinforce the sweeping claims about the decline of China that had gathered force in Britain following Macartney's embassy in 1792–93.[3] If the effects of the Tambora eruption did not decisively change British attitudes toward the Qing regime, the conditions they encountered in northeastern China tended to reinforce, for most members of the British embassy, negative perceptions of the Qing regime and Chinese culture.

Climate and Catastrophe

In analyzing the 'famine poems' of the Yunnan poet Li Yuyang, Wood calls attention to an emerging genre in early modern, eighteenth-century,

---

[2] Wood, *Tambora*, p. 233.

[3] On the Macartney embassy and it significance, see James Hevia, *Cherishing Men from Afar: Qing Guest Ritual and the Macartney Embassy of 1793* (Durham, NC: Duke University Press, 1995); Jeng-Guo S. Chen, 'The British View of Chinese Civilization and the Emergence of Class Consciousness', *The Eighteenth Century: Theory and Interpretation*, 45 (2004), 193–205; and, for British attitudes toward China during the period, Peter J. Kitson, *Forging Romantic China: Sino-British Cultural Encounters, 1760–1840* (Cambridge: Cambridge University Press, 2013).

and Romantic studies – the literature of climatic disaster – that has taken on new significance in the twenty-first century as critics draw on understandings of global warming to investigate the profound, even apocalyptic anxieties provoked by storms, eruptions, and earthquakes centuries ago.[4] In the early nineteenth century, however, no scientific study of volcanoes existed, and a science of climatology as such had yet to emerge.[5] In 1816 the default assumption remained that the Earth was banded, since Creation, by distinct latitudinal climatic zones, even as the work of James Hutton on geology, Pierre Simon de la Place on the evolution of the solar system, and Georges Cuvier on species extinction challenged both biblical chronologies of the age of the earth and ideas of climate as inherently stable.[6] Yet, even among scientists, that there was no accepted manner to distinguish between long-term climatic change and short-term weather anomalies, and the discovery of 'deep time' coexisted in often bizarre ways with the five thousand-year timeframe of biblical history.[7] Texts about environmental disasters well into the nineteenth century invoked

---

[4] Wood, *Tambora*, pp. 106–15. On the literature of disaster in the eighteenth century, see Robert Markley, '"Casualties and Disasters": Defoe and the Interpretation of Climactic Instability', *Journal of Early Modern Cultural Studies*, 8 (2008), 102–24; Eric Gidal, '"O happy Earth! reality of Heaven!": Melancholy and Utopia in Romantic Climatology', *Journal of Early Modern Cultural Studies*, 8 (2008), 74–101; and Jayne Elizabeth Lewis, *Air's Appearance: Literary Atmosphere in British Fiction, 1660–1794* (Chicago: University of Chicago Press, 2012). More generally, see Katharine Anderson, *Predicting the Weather: Victorians and the Science of Meteorology* (Chicago: University of Chicago Press, 2005), and Jan Golinski, *British Weather and the Climate of Enlightenment* (Chicago: University of Chicago Press, 2007).

[5] On the early history of climatology, see Richard Grove, 'The East India Company, the Raj, and the El Niño: The Critical Role Played by the Colonial Scientists in Establishing the Mechanisms of Global Climate Teleconnections 1770–1930', in *Nature and the Orient: The Environmental History of South and Southeast Asia*, ed. Richard H. Grove, Vinita Damodaran, and Satpal Sangwan (Delhi: Oxford University Press, 1998), pp. 301–23.

[6] See Robert Markley, 'A Brief History of Chronological Time', *Danish Yearbook of Philosophy*, 44 (2009), 59–75; Martin S. J. Rudwick, *Bursting the Limits of Time: The Reconstruction of Geohistory in the Age of Revolution* (Chicago: University of Chicago Press, 2005), and Rudwick, *Worlds before Adam: The Reconstruction of Geohistory in the Age of Reform* (Chicago: University of Chicago Press, 2008); and Ralph O'Connor, *The Earth on Show: Fossils and the Poetics of Popular Science, 1802–1856* (Chicago: University of Chicago Press, 2007).

[7] See Paolo Rossi, *The Dark Abyss of Time: The History of the Earth and the History of Nations from Hooke to Vico*, trans. Lydia G. Cochrane (Chicago: University of Chicago Press, 1984).

the typology of Noah's flood to interpret catastrophic events as evidence of God's displeasure with sinful populations and corrupt regimes.[8] This theological framework, however, carried with it (at least implicitly) the idea of a reversion to a norm: the covenant symbolized by the rainbow arching over receding waters promised a divinely orchestrated return to climatic stability. There was, as Wood argues persuasively, no analytical vocabulary beyond the theological rhetoric of sin, disaster, and retribution to make sense of a worldwide environmental crisis. Not surprisingly, then, the British travelers in 1816 China assume that they were encountering the 'normal' conditions of a stable, if alien, climate.

The published accounts of the Amherst embassy are, in many ways, atypical of the apocalyptic literature of 1816–18. The complex effects of the eruption – specifically, the interactions of the volcanic plume with the El Niño–Southern Oscillation – largely shielded eastern China from the terrors of failed harvests and killing frosts that decimated the rice crop in Yunnan. Consequently, the accounts of the embassy that I discuss may seem pedestrian compared to other works, like Mary Shelley's *Frankenstein*, produced in the aftermath of Tambora. Nonetheless, the narratives of John Francis Davis, Clarke Abel, Robert Morrison, and George Thomas Staunton reveal how nineteenth-century perceptions of China both influenced and were influenced by the entwined discourses of climate, agriculture, politics, and culture. As these accounts of Amherst's embassy suggest, the mutually constitutive discourses of climate and culture extend beyond ecological catastrophes to register complex, multivalent responses to alien environments and unfamiliar agricultural practices.

The Tambora Eruption: Climatological Effects in Eastern China

Twenty-five years ago, Tambora was (at best) a footnote in analyses of early nineteenth-century history. But with the eruption of Mount Pinatubo in the Philippines in 1992, volcanologists had their first opportunity to map and analyze data collected by satellites from a major volcanic event. This watershed in the study of the atmospheric responses to volcanoes produced hundreds of scientific papers on the chemical composition of aerosol sulfates injected into the stratosphere, the behavior of volcanic plumes when they reached the stratosphere, decreases in solar insolation

---

[8] See Stuart Peterfreund, "'Great Frosts and ... Some Very Hot Summers'": Strange Weather, the Last Letters, and the Last Days in Gilbert White's *The Natural History of Selbourne*', in *Romantic Science: The Literary Forms of Natural History*, ed. Noah Heringman (Albany, NY: SUNY Press, 2003), pp. 85–108.

in the northern hemisphere, and the complex effects of these phenomena on temperatures and precipitation in the northern hemisphere. As significantly for environmental historians, the computer models volcanologists developed could be adapted to study the effects of the Tambora eruption, an order of magnitude greater than Pinatubo.[9] In the past decade, numerous teams of scientists have sought to reconstruct the effects of volcanic eruptions on temperature and precipitation, recognizing that in an era of global warming the interactions between volcanic eruptions and climatic conditions have taken on new urgency. As the most powerful volcanic eruption recorded in tree-ring evidence, Tambora provides a test case for short-term responses to major climatic disruptions, and demonstrates that a global climatic event can have very different regional effects on timescales ranging from one to ten years.

At the risk of simplifying a dynamic area of ongoing scientific investigation, the computer models of the Tambora eruption suggest that different states of the El Niño–Southern Oscillation (ENSO) in the years immediately after the eruption would have produced substantially different short-term effects on weather patterns in eastern China.[10] ENSO refers to the complex atmospheric and oceanic interactions triggered by changes in sea surface temperatures in the western Pacific, and it is a primary driver of the global climate particularly in the tropics and subtropics. If sea surface temperatures warm in the eastern Pacific Ocean, much of the Pacific and Indian Ocean regions experience El Niño effects, including more precipitation during warmer summers over much of eastern China; if sea surface temperatures cool in the eastern Pacific and drive warm waters westward, La Niña effects dominate, with lower temperatures across South

---

[9] Pinatubo registered 6 on the Volcano Explosivity Index, the exponential scale used by volcanologists, and Tambora a 7.

[10] I draw on the following articles for this overview of recent research: K. J. Anchukaitis et al., 'Influence of Volcanic Eruptions on the Climate of the Asian Monsoon Region', *Geophysical Research Letters*, 37 (2010), L22703; D. Zanchettin et al., 'Background Conditions Influence the Decadal Climate Response to Strong Volcanic Eruptions', *Journal of Geophysical Research: Atmospheres*, 118 (2013), 4090–4106; C. E. Iles et al., 'The Effect of Volcanic Eruptions on Global Precipitation', *Journal of Geophysical Research: Atmospheres*, 118 (2013); J. Kandlbauer et al., 'Climate and Carbon Cycle Response to the 1815 Tambora Volcanic Eruption', *Journal of Geophysical Research: Atmospheres*, 118 (2013), 12,497–12,507; Masamichi Ohba et al., 'Impact of Strong Tropical Volcanic Eruptions on ENSO Simulated in a Coupled GCM', *Journal of Climate*, 26 (2013), 5169–5182; and Z. Zhuo et al., 'Proxy Evidence for China's Monsoon Precipitation Response to Volcanic Aerosols over the Past Seven Centuries', *Journal of Geophysical Research: Atmospheres*, 119 (2014), 6638–6652.

and Southeast Asia and southern China, and a general decrease in precipitation.[11] Historical reconstructions of ENSO states have begun to rely
on aggregated historical accounts of yearly weather conditions for specific
regions – like the Yangtze River Delta – and then use general patterns of
anomalous weather to produce an optimal model, or what one might call
a best-fit scenario, to match narrative accounts of temperature and precipitation patterns with computer simulations.[12] Their optimal match in
terms of reported precipitation and temperatures for China indicate what
is called a neutral state for ENSO – that is, a year without El Niño or La
Niña temperature anomalies greater than one degree centigrade – between
1815 and 1818. Recent work by some scientific teams, however, has not
ruled out weather patterns characteristic of La Niña conditions in 1816
that would have exacerbated precipitation shortfalls occasioned by the
weakness of the East Asian monsoon.

While temperatures in Yunnan Province fell at least three degrees below
normal and monsoon rains failed, eastern China, the area traversed by
the members of the Amherst embassy, saw near-normal temperatures
but dry, if not drought, conditions during what typically are the wettest
months of the year, July and August.[13] John Francis Davis, one of the
mission's translators, reports that members of the embassy 'were surprised

[11] See E. R. Cook et al., 'Asian Monsoon Failure and Megadrought during the
Last Millennium', *Science*, 328, 5977 (2010), 486–9. For a pioneering study of
ENSO effects on agriculture and food supplies in nineteenth-century Asia, see
Mike Davis, *Late Victorian Holocausts: El Niño Famines and the Making of the
Third World* (London: Verso, 2001).

[12] T. Jian et al., 'Yangtze Delta Floods and Droughts of the Last Millennium:
Abrupt Changes and Long Term Memory', *Journal of Theoretical and Applied
Climatology*, 82 (2005), 131–41. Even sophisticated studies have to rely on fairly
basic analyses of regional gazettes (keyword searches for 'cold' and its synonyms).
Dan Zhang, Richard Blender, and Klaus Fraedrich, 'Volcanic and ENSO Effects
in China in Simulations and Reconstructions: Tambora Eruption 1815', *Climate of
the Past Discussions*, 7 (2011), 2061–88; Zhang, Blender, and Fraedrich, 'Volcanoes
and ENSO in Millennium Simulations: Global Impacts and Regional Reconstructions in East Asia', *Theoretical and Applied Climatology*, 111 (2013), 437–54; and
Ohba et al., 'Impact of Strong Tropical Volcanic Eruptions on ENSO Simulated
in a Coupled GCM', p. 5178.

[13] See Congbin Fu et al., 'Climate of China and East Asian Monsoon', in *Regional
Climate Studies of China*, ed. Congbin Fu, Zhihong Jiang, Zhaoyong Guan, Jinhai
He, and Zhongfeng Xu (Berlin: Springer Verlag, 2008), pp. 1–48; C. Shen et al.,
'Exceptional Drought Events over Eastern China during the Last Five Centuries',
Climate Change, 85, 3–4 (2007), 453–71; and Y. B. Peng et al., 'Modeling of
Severe Persistent Droughts over Eastern China during the Last Millennium',
Climate of the Past, 10 (2014), 1079–91.

by the extreme heat of the climate at [...]. forty degrees of north latitude' with temperatures at noon reaching 90°F during their stay at Tungchow, outside of Beijing. A month later, traveling south toward Canton, he describes 'weather [...] so hot during the course of the day as to render it impossible to take exercise except in the morning or evening'.[14] Although eastern China was not devastated like Yunnan, local supply bottlenecks, food shortages, and rising grain prices in the wake of Tambora necessitated large grain purchases in much of the country.[15]

Amherst's Embassy: Court and Countryside

The ships in the Amherst expedition left England on the 9 February 1816 and arrived at Hong Kong five months later on 11 July; the members of the embassy were at sea, and for much of the voyage in the southern hemisphere, during the cold, wet European spring. The men on board had no first-hand knowledge of weather conditions in England; even Morrison, Staunton, and Davis, who joined the expedition in Canton, had spent most of their time in the humid, subtropical climate of the port and had little firsthand knowledge of the country beyond the tiny foreign quarter. Although Abel describes a spectacular sunset in the South China Sea – the 'vivid glory expanding into paths of light of the most beautiful hues' – that captures the stunning effects of the volcanic haze, there are no references in his or his fellows' published writings to indicate they were concerned by the severe weather affecting Europe.[16] In the accounts of the embassy, then, the unrecognized effects of Tambora on Chinese agriculture and society are filtered through the perspective of long-standing, Anglocentric ideas about the natural world and the temperate climates of northwestern Europe.[17] As a result, China is doubly distanced from

[14] John Francis Davis, *Sketches of China; Partly during an Inland Journey of Four Months between Peking, Nanking, and Canton* (London: Charles Knight, 1841), 1. 176; 1. 200.

[15] See Pierre-Etienne Will, *Bureaucracy and Famine in Eighteenth-Century China* (Stanford: Stanford University Press, 1990); and Susan M. Jones and Philip A. Kuhn, 'Dynastic Decline and the Roots of Rebellion', in *The Cambridge History of China*, 15 vols, ed. John K. Fairbank et al. (Cambridge: Cambridge University Press, 1978), 10. 107–62.

[16] Clarke Abel, *Narrative of a Journey in the Interior of China, and of a Voyage to and from that Country, in the Years 1816 and 1817* (London: Longman, Hurst, Rees, Orme, and Brown, 1818), p. 58. Wood quotes and discusses this passage briefly (p. 97).

[17] On ideas of the natural world as they emerged in Britain during the long eighteenth century, see Keith Thomas, *Man and the Natural World: Changing Attitudes*

what the Englishmen considered agro-climatological norms. First, in the interior of China, far from the East India Company factory at Canton, the British struggled to describe unfamiliar environments and tended to treat them analogically, comparing Chinese rivers, marshland, and agricultural regions (unfavorably) to their own (idealized) visions of the English countryside. Second, the anomalous conditions of 1816 were assumed to be typical of the entire empire, and therefore the agricultural landscape could serve as a measure of China's sociopolitical, technoscientific, and economic status relative to England's. In short, the effects of Tambora are inscribed silently and unwittingly into British pronouncements about China's climate, culture, and people.

Less studied than the Macartney embassy in the early 1790s, Amherst's failed mission nonetheless played a significant role in solidifying British views of China as a corrupt and backward-looking regime.[18] Like Macartney, Amherst headed a diplomatic effort that had two primary goals, both championed by the East India Company: to expand British trade to Chinese ports besides Canton, and to secure a permanent British ambassador in Beijing to deal with a range of commercial issues. The embassy included several men who were fluent in Chinese and had lived at Canton for some years: the British missionary Robert Morrison, the official translator; George Thomas Staunton, the second commissioner of the embassy and the only person who, as a young boy, also had been in Macartney's entourage; and John Francis Davis, then twenty-one, a writer for the Company, and later, in the 1840s, governor of Hong Kong.[19] Their accounts, along with those of Henry Ellis, the third commissioner, and Clarke Abel, the medical officer and naturalist, constitute the most significant of the fifteen published accounts of the embassy. Yet, as Eun Kyung Min has argued, even with three men fluent in Chinese, the British were unable to bridge the gap between Western and Chinese ideas of commerce and civility.[20] The overriding commercial aims of the Amherst

---

in England 1500–1800 (London: Allen Lane, 1983), and, for the late eighteenth and early nineteenth centuries, Eric Gidal, Ossianic Unconformities: Bardic Poetry in the Industrial Age (Charlottesville, VA: University of Virginia Press, 2015).

[18] Gao Hao, 'The Amherst Embassy and British Discoveries in China', History, 99 (2014), 568–87.

[19] See Michael Greenberg, British Trade and the Opening of China (Cambridge: Cambridge University Press, 1951), and Hosea Ballou Morse, The Chronicles of the East India Company Trading to China 1635–1834, 5 vols. (Oxford: Clarendon Press, 1926, 1929).

[20] Eun Kyung Min, 'Narrating the Far East: Commerce, Civility, and Ceremony

mission, she notes, forced the British into the 'curious position of show-casing British opulence, grandeur, arts and knowledge' in order to further a commercial agenda that was at odds with Qing standards of social class, ethnic and national identity, and diplomatic status.[21]

In the eyes of the court, Great Britain could be acknowledged only as a tributary kingdom and its representatives subject to the ritual pro-tocols of deferential submission. With the experience of the Macartney embassy firmly in mind, members of the mission were divided on whether or not Amherst should perform the traditional *kow-tow* before the Jiaqing Emperor, given that his orders allowed him the leeway to do so if he could secure the concessions that the East India Company sought. As Davis observed, 'the welfare of the company's trade was really the chief object of the embassy', even though he remained opposed to 'a servile compliance with the demands of the imperial government' (1. 56–7) that would force Amherst to play the role of a tribute-bearing dependent rather than an ambassador negotiating to strengthen commercial relations between two equal and sovereign nations.

There are literally hundreds of pages in the accounts devoted to dis-secting the negotiations between the Chinese and the British during Amherst's journey, by riverboat and cart, from Tianjin to Beijing. Mor-rison's account of one such exchange en route to Beijing seems as though it could have been lifted from a Gilbert and Sullivan operetta; but it was taken with grim seriousness by both Qing officials, who were adamant about Amherst's performing the *kow-tow*, and the British, who wanted to avoid the symbolic deference of a tributary people:

> It was proposed that if some of his Imperial Majesty's Ministers would perform the Tartar ceremony [the *kow-tow*] before his Royal Highness the Prince Regent's picture, the Embassador [Amherst] would perform it before the Emperor; Kwang [a Qing minister] said, with a counte-nance half sneering and half dissatisfaction, 'To what are we to perform the ceremony? we are not sent to England – if we were, we would not object to perform it.' This last expression was taken hold of [by Amherst], and replied to thus: 'If the Emperor will in writing declare it to be his will, that, in case of [a Qing] Embassador going to England, that Embassador shall perform the Tartar ceremony, I [Amherst] will perform it to the Emperor.'

in the Amherst Embassy to China (1816–1817)', *Studies in Voltaire and the Eighteenth Century* (2004), 160–80.
[21] Min, 'Narrating the Far East', p. 167.

The fact is that all such propositions, as they imply a perfect equality, are more offensive to the Chinese and Tartars than declining to
perform their ceremony. (38–9)

The British concern with civility and 'perfect equality' structures
Morrison's and his fellows' response to what they considered the uncivil
treatment they received when they finally reached the court. As both
parties' obsession with protocol and 'ceremony' suggests, 'civility' is
performative, predicated on class-specific expectations about manners,
dress, comportment, courtesy, hospitality, domestic order, and national
and personal senses of honor. In international encounters, in particular,
the embodied practices of 'civility' work to mediate linguistic, religious,
and cultural differences and to promote the convenient fiction that
like-minded gentlemen – of whatever nation, religion, or race – share
fundamental socioeconomic values and therefore should be able to forge
imagined communities of sympathetic interest across the divides of religion, language, culture, and race.[22] By the time of Amherst's embassy,
'perfect equality' had assumed frankly commercial overtones, and British
expectations of 'civil' behavior hinged on both parties acknowledging
that the expansion of trade was an essential demonstration of transcultural 'understanding'. Civility, however, turned out to depend as well
on Amherst's and his retinue's embodied experience of unfamiliar and
apparently unexpected climatic conditions.

Although the embassy's primary focus was on the diplomatic goals
of their mission and the behavior of Qing officials, all of the published
accounts took time to record the writers' impressions of what they saw
as the poverty of Chinese peasants and what Morrison called the 'flat,
marshy, unproductive, gloomy region[s]' through which the embassy
traveled.[23] In narrative and ideational terms, it is difficult to separate Morrison's, or Staunton's, or Abel's accounts of the failure of their mission
from their descriptions of the Chinese countryside, infrastructure, and
people. The very condition of the land, in their eyes, reflects the values and
assumptions of a moral agro-geography shared, although in very different
idioms, by the Manchus, Chinese, and the British: a prosperous agricultural economy that produces abundant harvests reflects fundamental

22 Robert Markley, *The Far East and the English Imagination, 1600–1730*
(Cambridge: Cambridge University Press, 2006), pp. 104–34.
23 Robert Morrison, *A Memoir of the Principal Occurrences during an Embassy from
the British Government to the Court of China in the Year 1816* (London: Printed for
the Editor, 1820), p. 16.

principles of good government, social stability, and providential favour; in contrast, a stressed or failing agricultural system in 'unproductive, gloomy regions[s]' testifies to corrupt, inadequate, or incompetent government; to the moral and spiritual sins of the people themselves; and, for most of the British members of the expedition, to the technoscientific backwardness of a sclerotic empire.[24] The analytical vocabularies of climate and culture invariably overlap, and the British perceptions of Chinese sociopolitical culture are interwoven with observations about the empire's limitations in agriculture, transportation, and flood control. Significantly, at least in their narrative retellings after the events, Morrison and Staunton imply that the mission failed because the court was brutally insensitive to the effects of heat, dust, and travel on Amherst and his retinue.

The British accounts of the failure of the mission in Bejing dovetail so closely on the specifics they suggest the narratives may have been coordinated. Staunton and Morrison, the translators throughout the confrontation, report a similar sequence of rhetorical and even physical confrontations.[25] The party arrived after a bone-jarring ride across the uneven granite streets of Beijing, as Morrison says, with 'Lord Amherst, being really fatigued by traveling all night [on] a dangerous road' (56–7). Wearied by his travels through the unaccustomed August heat, the ambassador 'pleaded indisposition', trying to delay his audience with the emperor until the following day because, according to Morrison, 'he could neither see any person nor transact any business till he had taken rest' (57). After much importuning by court officials, however, Amherst 'alighted from his carriage and was led [...] to a small unfurnished dirty apartment' where 'a crowd of persons of all ages and ranks filled the room [...] The Embassador directed that the crowd should be desired to withdraw, and leave him alone. The crowd of Chinese and Tartar officers paid not the least attention, but continued to press forward to see the strangers' (57). Rather than a formal reception and hospitality that would allow the British to gather themselves for their audience, they are left 'disappointed, vexed, and weary, [sitting] down on [a] bench', while messengers to the audience

---

[24] See Mark Elvin, 'Who was Responsible for the Weather? Moral Meteorology in Late Imperial China', *Osiris*, 13 (1998), 213–37. On responses to the volcanic haze over Europe after the eruption of the Icelandic volcano Laki in the 1780s, see Peterfreund, '"Great Frosts and ... Some Very Hot Summers"', pp. 85–108; and Tobias Menely, '"The Present Obfuscation": Cowper's *Task* and the Time of Climate Change', *PMLA*, 127 (2012), 477–92.

[25] Davis was not in the chamber when Amherst refused to attend the Emperor, and his account follows Morrison's closely.

hall in the palace conduct indirect negotiations about when Amherst will appear before the emperor.

The Qing violations of what the British considered civil behavior are set into a different context by Staunton, an East India Company employee more discerning about social hierarchies than the lower-class British missionary. He describes 'two classes among the courtiers present, crowding into the room', 'the princes of the blood and the eunuchs'. From his perspective as an employee of the East India Company based in Canton, he assumes that 'nearly all of them [were] Tartars' (Manchus) because no 'assembly of the superior class, or indeed any class, of Chinese, would have shown themselves so totally regardless, not merely of the considerations of courtesy, but even of the common feelings of humanity'.[26] This effort to divide the court along ethnic lines reflects, in some measure Staunton's own divided reaction to China: respect for the decaying grandeur of a cultured and ancient civilization, and impatience with the failure of the Qing officials to conform to 'modern', European notions of diplomacy, social customs, and international commerce.

The court, however, had firm ideas of the deference expected from a tributary British mission, and Morrison describes the standoff that led to the embassy's abrupt dismissal several hours after it had arrived. After refusing an invitation from the empress's brother, 'Duke Ho', to conduct him to the court, Amherst

> begged to be led to the apartments intended for him. The Duke [the emperor's brother-in-law] then came himself, and said, he wanted to introduce the Embassador to his Majesty [...]. The Embassador without rising said, that he felt unwell, and begged his Imperial Majesty would graciously decline requiring him to attend that day. The Duke said, 'You shall use your own ceremony' [bowing on one knee, rather than the *kow-tow*]. The Embassador requested the Duke to supplicate his Majesty to decline requiring an audience. The Duke became very anxious. The perspiration stood on his face. He went out – came again – took the Embassador by the arm to urge him away; and told an attendant to help him. The Embassador shook them from him, and said he would not go so, repeating the request to the Duke that he would report his case to the Emperor, and entreat his Majesty's acquiescence. (57)

Although Amherst's excuses of ill health and fatigue might be taken at face value, Staunton suggests that there were other factors in play in the

---

[26] George Thomas Staunton, *Notes of the Proceedings and Occurrences during the British Embassy to Pekin, in 1816* (London: Havant Press, 1824), pp. 120–1.

ambassador's refusal – notably, the 'mortifying' prospect of the 'unexpected and vexatious exposure of eight or nine of the principal persons of the British Embassy, in their dusty travelling dresses of the preceding day, and under every disadvantage of health and appearance from their night travelling, to the gaze of the whole imperial court of China' (118). The 'disadvantage[s] of health and appearance' effectively cast the British into the role of the uncultured barbarians that the Qing officials want them to play. Although it is understandable that Amherst would have wanted to change into suitable clothes, he and his party felt aggrieved that they were being tricked into an audience, 'fraudulently brought to the doors of the palace' (59), as Morrison puts it, before they had a chance to rest and change into appropriate clothing. However fatigued Amherst may have been, his refusal to appear at the early morning audience was considered an insult by the emperor, and the embassy was dismissed summarily. Because the British ship that had brought the embassy from Canton already had departed from its anchorage near Tianjin, the British were escorted along a four-month-long route down rivers and the Grand Canal, through the interior of eastern China, to Canton.

The effects of Tambora appear in these narratives in the details noted by Staunton and Morrison, particularly in the way that the vexations of the British are framed. Staunton's attention to the party's 'dusty' clothes, and Morrison's description of the 'dirty' apartment and the 'perspiration' on the Duke's face suggest how the weather conditions appeared to Amherst, and even to long-time residents of Canton, like Morrison, Staunton, and Davis. Temperatures in early September in Beijing now average about 30° Centigrade, and even in the aftermath of Tambora during the Dalton Minimum,[27] a late summer in East Asia might seem unusually hot and tiring for Amherst. According to Davis, the 'thermometer in [his] boat read 87°' Fahrenheit the day the embassy reached Tianjin, and he later happily reports that morning temperatures fell to 70°, although they rose above 80° in the afternoons throughout their journey to Beijing.[28] The consensus scientific models of the volcanic veil over the region indicate a decrease in precipitation over eastern China in the aftermath of Tambora, and the dust and dirt that seem to be everywhere in the Forbidden City register

[27] On the Dalton Minimum at the end of the Little Ice age, see Brian Fagan, *The Little Ice Age: How Climate Made History 1300–1850* (New York: Basic Books, 2000).
[28] Davis, *Sketches*, 1. 59. Robert Markley, 'Monsoon Cultures: Climate and Acculturation in Alexander Hamilton's *A New Account of the East-Indies*', *New Literary History*, 38 (2007), 527–50.

the effects of a drought which, while not as severe as in Yunnan, affected travel, decorum, and accommodations.[29] On 18 August, Davis found the ground on the riverbanks 'hard and dry' (98), although he records rain that afternoon, a significant storm a few days later, and rain again on the 30th of the month when the embassy left Beijing. In this context, the litany of adjectives in the British accounts – 'dirty', 'dusty' – register conditions in eastern China during the comparatively dry August of 1816 – typically the wettest month of the year in the Beijing–Tianjin region. The striking difference in conditions in eastern China from Yunnan in the southwest may help suggest why the court was slow to react to reports that poor harvests in the south and west were driving up grain prices: given the tenets of the 'moral meteorology' prevalent in Confucian thought, it was difficult to explain how the still-prosperous regions around Beijing could be culpable for cold summers and failed monsoons a thousand miles and more to the southwest.[30] Although Davis attributed the Emperor's rejection of Amherst's request to postpone his audience to the 'more than Machiavellian tortuosities and bad faith of that prince of Chinese jugglers, Duke Ho' (161), the court had more important matters to attend to than barbarians seeking additional ports to offload their opium. Worried about the depredations of pirates in the South China Seas and dealing with the unrest provoked by a second year of poor harvests, grain shortages, and widespread hunger, the Jiaqing Emperor was more zealous than his predecessor, the Qianlong Emperor, in trying to restrict foreign influences to Macao and Canton.[31]

However humiliating their dismissal from court, the journey to Canton gave members of the British embassy a rare opportunity to observe the countryside and its peoples without the pomp, circumstance, and obligations that attend diplomatic missions. Different accounts offer different perspectives on the people and the countryside: Staunton, a staunch defender of the East India Company's monopoly on the Canton trade, offers harsh views of the countryside and its inhabitants; Davis, ultimately

---

[29] Davis, *Sketches of China*, 1. 43, notes 'tempestuous' weather on 7–8 August, which delayed the embassy as it was about to embark on its river journey.

[30] See Elvin, 'Who was Responsible for the Weather?', pp. 213–37.

[31] On grain purchases and fluctuations in reserves during this period, see Pierre-Etienne Will and R. Bin Wong, *Nourish the People: The State Civilian Granary System in China, 1650–1850* (Ann Arbor, MI: University of Michigan Press, 1991), pp. 77–82. On the response to piracy and British attempts in 1802 and 1807 to seize the Portuguese trading entrepot of Macao, see Wensheng Wang, *White Lotus Rebels and South China Pirates: Crisis and Reform in the Qing Empire* (Cambridge, MA: Harvard University Press, 2014), pp. 209–52.

a firm supporter of 'free trade', paradoxically, for the future Governor of Hong Kong, is an often sympathetic observer of Chinese socioeconomic and political culture. Abel frequently vents his frustration with the Chinese restrictions on his observations; Davis, while registering complaints about food beneath the dignity of the British embassy and the bone-jarring ride to the Forbidden City in 'wretched little Chinese tiled carts ... on the ruined granite road' (148), nonetheless has a far more positive view of the people, culture, and landscapes he encounters.

As the only member of the embassy who could compare conditions in 1816 to those he witnessed as a boy on Marcartney's journey, Staunton maintained that 'the prosperity of [the Chinese] empire has been on the decline under the government of the present emperor' (157). He peppers his account of the journey from Beijing to Canton with descriptions of decay and poverty: 'These hills [in Jiangxi Province] are perfectly barren, and destitute even of trees – no signs whatever of cultivation or inhab- itants, except at their feet near the river, or in the lowest parts of the intervening vallies' (380).[32] At least some members of the embassy echo this view of the Chinese countryside, even as they exhibit what may seem, from a western, twenty-first- century perspective, a naïve and parochial understanding of a natural environment different from England's. Abel, the expedition's naturalist, compared the low-lying marshlands south and east of Tianjin to the environmental conditions familiar to his British readers:

> No country in the world can afford, I imagine, fewer objects of inter- est to any species of traveller, than the banks of [the] Pei-ho (Haihe River) [....] The land is marshy and sterile, the inhabitants are poor and squalid, their habitations mean, dirty, dilapidated, and the native productions of the soil are few and unattractive. (75)[33]

Traveling along the Haihe River as it winds through wetlands, Abel voices a deep-seated and long-standing British suspicion of marshes and swamps. The Scots historian William Robertson gave voice to these suspicions in his *History of the Americas*: 'The northern provinces of America', he wrote,

---

[32] Gao offers an extended discussion of this passage.

[33] In the regions of East China, between Tianjin and Beijing, Kandlbauer and his collaborators' model of the carbon cycle actually suggests an *increase* in plant productivity, if one assumes a neutral ENSO state. This increase, of course, could include non-crop plants and energetic plant growth in Abel's 'sterile' marshes (Kandlbauer et al., 'Climate and Carbon Cycle Response to the 1815 Tambora Volcanic Eruption', p. 12,501).

'wear [an] uncultivated aspect', where 'prodigious marshes overspread the plains, and few marks appear of human activity in any attempt to culti-vate or embellish the earth.' Like Englishmen seeing the Chinese land-scape for the first time, seventeenth-century colonists 'were astonished at their first entrance to the New World. It appeared to them waste, soli-tary, uninviting.'[34] Rather than seeing wetlands as ecologically diverse and resource-rich areas – important to local diets and economies – English nature writers in the seventeenth and eighteenth centuries register their horror for regions that were difficult to mark by property lines, expen-sive and time-consuming to drain, supposedly prone to the 'bad air' that caused disease, and resistant to agricultural 'improvement'.[35] For Abel, the marshlands along the river are inhospitable to the kind of agricultural stewardship that the English considered as firm evidence of prosperity.

Underlying his observations about the countryside are incipient, half-formed analogies between East and West. At times, when Abel finds himself in landscapes that remind him, in at least some respects, of more familiar environments, the tone of his descriptions changes markedly. As the embassy travels upriver, leaving behind what Davis calls 'the flat dis-tricts near the sea [and their] extensive salt-works' (51), Abel finds that

> the country gradually, though, slowly improved. The patches of millet became of greater extent; and we saw a greater number of people per-fectly clothed. This alteration of character was still more apparent when we approached with a few miles of Tien-sing [Tianjin]. Large fields of corn and pulse were now frequently contiguous, the dwellings more substantial, and the inhabitants more healthy and robust than any we had observed before. (77)

In the agricultural region outside of Tianjin, China, in Abel's eyes, takes on the appearance of propertied and productive land. The fields are 'contiguous', indicating property divisions; the houses are 'substantial', implying a landowning class invested in the agricultural 'improvement' of the region; and the people 'healthy and robust', as though they were counterparts of British gentry and yeomanry. Viewing China through the prism of Anglocentric expectations, Abel briefly finds socionatural markers in the landscape that conform to his assumptions and values

---

[34] William Robertson, *History of America* (London: Strahan and Caddell, 1777), 1. 257–8.
[35] See Andrew McRae, *God Speed the Plough: The Representation of Agrarian England, 1500–1660* (Cambridge: Cambridge University Press, 1996).

about agro-political prosperity. For his part, writing his narrative of the embassy a quarter- century later, Davis describes 'the vast numbers of grain junks' in 'close contiguity' (80) that are moored along the riverbank and stretch for miles. Without realizing that he is witnessing a boom market in grain shipments in the aftermath of Tambora, he interprets the commercial traffic on the river as evidence of a material prosperity that exists in a realm distinct from the palace intrigues that doomed the diplomatic mission.

Yet as the party moves inland towards Beijing, Abel is struck by what he assumes is the inability of the Chinese to transform wetlands into productive fields of grain. Sorghum 'clothed the bank of the river', he acknowledges, but

> its high and thickly planted stems had prevented our seeing the country beyond ... and had led us to suppose that it was generally well cultivated. I now found it to consist of a sterile marsh, extending to an undefinable distance. The soil collected from the river, and sometimes deposited by its overflow, frequently rendered its immediate precincts productive, whilst all beyond was untouched by the hand of the cultivator [...] [A]s the Chinese may excel in obtaining abundant products from land naturally fertile, they are much behind other nations in the art of improving that which is naturally barren. (87)

In passages such as these, Abel's descriptions of the sterility of the land restrict the evidence for 'civilized' agricultural cultivation to those cereal crops valued by the British at the expense of salt fields. His term, 'sterile marsh', does not suggest so much that the wetlands are a biological desert but an unfamiliar ecological region on the verges of salt marshes that have not been drained, manured, and planted with grain. In 1816, with wetlands suffering from an unusually dry summer, salt marshes and silted wetlands appear to Abel as though they were mud flats. At a time when China's population was close to 350 million, and Britain's just over 13 million, the idea that *any* land could remain uncultivated in so populous a nation suggests to Abel, as it does to Staunton, a web of interlocking administrative, governmental, and technoscientific failures. In turn, the implications of these 'sterile marsh[es]' are projected on to Chinese civilization itself as evidence of its socioeconomic, agricultural, and moral shortcomings.

The people themselves, like the land they inhabit, therefore appear to Abel uncultivated. He is troubled by the differences he observes among people of different classes, particularly the variations of skin colour that make the Chinese appear to be the 'inhabitants of different climates [rather] than of the same district' (78). As an Englishman versed in the emerging scientific racism of his day, he is shocked that the labourers pulling the boats along the Grand Canal are tanned by the sun: 'The dark copper colour of those who were naked contrasted so strongly with the paleness of those who were clothed, that it was difficult to conceive such distinct hues could be the consequence of greater or lesser exposure to the same degree of solar and atmospheric influence' (78).[36] The sun-tanned skin of the laborers suggests how different the effects of Tambora were in eastern China from those in Western Europe or Yunnan: there was no Year without a Summer, but a warm, prolonged period of dry weather. Abel can 'conceive' of the effects of ultraviolet radiation only when some of the laborers strip to swim out to the embassy's boats, and he observes that their legs make them appear 'to have on a pair of light-coloured pantaloons' (78). Troubled by the differences in skin tone and the varying facial features of the Chinese, Abel asks a question fundamental to the tenets of late eighteenth- and early nineteenth-century racial climatology of the sort popularized by Montesquieu and the Comte de Buffon: 'Can these modifications of physical character depend on varied circumstances of individual habits in the same climate'? (79). For Abel, the sun-tanned laborers destabilize the emerging idea of distinct racial categories at a time when racial classifications in Europe were hardening into scientific racism.[37] Climate is written on foreign bodies not as the immutable generalizations of armchair savants in Europe but as the contingent and multi-vectored effects that destabilize the values and assumptions of climatological determinism.

Such uncomfortable questions may help to explain Abel's aggressively hostile – and defensive – attitude toward the living conditions he observed among peasants. Chinese villages between Tianjin and Beijing, he declares, are characterized by 'dirt, squalidness, and extreme poverty' (87). Although troubled by the physiological differences he observes between the upper and lower classes, Abel apparently feels himself on firmer ground in judging the living conditions of peasants as evidence of Chinese backwardness: their 'habitations were miserable beyond any thing

[36] Roxanne Wheeler, *The Complexion of Race: Categories of Difference in Eighteenth-Century British Culture* (Philadelphia: University of Pennsylvania Press, 2000); and Felicity A. Nussbaum, *The Limits of the Human: Fictions of Anomaly, Race, and Gender in the Long Eighteenth Century* (Cambridge: Cambridge University Press, 2003).

[37] See Michael Keevak, *Becoming Yellow: A Short History of Racial Thinking* (Princeton: Princeton University Press, 2011).

which England can exemplify. Built of mud, and divided into unfurnished rooms, ventilated by several apertures,' he continues, 'they looked more like the dens of beasts than the habitations of men' (87). By comparing Chinese peasants to foxes – the most notable den-dwelling 'beasts' indigenous to nineteenth-century England – Abel casts at least the lower classes beyond the pale of a transcultural idea of the human. As significantly, the vehemence of his language serves a compensatory function by directing his anger (and his embarrassment at the embassy's failure) toward the 'uncivilised' qualities of the Chinese. Rather than trying to imagine what Bruno Latour terms a 'reciprocal anthropology', Abel merely complains, without noting the stunning irony, that the Chinese 'looked upon us as a strange species of animal, whom it was curious to observe, but as beings without the pale of civilised treatment' (106).[38] In effect, he projects on to the Chinese the same prejudices that he voices; the conflicting views on commerce and civility described by Min both inform and are informed by reciprocal efforts to enforce distinctions between civilized and barbarian peoples, between humans and subhumans. To underscore his orientalist distinctions between the English and the Chinese, Abel must treat the conditions he observes during the summer of 1816 – the knock-on economic effects of Tambora – as both the occasion for and evidence of his views about topography, climate, racial physiology, and the downward spiral of the Qing Empire.

Davis and the Ecologies of China

Morrison, Staunton, and Abel published their accounts within a few years of the embassy, but Davis's *Sketches* did not appear until 1841, after the beginning of the First Opium War. By the time of its publication, Davis had established a reputation as one of Britain's most knowledgeable commentators on China, having produced translations of Chinese literary texts and a two-volume study, *The Chinese: A General Description of the Empire of China and Its Inhabitants* (1836), among the more measured and influential works about the Middle Kingdom published in the prelude to war. His retrospective description of the embassy is interspersed with suggestions about the military vulnerability of Tianjin and the potential use of rivers as conduits for British troops and weaponry; yet the first volume of *Sketches*, in particular, assumes the generic character of a travel

---

[38] Bruno Latour, *We Have Never Been Modern* (Cambridge, MA: Harvard University Press, 1993).

narrative through China, a familiar genre for more than two hundred years in Europe.[39] In contrast to some of his criticisms in *Sketches* of the court's behavior and the machinations of the emperor's advisors, notably 'Duke Ho', Davis resists the tendency to generalize from his experiences in 1816. In contrast to Abel, Morrison and Staunton, he separates his affective responses to the suspect morality of some Qing officials from the racial and ethnic typologies that colour the others' portraits of the empire.

While critical of the policies of the Qing government and insistent in defending his position that Amherst should not have kow-towed to the emperor, Davis takes pains to emphasize that 'upon the whole, the Chinese [are] among the most good-humoured people in the world, and the most peaceable; and the chief causes of this must be sought in their political and social institutions'.[40] Significantly, Davis attributes what he has seen 'of extreme poverty and destitution' in China to demographic and ecological pressures rather than racial or technoscientific inferiority: 'Whatever there is in the country of extreme poverty and destitution arises solely from the unusual degree to which the population is made to press against the means of subsistence [...] and not from any fault in the *distribution* of wealth, which is perhaps far more equal here than in any other country' (1. 242). This rejection of orientalist biases allows Davis to envision at least an incipiently 'modern' China waiting to emerge from Confucian traditionalism. Ecological and demographic constraints produce, in his eyes, the paradoxes that define late Qing society. The comparative poverty of the upper classes leads to a widespread obsession with 'the ranks and conditions of men' to compensate for the fact that there 'is much less inequality in fortunes' (1. 242) in China than in Britain. In praising the '*cheerful* industry' of the people as the 'best proof in the world that [they] possess their full share of the results of their own labour' (1. 194), Davis attributes to the Chinese the capacity and incentive for individual initiative that Adam Smith and David Ricardo describe as a fundamental mechanism for economic progress.[41] In mirroring the practices and desires of free-born

---

[39] See Donald Lach, with Edwin J. van Kley, *Asia in the Making of Europe*. 3 vols (Chicago: University of Chicago Press, 1965–93).

[40] John Francis Davis, *The Chinese: A General Description of the Empire of China and Its Inhabitants*. 2 vols (London: Charles Knight, 1836), 1. 199.

[41] On the comparative 'modernity' of the Chinese economy through the eighteenth century, see R. Bin Wong, *China Transformed: Historical Change and the Limits of European Experience* (Ithaca, NY: Cornell University Press, 1997); Kenneth Pomeranz, *Europe, China, and the Making of the Modern World Economy* (Princeton: Princeton University Press, 2000); and Pomeranz, 'Their Own Path to Crisis? Social Change, State-Building, and the Limits of Qing Expansion,

Englishmen, the Chinese, if not their isolationist government, become, for Davis, part of an imagined civil polity that – in 1836 – suggests how amenable they would be to an accommodation with Britain's expansionist policies of 'free-trade'.[42] In this respect, the entrenched conservatism of the ruling elites offers opportunities for future legions of British engineers and investors to modernize China's infrastructure as well as its trade policies.

Although Davis resists the tendency to impose a racialist, climatological determinism on the Chinese by rejecting the widespread European notion that China's demographic pressures stem from systemic technoscientific and political failures, he remains critical of much of the infrastructure he encounters.[43] One of the possible, if hard to document, effects of the Tambora eruption in eastern China may have been increased silting in major rivers as a consequence of two related factors. First, the failures of the monsoon to the west, near the headwaters of the Yellow River (for example) may have slowed the flow of water to the sea, thereby allowing sediments to build up rapidly in shallow sections.[44] As sediments clogged tributaries and smaller rivers, even below-average rainfalls might have triggered flooding. Second, the cold, post-Tambora winter of 1815 meant a much-delayed and uneven spring thaw, and a late snow melt might in the west may have increased the silt carried downriver to the east. More silt, more flooding.[45] On 30 September, Davis observed a flooded countryside in Shandong Province as the party navigated the Grand Canal:

> the swamps increased rapidly, until the whole country, as far as the eye could reach, displayed the effects of a most extensive recent inundation.

c.1770–1840', in *The Age of Revolutions in Global Context, c. 1760–1840*, ed. David Armitage and Sanjay Subrahmanyam (Basingstoke: Palgrave Macmillan, 2010), pp. 189–208.

[42] Robert Markley, 'China and the English Enlightenment: Literature, Aesthetics, and Commerce', *Literature Compass*, 11 (2014), 517–27.

[43] Michael Adas, *Machines as the Measure of Men: Science, Technology, and Ideologies of Western Dominance* (Ithaca, NY: Cornell University Press, 1989).

[44] See the explanation of the canal system in Randall A. Dodgen, 'Hydraulic Evolution and Dynastic Decline: The Yellow River Conservancy, 1796–1855', *Late Imperial China*, 12 (1991), 36–63. On sedimentary build-up over the last millennium and its complex consequences for understanding riverine dynamics, see Mark Elvin and Su Ninghu, 'Action at a Distance: The Influence of the Yellow River on Hangzhou Bay since A. D. 1000', in *Sediments of Time: Environment and Society in Chinese History*, ed. Mark Elvin and Liu Ts'ui-jung (Cambridge: Cambridge University Press, 1998), pp. 344–407.

[45] See Robert Marks, '"It Never Used to Snow": Climatic Variability and Harvest Yields in Late Imperial South China, 1650–1850', in *Sediments of Time*, pp. 411–46.

The waters were on a level with those of the canal, and there was no need of dams, which were themselves nearly under water [....] Clumps of large trees, cottages, and towers, were to be seen on all sides, half under water, and deserted by the inhabitants. The number of these towers led to the inference that they were provided as places of refuge in case of inundation, which must here be very frequent [....] All within range of the eye was swamp, and coldness, and desolation – if fact, a vast inland sea, as many of the large boats at a distance were *hull down*, or invisible except their masts. (1. 257–8)

Davis's assumption that the towers serve as a place of refuge for the victims of frequent 'inundation' normalizes what, to many of his readers, would seem a climate of catastrophic extremes. The flooding of 1816, perhaps exacerbated by the effects of the Tambora eruption, marks both the technoscientific limitations of hydraulic engineering in China and the resiliency of a people of 'the highest perseverance and industry' able to maintain the canal against 'incalculable' difficulties (1. 258). The 'coldness' and 'desolation' of the flooded landscape marks the limits of Davis's praise of the Chinese and their culture. In 1816, the empire remains at the mercy of its climate of extremes: heat and dust in the north, and a 'vast inland sea' flooding the countryside north of the Yellow River.

If Amherst's failed embassy testifies to the gaps between Chinese and British ideas of commerce, civility, and diplomacy, it also suggests the inseparability of climate and culture. The difficulties that the British had in acclimating to the unexpected heat, 'dirt', and fatigue of a late Chinese summer at the fortieth latitude are as much a part of their narratives as the protocols of the *kow-tow*. Had Amherst not been exhausted by weeks of traveling through 30°C heat, had he been willing to kneel in less dusty attire and bow his head nine times to the Jiaqing Emperor, the generalizations about the Chinese empire and its people in the run-up to the First Opium War may have been a little less sweeping and a little more nuanced. As Wood argues, one of the effects of failed grain harvests and inadequate relief efforts in Yunnan Province in the years after Tambora was the rapid growth of domestic opium cultivation and increasing pressure on the Qing bureaucracy to combat an illegal and lucrative trade. The cascading effects of this illicit commerce shadowed the areas of eastern China seemingly unaffected by Tambora and hardened the differences between the Qing court and Britons single-mindedly focused on commercial expansion. Wearied by climatic conditions they could neither adjust to nor truly comprehend, the embassy returned to Canton more skeptical than ever about a dialogue between equals.

Tea and the Limits of Orientalism in De Quincey's Confessions of an English Opium-Eater

EUGENIA ZUROSKI-JENKINS

[H]appiness [...] in my judgment, enters the room with the tea-tray: for tea, though ridiculed by those who are naturally of coarse nerves, or are become so from wine-drinking, and are not susceptible of influence from so refined a stimulant, will always be the favourite beverage of the intellectual: and, for my part, I would have joined Dr. Johnson in a *vellum internecinum* against Jonas Hanway, or any other impious person, who should presume to disparage it.[1]

Thomas De Quincey would cut a very different figure in literary history if he had authored *Confessions of an English Tea-Drinker*. The text he did write, *Confessions of an English Opium-Eater* (1821), reveals the opium-eater to be equally dedicated to drinking tea, but, unlike opium use, tea-drinking simply is not the stuff of 'confession'. Samuel Johnson made just this point in the piece to which De Quincey refers, a scoffing review of Jonas Hanway's 1756 diatribe against the British tea habit.[2] In his *Essay on Tea*, Hanway had argued at length that Britons of all social ranks had developed a 'wild infatuation' with the fashionable beverage, to the detriment of the nation.[3] Employing xenophobic and medical rhetoric to posit tea as a foreign invader and its consumption a form of malady, Hanway claimed that the tea trade was as bad for the British economy as tea-drinking was pernicious to Britons' health. Tea, he wrote, is a 'Chinese drug', an 'intoxicating liquor', and a 'slow poison'; it is no less than 'a

---

[1] Thomas De Quincey, *Confessions of an English Opium-Eater and Related Writings*, ed. Joel Faflak (Peterborough, ON: Broadview Editions, 2009), p. 111. All references are to this edition.

[2] Samuel Johnson, 'Review of ... An Essay on Tea', in *Samuel Johnson: The Major Works*, ed. Donald Greene (New York: Oxford University Press, 2000), pp. 509–17.

[3] Jonas Hanway, *A Journal of Eight Day's Journey from Portsmouth to Kingston Upon Thames ... To Which Is Added, An Essay on Tea* (London, 1756), p. 245.

seven-headed monster, which devours [...] the best fruits of this land'.[4] While the tea trade holds Britain in thrall to the Chinese – 'the most effeminate people on the face of the whole earth' – the consumption of tea 'is an epidemical disease' and 'universal infection'.[5] 'Habit reconciles us to tea,' Hanway warns, 'as it does Turks to opium,' and makes the British 'act more wantonly and absurdly than the Chinese themselves'.[6] Johnson countered the fervor of Hanway's claims by declaring himself 'a hardened and shameless tea-drinker, who has, for twenty years, diluted his meals with only the infusion of this fascinating plant, whose kettle has scarcely time to cool, who with tea amuses the evening, with tea solaces the midnights, and, with tea, welcomes the morning'.[7] His suggestion that any amount of tea consumption could be thought 'shameful' is, of course, tongue-in-cheek; Johnson refutes Hanway's warning about the dire effects of Britain's 'infatuation' with the 'Chinese drug' known as tea by offering himself as living evidence of tea's congruity with normal routines and general English well-being.[8]

Johnson's response to Hanway demonstrated how fluidly certain Chinese imports were accommodated as icons of English identity in the eighteenth century, even as Hanway's essay gave voice to emergent anxieties about English accommodation of and dependence on Chinese goods. When De Quincey alludes to this debate in *Confessions of an English Opium-Eater*, he registers the ambivalence that characterized British attitudes toward Chinese commodities in general since they became ubiquitous in the previous century.[9] By siding so definitively with Johnson in

4 Hanway, *Essay on Tea*, pp. 246, 215, 230, 245.
5 Hanway, *Essay on Tea*, pp. 213, 244.
6 Hanway, *Essay on Tea*, pp. 222, 213.
7 Johnson, 'Review', p. 509.
8 In a follow-up 'Reply' to Hanway, Johnson repeats this point: 'Of tea, what have I said? That I have drank it twenty years, without hurt, and, therefore, believe it not to be poison.' Johnson, 'Reply to a Paper in the *Gazetteer* of May 26, 1757', in Greene, ed., *The Major Works*, pp. 517–21 (p. 518). For an extended discussion of Hanway and Johnson's debate on tea, see Eugenia Zuroski Jenkins, *A Taste for China: English Subjectivity and the Prehistory of Orientalism* (New York: Oxford University Press, 2013), pp. 152–8.
9 There is a growing scholarly literature on the significance of China and chinoiserie to British culture and self-definition in the long eighteenth century and beyond. See, for example, David Porter, *Ideographia: The Chinese Cipher in Early Modern Europe* (Stanford: Stanford University Press, 2001), and *The Chinese Taste in Eighteenth-Century England* (Cambridge: Cambridge University Press, 2010); Robert Markley, *The Far East and the English Imagination, 1600–1730* (Cambridge: Cambridge University Press, 2006); Yu Liu, *Seeds of a Different Eden:*

defense of English tea-drinking, however, De Quincey performs a sleight of hand that directs our attention to the singular problem of opium; focusing on opium's narcotic effects allows him to frame Britain's ambivalence about foreign goods as a matter solely of *opium* addiction. The substance of opium is held accountable for the mixture of desire and horror with which De Quincey's narrator responds to it; the well-known descriptions of the Opium-eater's 'oriental dreams' in the text's final pages suggest that the drug itself comes to impose 'Asiatic scenes' on the narrator's imagination by exercising a 'fascinating power' over him.[10] Thus, he concludes, 'Not the opium-eater, but the opium, is the true hero of the tale; and the legitimate centre on which the interest revolves. The object was to display the marvellous agency of opium, whether for pleasure or for pain: if that is done, the action of the piece is closed'.[11]

In short, by making opium 'the true hero of the tale', De Quincey establishes a prototypical narrative of drug abuse that invites us to see the complicated effects of Britain's metabolization of global trade as a form of psychological confusion caused literally by the ingestion of a foreign substance.[12] *Confessions* can only tell this story of opium's 'marvellous

---

Chinese Gardening and a New English Aesthetic Ideal (Columbia, SC: University of South Carolina Press, 2008); Eric Hayot, Haun Saussy, and Steven G. Yao, eds, *Sinographies: Writing China* (Minneapolis, MN: University of Minnesota Press, 2008); Eric Hayot, *The Hypothetical Mandarin: Sympathy, Modernity, and Chinese Pain* (New York: Oxford University Press, 2009); Elizabeth Hope Chang, *Britain's Chinese Eye: Literature, Empire, and Aesthetics in Nineteenth-Century Britain* (Stanford: Stanford University Press, 2010); 'China and the Making of Global Modernity', ed. Robert Markley, special issue of *Eighteenth-Century Studies*, 43 (2010); Chi-ming Yang, *Performing China: Virtue, Commerce, and Orientalism in Eighteenth-Century England, 1660–1760* (Baltimore, MD: Johns Hopkins University Press, 2011); Zuroski Jenkins, *A Taste for China*; and Peter J. Kitson, *Forging Romantic China: Sino-British Cultural Exchange, 1760–1840* (Cambridge: Cambridge University Press, 2013).

10 De Quincey, *Confessions*, pp. 124–9.

11 De Quincey, *Confessions*, p. 129.

12 Robert Morrison argues that 'De Quincey *created* what we now recognize as the contemporary experience of opiate use and abuse, both in his descriptions of opium as a profoundly paradoxical substance that simultaneously deepens and eviscerates subjectivity, and in his many narratives which represent the drug as an invasive force that terrorizes the body'. Robert Morrison, 'De Quincey's Addiction', *Romanticism*, 17 (2011), 270–7 (p. 270). Barry Milligan similarly points out that the vocabulary we continue to use today to discuss drug use and addiction derives from mid-nineteenth-century anti-opium movements. *Pleasures and Pains: Opium and the Orient in Nineteenth-Century British Culture* (Charlottesville, VA: University of Virginia Press, 1995), p. 22.

agency', however, against a backdrop of commonplace, unaltered English life, which De Quincey relies on the recurrent trope of tea to depict. Tea is ever-present in the text; what the Opium-eater calls at one point the 'eternal tea-pot' – an echo of Johnson's eternally warm kettle – is perhaps its most potent signifier of a vision of English life uncompromised by opium's 'fascinating power'.[13] 'The favourite beverage of the intellectual' defines the world to which the English opium-eater aspires to belong, and from which he finds himself increasingly alienated. Readers are encouraged to read tea as a counterpoint to opium, an icon of domestic normality that helps the text dramatize the disruptive and disorienting effects of opium as it insinuates itself into daily habits, alienating English culture from English identity. But tea is also latently present in its supposed opposite, opium: De Quincey's 'Chinese drug' and its terrifying effects on the English psyche are modeled on Hanway's hyperbolic account of tea. The mention of Hanway's essay (ostensibly to dismiss it, but in effect bringing it into the frame) introduces a minute tear in the seam of the text's vision of ideal English life, a fissure that destabilizes the fantasy of domesticity that frames the troubled subjectivity of the opium addict. While the text indicts opium for the narrator's flights from norms of reason, moderation, and self-possession that define English selfhood, the historical fluctuation of the trope of tea in English writing disturbs these standards of normativity from within.

Confessions' semiotic entanglement of the two commodities mirrors their convolution in the vexed political economy between Britain and China in the era of the 'Opium Wars'. As Joel Black points out, '[i]t was Britain's insatiable tea habit, after all, that drove it to export Indian opium into China in the first place as a way of balancing its trade deficit with that nation'.[14] Black notes that 'De Quincey was clearly aware of Britain's

---

13 De Quincey, *Confessions*, p. 111.

14 Joel Black, 'National Bad Habits: Thomas De Quincey's Geography of Addition', in *Thomas De Quincey: New Theoretical and Critical Directions*, ed. Robert Morrison and Daniel Sanjiv Roberts (London: Routledge, 2008), pp. 143–64 (p. 156). On this topic, Black cites David A. Bello, *Opium and the Limits of Empire: Drug Prohibition in the Chinese Interior, 1729–1850* (Cambridge, MA: Harvard University Asia Center, 2005), p. 33, and Cannon Schmidt, 'Narrating National Addictions: De Quincey, Opium, and Tea', in *High Anxieties: Cultural Studies in Addiction*, ed. Janet Farrell Brodie and Marc Redfield (Berkeley: University of California Press, 2002), pp. 63–84 (pp. 77–8). See also Markman Ellis, Richard Coulton, and Matthew Mauger, *Empire of Tea: The Asian Leaf that Conquered the World* (London: Reaktion Books, 2015), pp. 213–19. 'The Anglo-Chinese conflict of 1840–42 was indeed an "opium war",' they write, 'but it was also a "tea war"'

dependence on China for tea', without which 'our daily life would, generally speaking, be as effectively ruined as bees without a Flora'.[15] Carol Margaret Davison has also pointed out the irony that while the popular association of opium with China 'ran contrary to historic fact' given that the vast majority of opium imported into Britain until the late nineteenth century came from Turkey, 'if a costly "addiction" actually existed that made Britain dependent on China, that "addiction" was the consumption of tea'.[16] By directing our attention to the problem of opium, De Quincey's narrative reproduces the scapegoating of opium for a host of cultural anxieties that can be traced to the history of British tea consumption. At the same time, however, the text displays a constant awareness of the stakes and pitfalls of precisely this kind of cultural reproduction – the retelling of certain stories, the reincarnation of particular ideals – and by allowing us to perceive his narrative as a reiteration of cultural myths, he – perhaps unwittingly – enables a critical perspective on the mythologies supporting modern English self-definition, and the ironies and internal contradictions that render them strange to their own task.

By emphasizing the text's awareness of the 'Chineseness' of its preferred icon of Englishness, this essay argues that the infamous orientalism of De Quincey's *Confessions*, far from consolidating a model of English identity secured by an aversion to foreign (and particularly Chinese) influence, instead reveals De Quincey's acute awareness of the ways in which British subjects of the early nineteenth century were fundamentally, to borrow Julia Kristeva's phrase, 'strangers to themselves', even in their most 'English' predilections.[17] While the hyperbolic orientalism of De Quincey's depiction of opium seems, to some extent, to preserve tea-drinking as part of an alternate world, in which English identity is secured against exotic influence and monstrous transformations, *Confessions'* tale

---

(pp. 218–19). For a discussion of how a 'tea and opium cycle' characterized Britain's belated entry into a global silver economy, see Dennis Owen Flynn and Arturo Giraldez, 'Cycles of Silver: Global Economic Unity through the Mid-Eighteenth Century', *Journal of World History*, 13 (2002), 391–427 (p. 411).

[15] Black, 'National Bad Habits', p. 162n22. De Quincey quotation is from Thomas De Quincey, *Articles from Hogg's Instructor and Titan, 1853–58*, ed. Edmund Baxter, *The Works of Thomas De Quincey*, vol. 18 (London: Pickering and Chatto, 2001), p. 155.

[16] Carol Margaret Davison, '"Houses of Voluntary Bondage": Theorizing the Nineteenth-Century Gothic Pharmography', *Gothic Studies*, 12 (2010), 68–85 (p. 71).

[17] Julia Kristeva, *Strangers to Ourselves*, trans. Leon S. Roudiez (New York: Columbia University Press, 1991).

of addiction inevitably poses questions about the dependencies both material and conceptual that structure even the most apparently self-sufficient forms of English life and identity. At stake is not only the validity of Britain's tea habit but the whole premise of a national culture made of consumer habits that acquire the status of tradition: the material reproduction of Englishness through routines of imitation and repetition. The pervading 'Chineseness' of one of England's most sacrosanct rituals provides De Quincey a way of considering the abiding strangeness of English self-representation in general.

There is, of course, a vast body of scholarship on De Quincey that examines the pervasive problem of self-coherence in his writing, including a number of psychoanalytic readings that show how various pressures of empire manifest as apparent pathologies in his narratives.[18] *Confessions'* trope of opium addiction has proven extremely generative ground for accounts of how orientalism simultaneously compels and destabilizes British concepts of self. Rajani Sudan, for example, pointing to De Quincey's 'exceedingly convoluted representation of the self', reads the Opium-eater's addiction as 'a domesticating habit: it denatures tigerish ferocity and recontextualizes the whole scope of "an obscure and imaginary oriental ferocity" within the security of the English household'.[19] As a result, 'opium and its attendant potential for invoking oriental fantasy and horror have a curiously *familial* place in De Quincey's household'; the imagined oriental 'other', rather than being abjected from English domesticity and selfhood, is 'introjected' into them, instilling a fundamental strangeness at the heart of that which is most familiar – a psychological phenomenon that Freud later called the unconscious.[20] Sanjay Krishnan

18 The most influential of these studies is John Barrell, *The Infection of Thomas De Quincey: A Psychopathology of Imperialism* (New Haven, CT: Yale University Press, 1991). See also Nigel Leask, *British Romantic Writers and the East: Anxieties of Empire* (Cambridge: Cambridge University Press, 1992); Milligan, *Pleasures and Pains*; Alan Bewell, *Romanticism and Colonial Disease* (Baltimore, MD: Johns Hopkins University Press, 1999); and Rajani Sudan, *Fair Exotics: Xenophobic Subjects in English Literature, 1720–1850* (Philadelphia: University of Pennsylvania Press, 2002). See also Robert Morrison, '"Earthquake and Eclipse": Radical Energies and De Quincey's 1821 *Confessions*', in *Thomas De Quincey*, pp. 63–80. Morrison focuses on inconsistencies in De Quincey's 'attitude toward class, race, imperialism, and political violence' in order to show how 'De Quincey's delighted confidence in his own Englishness is frequently undermined by sympathies that disrupt the political and social ideologies he is ostensibly bent on affirming' (pp. 63–4).

19 Sudan, *Fair Exotics*, pp. 69, 71.

20 Sudan, *Fair Exotics*, pp. 71–3. For a different reading of *Confessions'* relationship

demonstrates how the vocabulary cultivated in psychoanalytic readings of the Opium-eater opens up formal analyses not only of subjectivity but also of the material world that subjects inhabit. Also focusing on 'the work of opium' in the text, Krishnan shows how it 'forces a relationship between things alien or repugnant to one another'.[21] In its character as a narcotic, Krishnan argues, opium 'shows up the alien as the effect internal to the modalities of the commodity regime', revealing how heterogeneity 'is not ... in "excess" of the comprehensible or thematizable' within Britain's empire but rather 'gnaws at the system from within'.[22] The contradictory functions of opium – as a narcotic, it 'pushes the self toward the terrors and possibilities opened up by difference', while as a commodity, it 'functions as part of a material process to make homogeneous through mechanisms of discipline and "exchange" the different temporalities and histories of the non-European world' – have the same paradoxical effect on the empire that they have, in Sudan's reading, on the imperial subject, 'pointing to the activation of difference within a world that has ostensibly been made safe in being made the same'.[23]

But the dynamic that both Sudan and Krishnan locate in opium – the resonance of strangeness in an object designed, whether by habit or economic imperative, to serve English normality – could also be identified

to Freudian theory, see Humberto Garcia, 'In the Name of the "Incestuous Mother": Islam and Excremental Protestantism in De Quincey's Infidel Book', *Journal for Early Modern Cultural Studies*, 7 (2007), 57–87.

[21] Sanjay Krishnan, 'Opium and Empire: The Transports of Thomas De Quincey', *boundary 2*, 33.2 (2006), 203–34 (p. 204).

[22] Krishnan, 'Opium and Empire', p. 232.

[23] Krishnan, 'Opium and Empire', p. 234. For other readings of the problem of British self-coherence in De Quincey's depiction of addiction, see Black, 'National Bad Habits'; Davison, 'Houses of Voluntary Bondage'; Daniel O'Quinn, 'Ravishment Twice Weekly: De Quincey's Opera Pleasures', *Romanticism on the Net*, 34–35 (2004), DOI: 10.7202/009436ar; Elizabeth Fay, 'Hallucinogesis: Thomas De Quincey's Mind Trips', *Studies in Romanticism*, 49 (2010), 293–312; George C. Grinnell, 'Multiple Personality: De Quincey's Political Economies of Infirmity', in *The Age of Hypochondria: Interpreting Romantic Health and Illness* (London: Palgrave Macmillan, 2010), pp. 120–48; and Milligan, 'Brunonianism, Radicalism, and "The Pleasures of Opium"' in *Thomas De Quincey*, pp. 45–62. Milligan argues that De Quincey's 'emphasis upon opium's ability to blur [...] boundaries and increase their permeability' allows him to present himself as a 'far more slippery political commentator than the High Tory mouthpiece who has often emerged from De Quincey criticism and biography' (p. 58). For a reading of De Quincey's exploration of 'absolute habituation' as a philosophical engagement with Kant, see David L. Clark, 'We "Other Prussians"': Bodies and Pleasures in De Quincey and Late Kant', *European Romantic Review*, 14 (2003), 261–87 (p. 261).

in tea. In a way, tea supports the argument even better than opium does: tea's supposed stability as a symbol of English domesticity heightens the uncanniness of its own Chinese origins. In tea, the exotic does not arrive, like the traveling Malay in one of *Confessions'* most oft-cited episodes, at the Englishman's door; it already occupies – indeed, defines – the home. How does the account of Chinese influence on, and infiltration of, English culture and identity change when the alibi of addiction is taken away, when the boundaries that define impropriety cannot be located? In the figure of tea, does *Confessions'* orientalism confront its own limit in the form of a Chineseness that cannot be imaginatively estranged from English selfhood?

G. G. Sigmond opens his 1839 history of tea, *Tea; Its Effects, Medicinal and Moral,*

> Man is so surrounded by objects calculated to arrest his attention, and to excite either his admiration or his curiosity, that he often over-looks the humble friend that ministers to his habitual comfort; and the familiarity he holds with it almost renders him incapable of appreciating its value.[24]

Such is the case, he argues, with the British and their tea. Julie E. Fromer, reading Sigmond, suggests that tea's history as an exotic import, intro-duced into Britain in the late seventeenth century and popularized in the eighteenth, is radically sublimated in Victorian culture's embrace of it as a symbol of everyday, quintessentially English life.[25] Only a few decades before Sigmond remarks on the unremarkability of tea in British culture, it was being marketed to British consumers as a 'Chinese' luxury. Markman Ellis, Richard Coulton, and Matthew Mauger have shown that mid-eight-eenth-century trade cards advertised tea 'as an exotic commodity brought to London by the remarkable transoceanic reach of British mercantile activity', and that the majority of surviving trade cards from the late eight-eenth century 'make use of a series of stock images representing oriental gardens, tea bushes, pagodas, harbours, Chinese labourers and merchants' (Fig. 3).[26] 'This apparent exoticization of tea', they point out, 'paradoxi-cally demonstrates its increasing naturalization in Britain' as 'consumers

---

[24] G. G. Sigmond, *Tea; Its Effects, Medicinal and Moral* (London, 1839), p. 1.
[25] Julie E. Fromer, *A Necessary Luxury: Tea in Victorian England* (Athens, OH: Ohio University Press, 2008). Fromer quotes the passage from Sigmond on p. 1.
[26] Ellis et al., *Empire of Tea*, pp. 132–4.

Figure 3: British trade card for 'Fine Tea' (1733–1769)

were increasingly being asked to re-interpret their own newly acquired cultural practices [...] as the luxurious (yet commonplace) habits of the inhabitants of a trading superpower'.[27] Consumers are apparently asked to reinterpret their tea habit yet again in the early decades of the nineteenth century, as representations of tea as an exotic yet accessible luxury give way to Sigmond's 'humble friend that ministers to [one's] habitual comfort'; according to Fromer, 'Victorian novels focus exclusively on the domestic resonances of tea-drinking.'[28]

This naturalization of tea's place in British culture took place, ironically, amid swelling strains of sinophobia in British popular culture. In the early nineteenth century, cartoonists elaborated popular chinoiserie designs into monstrous caricatures designed to humiliate Chinese political pretensions and persuade viewers, through a combination of mockery and fear-mongering, of the absolute incompatibility of British and Chinese cultures. Satires like George Cruikshank's 'The Court at Brighton à la Chinese!!' (1816), which depicts the Prince Regent as a Chinese despot, supported the popular idea that the more Chinese things Britons consume, the more Britons are consumed by a virulent Chineseness (Fig. 2; see p. 72).[29] This

27 Ellis et al., *Empire of Tea*, pp. 135–7.
28 Fromer, *A Necessary Luxury*, p. 293.
29 On the orientalization and racialization of the Chinese in British culture of the eighteenth and nineteenth centuries, see Michael Keevak, *Becoming Yellow: A Short*

vicious orientalization of the 'Chinese taste' largely bypassed tea and porcelain, flourishing instead in representations of opium addiction.[30] But
the extraordinary effort that British culture invested in generating specters of Chinese menace through the trope of opium addiction preserved a
latent form of exoticism even in seemingly domesticated objects like tea-
things. Together with the porcelain vessels in which it was typically served,
Chinese tea was, by the nineteenth century, perhaps the best example of
what Elizabeth Hope Chang calls the 'familiar exotic': an object that is
simultaneously 'a comforting icon of British domesticity and a dangerous token of visual difference'.[31] While tea may never have appeared as
dangerous a substance as opium in Victorian culture, as a cultural object
it possessed the uniquely unsettling capacity to admit occasional glimpses
of its foreign origins and once-exotic aura from its position as a mundane
fixture of ordinary British life. As orientalist caricatures like *The Brother
to the Moon's Visit to the Court of Queen Vic* (1843) illustrate, the familiar
form of the teapot could be recruited to participate in siniphobic visual
satire (Fig. 4).

De Quincey participated explicitly in Britain's anti-Chinese discourse
in his writings on the 'Opium Wars'. In 'The Opium and the China
Question' (1840) he urged 'armed interference' to preserve British trading
interests in China, specifically the export of opium to support the British
import of tea, referring to the Chinese as 'vagabonds' and 'idolaters', and
citing a 'horrible Chinese degeneration of moral distinctions' in Canton.[32]
He defines the English by 'our indomitable energy, and our courageous
self-dependence' in imperialist endeavors; Englishmen are characterized
by a capacity for 'relying upon themselves against all enemies [...] with
a reverence for laws – with constitutional energy, and, above all, with a
pure religion'. 'Now, what we are in the very supreme degree', De Quincey
declares, 'that is China in the lowest'.[33] 'Oriental powers like China', he

History of Racial Thinking (Princeton: Princeton University Press, 2011), and Peter
J. Kitson, *Romantic Literature, Race, and Colonial Encounter* (Basingstoke: Palgrave
Macmillan, 2007).

[30] See Milligan, *Pleasures and Pains*; Black, 'National Bad Habits'; Davison,
'Houses of Voluntary Bondage'; Chang, *Britain's Chinese Eye*, pp. 111–40; and
Krishnan, 'Opium and Empire'.

[31] Chang, *Britain's Chinese Eye*, p. 73.

[32] Thomas De Quincey, 'The Opium and the China Question' and 'Postscript
on the China and the Opium Question', in *The Works of Thomas De Quincey*,
Volume 11: *Articles from* Tait's Magazine *and* Blackwoods Magazine, ed. Julian
North (London: Pickering and Chatto, 2003). 532–72 (pp. 561, 552).

[33] De Quincey, 'The Opium and the China Question', p. 545.

Figure 4: Cover image to book of etchings by Richard Doyle, *The Brother to the Moon's Visit to the Court of Queen Vic* (London: Fores, 1843)

insists, are 'incapable of a true civilization, semi-refined in manners and mechanic arts, but incurably savage in the moral sense'.[34] Indeed, one of the reasons *Confessions* has received such immense critical attention is because of the ways, as a self-indictment of a certain kind of English character under 'oriental' influence, the memoir both introduces and complicates the orientalist vocabulary De Quincey calls upon in these later defenses of English character and British national honor.[35] The confidence with which the author of the political essays proclaims, following his list of cultural and political virtues, 'Such are we English people – such is the English condition,' while disparaging Chinese cultural and moral integrity, cannot take root in *Confessions*. This is not only, as many readers have already shown, because the English narrator's own addiction to opium compromises his claim to English virtue and moral purity. It is also because *Confessions'* depiction of the cultural sites where 'the English condition' is materially reproduced reveals them to be saturated with the 'familiar exotic': forms, like tea, that flicker with a potentially alien agency,

---

[34] De Quincey, 'The Opium and the China Question', p. 554.
[35] For a reading of the 'Opium War' essays that complicates the conventional view of them as 'garden-variety, jingoistic war-mongering', see Charles Rzepka, 'The Literature of Power and the Imperial Will: De Quincey's Opium War Essays', *South Central Review*, 8 (1991), 37–45 (p. 42).

and fail to sustain a subject marked by genuine and undiluted 'English character'.

Opium may be the 'hero of the tale' but tea is essential to the setting in which *Confessions'* 'action' takes place. De Quincey repeatedly uses the ritual of tea to demarcate the world of domestic comforts that opium addiction ruptures, a world he identifies as distinctly English in contrast to the orientalized dreamscapes into which opium plunges him. 'Surely everybody is aware of the divine pleasures which attend a winter fire-side', he writes, establishing the atmosphere of a typical English cottage:

> ... candles at four o'clock, warm hearth-rugs, tea, a fair tea-maker, shutters closed, curtains flowing in ample draperies on the floor, whilst the wind and rain are raging audibly without,
>
> And at the doors and windows seem to call
> As heav'n and earth they would together mell;
> Yet the least entrance find they none at all;
> Whence sweeter grows our rest secure in massy hall.
>   — *Castle of Indolence*
>
> All these are items in the description of a winter evening, which must surely be familiar to every body born in a high latitude.[36]

The most common pleasures of English domestic life may be efficiently rendered by the mention of tea, a metonym for hearth and home so familiar to nineteenth-century British readers that it anchors a vision of intimate English well-being insulated from whatever hostile forces rage beyond the threshold.[37]

While this vision is proffered as a self-explanatory, universally familiar image to British readers — this is precisely Sigmond's realm of 'habitual comfort' — it wavers immediately under scrutiny. As David Simpson has pointed out, De Quincey refers here not simply to recognizable tropes

---

[36] De Quincey, *Confessions*, p. 110. The quoted verse is from James Thomson, *The Castle of Indolence* (1748), ll. 43.6–9.

[37] As many studies of tea in British culture have shown, the role of 'the fair tea-maker' — the woman responsible for making and serving tea in the home — is crucial to the semiotics of English domesticity. In addition to Fromer, see Marcia Pointon, *Strategies for Showing: Women, Possession, and Representation in English Visual Culture, 1665–1800* (Oxford: Oxford University Press, 1997), pp. 15–58; Elizabeth Kowaleski-Wallace, *Consuming Subjects: Women, Shopping, and Business in the Eighteenth Century* (New York: Columbia University Press, 1996), pp. 19–36; and Zuroski Jenkins, *Taste for China*, pp. 132–39.

of domesticity but to particular literary deployments of them. Not only does the passage explicitly invoke James Thomson's verse, but the scene, Simpson writes, 'recalls Cowper and Coleridge with uncanny exactness [...] This fireside is a very literary, almost tongue-in-cheek fireside; it is Leigh Hunt's sociable scene, and in its specification of a "winter evening" it cites [...] of course, the title of the fourth book of Cowper's *The Task*'.[38] As Marie Odile-Bernez has shown, novels too relied on this mytholo-gized interior scene to naturalize commodities like tea, once considered 'luxuries,' as middle-class domestic 'comforts': 'Novelists concentrated on some essential elements: an independent house, often a farm or cottage, pleasantly situated in the country, and a happy family life, with the wife at the center of an array of domestic material objects'.[39] The repetition of details like tea in this shared vision not only propagates a particular image of domestic comfort as the representation of 'English life', but also makes recognition of this image the basis of English literary tradition. As many critics have observed, De Quincey was preoccupied throughout his career with his own relationship to the English literary canon, and the writers generating it; he documented his own determined pursuit of a friendship with Wordsworth in his essays on the poet, published in *Tait's Magazine* in 1839,[40] and he was keenly aware of the way his Opium-eater persona drew on Coleridge's reputation.[41] The 'very literary, almost tongue-in-cheek' quality Simpson points to in this passage is characteristic of De Quincey's consistently overwrought way of representing his own relationship to the

[38] David Simpson, *Romanticism and the Question of the Stranger* (Chicago: University of Chicago Press, 2013), pp. 73–4.

[39] Marie Odile-Bernez, 'Comfort, the Acceptable Face of Luxury: An Eighteenth-Century Cultural Etymology', *Journal for Early Modern Cultural Studies*, 14. (2014), 3–21 (p. 8).

[40] Thomas De Quincey, 'William Wordsworth', in *Recollections of the Lakes and the Lake Poets* (New York: Cambridge University Press, 2013), pp. 123–210.

[41] Leask reads *Confessions* as a rewriting of the *Biographia Literaria* in which De Quincey self-consciously and anxiously presents himself as a 'double' of Coleridge; David Stewart argues that De Quincey models himself on Coleridge 'most particularly in using a distinctively Coleridgian paradox to integrate himself into the marketplace'. *Romantic Writers and the East*, pp. 170–228; David Stewart, 'Commerce, Genius, and De Quincey's Literary Identity', *SEL: Studies in English Literature*, 50 (2010), 775–89 (p. 781). Robert Morrison has argued that 'as De Quincey borrowed from Coleridge, others borrowed from him: Maginn, Knight, Wainwright, Wilson, Poe, Musset, Baudelaire, and a host of others all saw in the Opium-Eater construct the potential for notoriety and profit'. Morrison, 'De Quincey and the Opium-Eater's Other Selves', *Romanticism*, 5 (1999), 87–103 (p. 101).

'geniuses' of Romanticism; Margaret Russett has called this his 'grandiose humility', noting that at the same time that it 'marks him [...] as a writer of putatively diminished powers, it also suggests that to publish another's genius is to replicate oneself, even while instantiating the devious turns of what Pierre Bourdieu calls "reproduction"'.[42]

These 'devious turns' in the processes of material cultural production are in evidence in this self-consciously literary fireside scene. In order to examine the formal effects of the tea De Quincey places at the center of the image, it is worth examining the way the passage undermines its own claim to present a stable image of Englishness through its convoluted evocation of other English authors, particularly Wordsworth. The period of De Quincey's life that corresponds to this episode in *Confessions* finds De Quincey living at Dove Cottage, Wordsworth's house in Grasmere, which De Quincey occupied – having finally forged a personal relationship with the poet (which went from close to strained) – from 1809 to 1820. Thus when the Opium-eater declares, 'Let there be a cottage', adding in the course of his description of this cottage that in his details, 'I must abide by the actual scene', we seem to have every reason to believe that this is an 'actual' description of Dove Cottage, and that we are being given a glimpse of De Quincey occupying the position of Wordsworth. In an editorial note in the Oxford World Classics edition of *Confessions*, Grevel Lindop asserts unequivocally that the description of the house that contains the idyllic fireside scene 'is of Dove Cottage, Grasmere'.[43] As Daniel O'Quinn has argued, however, De Quincey never names the cottage in *Confessions* and, indeed, goes to formal lengths to present it as an explicitly fictional creation: 'Let there be a cottage, standing in a valley, 18 miles from any town', he opens.[44] In O'Quinn's words, 'Throughout the "analysis of happiness" the Opium-eater has produced a representation which makes sense but which eludes direct referentiality'; Lindop's note 'solves a critical problem at this point in the text: namely he ensures the

---

42 Margaret Russett, *De Quincey's Romanticism: Canonical Minority and the Forms of Transmission* (Cambridge: Cambridge University Press, 1997), p. 2. Fromer also refers to Bourdieu, using his theory of 'habitus' to read the site of the tea table in Britain. Fromer, *Necessary Luxury*, pp. 8–9. See Pierre Bourdieu, *The Logic of Practice* (Stanford: Stanford University Press, 1980) and *The Field of Cultural Production: Essays on Art and Literature* (New York: Columbia University Press, 1993).

43 Thomas De Quincey, *Confessions of an English Opium-Eater and Other Writings*, ed. Grevel Lindop (New York: Oxford University Press, 1998), p. 242n58.

44 De Quincey, *Confessions*, p. 109.

referentiality of the "picture"'.[45] The reader's will to interpret this 'cottage, standing in a valley, 18 miles from any town' as Dove Cottage, in other words, tries to close a gap that the text leaves provocatively open between the scene it paints and the 'actual' site to which it refers.

Over the entire, extended passage in which the Opium-eater directs us to imagine him within this cottage, at the fireside with his tea, the question of whether this is a vision of Wordsworth's house hovers. If his opium addiction aligns the narrator with Coleridge, his 'oriental dreams' calling to the reader's mind an image of 'Kubla Khan', then the gesture of installing himself in Wordsworth's cottage with a pot of tea seems to counter the orientalism of opium, grounding the narrator in a scene that could not be more typically English. This binary has been set up by Coleridge himself, who opens 'Kubla Khan: Or, A Vision in a Dream. A Fragment' with a preface explaining that the dream occurred in another version of the typical English cottage, 'a lonely farm-house between Porlock and Linton, on the Exmoor confines of Somerset and Devonshire'.[46] But where Coleridge's poem attributes the poet's oriental visions to a combination of opium and reading Chinese scenes in the travel narrative *Purchas His Pilgrimage* (1613), *Confessions* traces the disruptive alienation associated with opium to the narrator's own uneasy impersonation of Wordsworth. Charles Rzepka has suggested that 'De Quincey, as tenant of what was gradually becoming something of an unofficial shrine to Wordsworth, often found himself placed in the position of a false "English idol" by pilgrims to the Lakes more recent than himself.' The Malay who arrives at the cottage and exposes the Opium-eater's limitations as both host and linguist dramatizes, for Rzepka, De Quincey's awareness that 'he had disappointed hopeful pilgrims to Dove Cottage', his awareness of 'the flimsiness of [his own] pretensions to authorship' compared to Wordsworth, but also his own perception of Wordsworth, now an estranged friend, as a 'fallen god of poetry'.[47] Regardless of the extent to which we agree that these biographical details 'explain' the imagery of *Confessions*, it is clear that the text teases us into imagining Wordsworth's spectral presence under the pretense of anchoring us in a scene of unwavering Englishness,

[45] Daniel O'Quinn, 'Murder, Hospitality, Philosophy: De Quincey and the Complicitous Grounds of National Identity,' *Studies in Romanticism*, 38 (1999), 135–70 (p. 157n26).

[46] Samuel Taylor Coleridge, *Poetical Works*, ed. Ernest Hartley Coleridge (Oxford: Oxford University Press, 1986), pp. 295–98 (p. 295).

[47] Charles Rzekpa, 'De Quincey and the Malay: Dove Cottage Idolatry', *The Wordsworth Circle*, 24 (1993), 180–5 (p. 183).

and then refuses to let this supposed cultural anchor hold anything fast: the narrator is hardly Wordsworth, Wordsworth himself is hardly Wordsworth, the scene is not quite Dove Cottage. De Quincey's own admiration and imitation of Wordsworth give way to an unsettling 'idolatry' that finds expression in the 'monstrous scenery' of the Opium-eater's 'oriental dreams', in which 'I was the idol; I was the priest; I was worshipped; I was sacrificed'.[48]

Rzepka's reading helps us see how *Confessions* frames the exotic less as a flight away from the familiar than as a persistent, disruptive sense that the familiar is fundamentally strange. The text may try to displace exoticism on to the traveling Malay who appears at the door, or the physiological influence of opium, but it cannot help tracing its disorienting effects back to the narrator's efforts to inscribe himself within a fantasy of Englishness. We may furnish this cottage, standing in a valley, 18 miles from any town, with 'items [...] which must surely be familiar to every body born in a high latitude', but the fact remains that we have no idea where we actually are, or on what ground the text's subject stands. In the same way that he thus opens a version of Coleridge's orientalized 'romantic chasm'[49] in his own relationship to his English idols, De Quincey uses tea's potent status in English culture to emphasize that the most mundane signifiers of familiar life operate mysteriously. At the height of his opium addiction, the narrator describes his attempt to simulate a normal domestic routine comprising tea and poetry with his wife, 'M.': 'A young lady sometimes comes and drinks tea with us: at her request and M.'s I now and then read W[ordsworth]'s poems to them.'[50] The poignancy of this particular confession – that the narrator ritualistically goes through the motions of this ideal form of English life while being psychologically distanced from it by his opium use – draws on one of the text's signature moves, which is to depict English culture as having a sheltered 'inside' by dramatizing the narrator's torment at not being able fully to inhabit it. Counter to Thomson's image of sweet 'rest secure at massy hall', De Quincey's interiors have already been punctured by something that does not belong: the Opium-eater himself, the stranger who corrupts the sanctity of English space by imperfectly embodying a mastery of its terms. Here, yet again, he is merely impersonating Wordsworth. Summoning his characteristic combination of self-aggrandizement and self-deprecation, the narrator notes

---

48 De Quincey, *Confessions*, p. 125.
49 Coleridge, 'Kubla Khan', line 12.
50 De Quincey, *Confessions*, p. 115.

that 'reading [aloud] is an accomplishment of mine; and, in the slang use of the word *accomplishment* as a superficial and ornamental attainment, almost the only one I possess: and formerly, if I had any vanity at all connected with any endowment or attainment of mine, it was with this; for I had observed that no accomplishment is so rare'. He adds, 'W[ordsworth], by the bye, is the only poet I ever met who could read his own verses: often indeed he reads them admirably.' He thus frames his greatest 'accomplishment' as the art of imposture: the one measure by which he might slightly surpass Wordsworth is in the art of *imitating Wordsworth*.[51]

The narrator's rehearsal of the tea-and-Wordsworth routine echoes the text's rehearsal of the typical tea-and-hearth scene, revealing that the signs and rituals that define English culture are established precisely through such patterns of repetition, but also registering an anxiety that this mode of reproduction hollows out the culture it is supposed to fortify. De Quincey relies on the trope of tea to apprehend a version of 'true' English culture, even as his narrator suffers the awareness that a reliance on tropes is what removes him from a state of authenticity. In the Opium-eater's hands, like the figure of Wordsworth to which it is attached, tea's iconic relationship to Englishness begins to take on a cast of obsessive idolatry. The text therefore attempts to stabilize its representation of Englishness by erasing all traces of tea's status as a *figure*: while opium is hyperbolically inflated as a literary creature, taking center stage as the 'hero' of *Confessions*' gothic tale, tea eschews the reader's scrutiny even as it continually crops up. It is all but buried in the concatenation of 'candles at four o'clock, warm hearth rugs, tea, a fair tea-maker, shutters closed, curtains flowing in ample draperies on the floor', hiding in plain sight at the very center of the 'divine pleasures' afforded by the English domestic scene.

Through such barely visible repetitions, De Quincey's text insists that tea is hardly worth mentioning, though to live without it is to test the bounds of English civilization itself. When the narrator finds himself, as a young man, wandering through Wales with only enough money for one meal per day, 'the single meal, which I could venture to order, was coffee or tea'.[52] These imported beverages are the Englishman's last tether to social autonomy; when he can no longer afford them, he is reduced to a kind of feral grazing, 'subsist[ing] either on blackberries, hips, haws, etc.

---

[51] De Quincey, *Confessions*, pp. 114–15.
[52] De Quincey, *Confessions*, p. 64.

or on the casual hospitalities' of compassionate strangers.[53] Tea appears again to mark a distinction between 'respectable' domestic life and the seedy existence of the Opium-eater's early years in London. Narrating his difficult years squatting in a derelict house with an orphan girl who is convinced the site is haunted, he notes that upon returning to the house years later he found it:

> now occupied by a respectable family; and, by the lights in the front drawing-room, I observed a domestic party, assembled perhaps at tea, and apparently cheerful and gay. Marvellous contrast, in my eyes, to the darkness – cold – silence – and – desolation of that same house eighteen years ago, when its nightly occupants were one famishing scholar, and a neglected child.[54]

Each of these mentions of tea is designed to come across as merely incidental. Here, tea need not even be directly observed; its presence is implied by the 'cheerful' family scene. The conditional adverb 'perhaps' attaches tea to English domestic happiness with the lightest touch, insulating the tea-table from the full charge of a metonym (which would allow tea to substitute for happiness) while simultaneously naturalizing the association. Unlike opium, in which the narrator identifies a 'marvellous agency [...] whether for pleasure or for pain', tea performs its cultural work by receding into the background: its presence attests to nothing more than a normal order of things in English spaces, where no object exercises the 'fascinating power' that opium wields over its addicts. This was precisely Dr Johnson's argument about tea: that 'as it neither exhilarates the heart, nor stimulates the palate, it is commonly an entertainment merely nominal, a pretence for assembling to prattle, for interrupting business, or diversifying idleness [...] indeed, there are few but discover, by their indifference about it, that they are brought together not by the tea, but the tea table'.[55] The English can take or leave tea, Johnson suggests; it just so happens that many of them choose to take it. In contrast to opium, tea signifies a world in which the English subject commands his own space and the things within it, which are there quietly, tacitly, to serve his own comfort.

Even as he draws this distinction, however, De Quincey unsettles it by

---

53 De Quincey, *Confessions*, p. 64.
54 De Quincey, *Confessions*, pp. 69–70.
55 Johnson, 'Review', p. 512.

introducing a kind of rhetorical excess that taints the reassuringly prosaic quality of the domestic scene. The 'marvellous contrast' the scene illustrates presages the 'marvellous agency' the text later attributes to opium. By revealing that such a mundane image generates, 'in [his] eyes', effects on the order of 'marvellous', the narrator gives us to understand that the domestic scene assembled (perhaps) around everyday tea-drinking exercises the same grip on his imagination that opium does. Even as it quells the material significance of tea to the scene – perhaps there is tea, perhaps there is not – the passage registers the power of tea as a cultural symbol. Does not the phrase 'perhaps at tea' display a kind of 'marvellous agency' in its ability to transform household space so dramatically, demarcate the quality of life so starkly, and render so efficiently the shape and substance of English happiness?

The 'outsider' status that the Opium-eater assigns himself not only removes him from the comfort and stability afforded by the scene in the window, but allows him, despite himself, a perspective on the scene from which it appears first and foremost as a representation of something. The comforts such scenes comprise are, from his perspective, less actual comforts than they are signs of comfort; while tea presents itself within the scene as 'the humble friend that ministers to [the Englishman's] habitual comfort', to the Opium-eater who watches from beyond the window, tea remains a stranger. Even when the Opium-eater manages to install himself in one of these fabled interiors, and partake of the pleasures of tea, poetry, and female company, he presents himself as going through the semiotic motions of normality in a way that is anathema to 'being normal'.

The narrator's strange relation to the representation of Englishness, which exposes a strangeness *in* the representation of Englishness, culminates in the odd way in which the Opium-eater finally inserts himself into the interior scene of the cottage that both is and is not Dove Cottage. Daniel O'Quinn has analyzed the 'complex distantiation' that De Quincey achieves in the final paragraphs of this section, when, in order to place himself in the scene, he shifts from describing the interior of a cottage to giving directions to an imaginary painter of the scene: 'But here, to save myself the trouble of too much verbal description, I will introduce a painter; and give him directions for the rest of the picture.'[56] From this point, O'Quinn writes, 'The Opium-eater separates an addressee from the reader and places the reader in the position of a spectator or accessory. This spectatorship is, of course, metaphorical – this is still a reading

---

[56] De Quincey, *Confessions*, p. 111.

practice – but the reader is separated from a scene of representation and becomes a witness to a verbal action.'[57] This device, in other words, puts the reader in the very position into which the Opium-eater finds himself perpetually slipping: at just enough of a cultural distance from the scene that its contours lend themselves to analysis but not occupation. While, from this perspective, certain formal qualities of the scene come into focus – as both O'Quinn and Simpson point out, these passages mimic still life in the way they focus on the particular material things that domesticity comprises – the human subject of the virtual painting, the person defined by domestic order, refuses to take shape.[58] 'Paint me, if at all, according to your own fancy', the Opium-eater instructs.[59] 'Two options are offered in this command', O'Quinn explains: 'either don't paint me at all or paint what suits you best. The first involves the refusal of representation; the second involves the refusal of a specific visual referent in favour of a delusion.'[60]

What is it, then, that we are being made to see here? First, let me ask, what might we make of the fact that the rhetorical shift described above, with the turn to a fictional painter, occurs immediately after the narrator, invoking Dr Johnson, defends tea 'against Jonas Hanway, or any other impious person, who should presume to disparage it'? In this context, the subsequent line 'But here, to save myself the trouble of too much verbal description, I will introduce a painter' serves as an argumentative tactic: it interrupts the defense of tea that is in progress by saying, in effect, 'Rather than state my case in so many words, let me *show* you.' The picture that the fictional painter is then instructed to paint is thus presented as if the image will speak for itself:

> Paint me, then, a room seven feet by twelve, and not more than seventeen and a half feet high [...] Make it populous with books: and, furthermore, paint me a good fire; and furniture, plain and modest, befitting the unpretending cottage of a scholar. And, near the fire, paint me a tea-table; and (as it is clear that no creature can come to see one such a stormy night,) place only two cups and saucers on the tea-tray:

57 O'Quinn, 'Murder, Hospitality, Philosophy', p. 156.

58 O'Quinn, 'Murder, Hospitality, Philosophy', p. 157. Simpson points out that the evocation of still life enhances the Opium-eater's status as a 'stranger', since still life formally dictates that 'the stranger always be kept out of the picture, even if always about to arrive'. Simpson, *Romanticism and Question of the Stranger*, p. 74.

59 De Quincey, *Confessions*, p. 112.

60 O'Quinn, 'Murder, Hospitality, Philosophy', p. 157.

and, if you know how to paint such a thing symbolically, or otherwise, paint me an eternal tea-pot – eternal *à parte ante*, and *à parte post*; for I usually drink tea from eight o'clock at night to four o'clock in the morning.[61]

The romantic interior drawn from Thomson, Cowper, and Coleridge has, through the addition of books and modest furniture, metamorphosed into Dr Johnson's study. Tea remains central: the 'eternal tea-pot' testifies that this room is occupied by one who, like Johnson, 'with tea amuses the evening, with tea solaces the midnight, and, with tea, welcomes the morning'. The spirit of Johnson joins the list of British authors summoned by the secure cottage interior; the still life has been reprised explicitly to refute Hanway's claims that Britain's homes have been invaded by a Chinese menace, and English lives threatened by an infectious addiction.

In this capacity, however, the tableau takes an odd turn when the narrator inserts himself into it: 'the next article should naturally be myself – a picture of the Opium-eater, with his "little golden receptacle of the pernicious drug", lying beside him on the table'.[62] The phrase 'pernicious drug' is taken from a novel the narrator cites earlier in a footnote: Thomas Hope's *Anastasius, or, Memoirs of a Greek* (1819).[63] But it also recalls Hanway's characterization of tea, which his essay (the very subtitle tells us) 'considered as pernicious to health'.[64] Two things occur simultaneously in this moment: the scene of scholarly tranquility becomes a portrait of addiction, and the case for tea is corrupted by the testimony of the Opium-eater's body. Johnson had supported his claims of English physiological 'indifference' to tea by offering his own body as evidence: in Hanway's warnings about the 'pernicious' effects of tea, Johnson writes, 'he has aggravated in the vehemence of his zeal', for 'after soliciting them by this watery luxury, year after year, I have not yet felt [them]'.[65] But

[61] De Quincey, *Confessions*, p. 111.
[62] De Quincey, *Confessions*, p. 112.
[63] De Quincey, *Confessions*, pp. 92–3.
[64] As De Quincey would have been well aware, the term 'pernicious' continued to adhere to tea in anti-luxury tracts of the late eighteenth century. Ellis et al. point out that an *Essay on Tea, Sugar, White Bread and Butter, Country Alehouses, Strong Beer and Geneva, and other Modern Luxuries* (Salisbury, 1777) claims that tea causes 'Indian melancholy', and that 'a puny race of children are the wretched consequences of this pernicious liquor' (pp. 14–27, quoted in Ellis et al., *Empire of Tea*, p. 188). Milligan quotes a 1795 lecture by Coleridge that refers to tea as a 'pernicious Beverage'. *Pleasures and Pains*, p. 31.
[65] Johnson, 'Review', p. 515.

the Opium-eater is defined by exactly the kind of relationship to Chinese substances against which Hanway sounded the alarm. The 'marvellous contrast' of worlds we have been led to expect by the juxtaposition of tea-drinking and opium-eating folds, in the figure of the Opium-eater himself, into an unsettling consonance. Even as opium usurps the role of protagonist from the narrator, the 'eternal tea-pot' exerts pressure on opium's own semantic autonomy. Its seemingly innocuous but ubiquitous presence, in challenging opium's prerogative to define the world into which the Opium-eater's agency disappears, threatens to come startlingly to the fore of the image.

This helps to explain why the narrator eschews direct representation of himself in the imagined painting, and directs our attention instead to the image of opium itself:

> As to the opium, I have no objection to see a picture of *that* [...] you may as well paint the real receptacle, which was not of gold, but of glass, and as much like a wine-decanter as possible. Into this you may put a quart of ruby-coloured laudanum: that, and a book of German metaphysics placed by its side, will sufficiently attest my being in the neighbourhood; but, as to myself, – there I demur. I admit that, naturally, I ought to occupy the foreground of the picture; that being the hero of the piece, or (if you choose) the criminal at the bar, my body should be had into court. This seems reasonable: but why should I confess, on this point, to a painter? or why confess at all? [...] No: paint me, if at all, according to your own fancy.[66]

At least since Johnson, the depiction of English culture, space, life, and subjectivity relied on emergent middle-class conventions of contrast: the opposition of suffering and comfort, vice and virtue, fantasy and reality, and, increasingly, East and West. In the Opium-eater, De Quincey has created a persona who persistently rattles these oppositions, not by trying to transgress or disrupt social norms and ideals but by trying too earnestly, and without success, to embody them. His own flawed reproduction of Englishness exposes the ideological structures and processes on which the effect of Englishness relies. He calls upon the figure of opium rather explicitly here to stand in for himself as the protagonist of the 'crime' upon English standards, a desperate gesture that tries to support the orientalist theory of some kind of external attack or infiltration of what would otherwise be a perfectly sound, self-same existence. The story that unfolds

66 De Quincey, *Confessions*, p. 112.

from this point forward, of opium's 'marvellous agency' that subsumes the narrator's own, can be read as a fiction in which opium is made to stand trial for the uncanny cultural effects that converge on the Opium-eater in his mission to embody Englishness.

Like all his other narrative tactics, this one is only partially successful, and is therefore not successful at all, in producing an uncompromised form of English identity. For in order to deflect accountability for English disorder away from himself and on to the orientalized culprit of opium, the Opium-eater must claim, finally, the level of intimacy between English subject and Eastern commodity that Johnson's version of Englishness disavows. The Opium-eater, in his attempt to ally himself with Johnson, ends up rehearsing the hysterical sinophobia of Hanway, and, moreover, embodying exactly the kind of cultural pollution that Johnson declared absurd. The Opium-eater's typically quixotic way of aligning himself with the great men who define English tradition and character, in this instance, unravels the whole set of images and associations that this tradition has woven into the *habitus* of modern English masculinity.

Habitus, a term introduced by Bourdieu, describes the 'systems of durable, transposable dispositions' specific to a given culture that structure individual subjectivities within the culture.[67] Cultural reproduction consists fundamentally of the reproduction of *habitus* over time, such that

> the *habitus*, a product of history, produces individual and collective practices – more history – in accordance with the schemes generated by history. It ensures the active presence of past experiences, which, deposited in each organism in the form of schemes of perception, thought and action, tend to guarantee the 'correctness' of practices and their constancy over time, more reliably than all formal rules and explicit norms.[68]

The Opium-eater again and again presents himself as clumsily embodying the threads of the English *habitus*: he is bound to and by them, but he deploys himself awkwardly, not quite achieving the 'correctness' or fluency of being that ought to be guaranteed by cultural coherence. By excessively

---

[67] *Habitus*, Bourdieu writes, consists of 'structured structures predisposed to function as structuring structures, that is, principles which generate and organize practices and representations that can be objectively adapted to their outcomes without presupposing a conscious aiming at ends or an express mastery of the operations necessary in order to attain them'. Bourdieu, *The Logic of Practice*, p. 53.

[68] Bourdieu, *The Logic of Practice*, p. 54.

reiterating the tropes of English domesticity through an incessant series of quotations, references, and aesthetically self-conscious gestures, *Confessions* ultimately generates, in the narrator's imagined painting, not an image of Englishness per se but of Englishness as *habitus*. It puts us in a position to see not only the confluence of postures that come together in modern English subjectivity, but the convoluted histories that demand graceful negotiation in the 'active presence' of subjectivity. The Opium-eater's lack of grace in this capacity disrupts the regeneration of *habitus* even as it participates in it, in the manner of a cultural mutation. As David Simpson puts it, 'It is hard not to suspect that in turning our attention to [Johnson's review of Hanway], De Quincey is artfully opening out the still-life painting of secure domesticity he is, with an equal knowingness, at the same time constructing.'[69]

The Opium-eater, in other words, is never at home in his own *habitus*. He is fully aware that cultural assimilation can only occur through material processes of repetitive habituation, but as he pursues the 'habitual comforts' that assimilate English rituals to a concept of English identity, he reveals the paradoxical way in which the very cycles of repetition that smooth out difference introduce their own processes of alienation. In *Suspiria De Profundis: Being a Sequel to the Confessions of An English Opium-Eater* (1845), De Quincey uses the formal model of 'involution' to describe something very like Bourdieu's *habitus*:

> Often I have been struck with the important truth – that far more of our deepest thoughts and feelings pass to us through perplexed combinations of *concrete* objects, pass to us as *involutes* (if I may coin that word) in compound experiences incapable of being disentangled, than ever reach us *directly*, and in their own abstract shapes.[70]

Tea and opium ultimately constitute one of these 'perplexed combinations' that mediates English subjectivity. In another late essay, 'The English Mail-Coach' (1849), De Quincey elaborates further on 'involuted' subjectivity, tracing the 'dream-horror' described in his earlier works to the principle of self-repetition:

> The dreamer finds housed within himself – occupying, as it were, some separate chamber in his brain – holding, perhaps, from that station a secret and detestable commerce with his own heart – some horrid

---

69 Simpson, *Romanticism and the Question of the Stranger*, p. 75.
70 De Quincey, *Confessions*, p. 151.

alien nature. What if it were his own nature repeated, – still, if the duality were distinctly perceptible, even *that* – even this mere numerical double of his own consciousness – might be a curse too mighty to be sustained. But how, if the alien nature contradicts his own, fights with it, perplexes it, and confounds it? How, again, if not one alien nature, but two, but three, but four, but five, are introduced within what once he thought the inviolable sanctuary of himself?[71]

The horrifying multiplications of 'alien natures' in the mix of selfhood is a formal consequence of becoming habituated to oneself in and through material cultures: the 'perplexed combinations of *concrete* objects' generate a self made of its 'own nature repeated' with the additionally alienating material supplement of foreign objects.

In this version of the narrative, not opium but tea proves the 'true hero of the tale'. Read as a tale less of addiction than of the paradoxically alienating effects of *habit*, *Confessions* seems directly to summon the very forebear it tries hardest to disavow: Jonas Hanway, who warned that 'habit reconciles us to tea, as it does Turks to opium'. When, in the 'Introduction to the Pains of Opium', the Opium-eater catalogues the kinds of 'concrete objects' that end up as 'involutes' that channel, from the outside, the innermost contents of the self, it is not exotic objects he names but the things so familiar to one's daily habits that they pass in and out of one's life without being accounted for. Among this set of objects, tea-things loom large:

My [student's] gown is, by this time, I dare to say, in the same condition with many thousands of excellent books in the Bodleian, viz. diligently perused by certain studious moths and worms: or departed, however (which is all that I know of its fate), to that great reservoir of *somewhere*, to which all the tea-cups, tea-caddies, tea-pots, tea-kettles, &c. have departed (not to speak of still frailer vessels, such as glasses, decanters, bed-makers, &c.) which occasional resemblances in the present generation of tea-cups, &c. remind me of having once possessed, but of whose departure and final fate I [...] could give, I suspect, but an obscure and conjectural history.[72]

In De Quincey's nightmarish revision of the Lockean mental storehouse, the part of the mind that defines the self contains things that one cannot

<hr>

71 De Quincey, *Confessions*, pp. 250–1.
72 De Quincey, *Confessions*, p. 101.

remember admitting. Locke theorized a self that assimilates foreign objects to itself in the form of ideas acquired through the senses and made 'familiar';[73] De Quincey inverts this model to imagine a self in which familiar objects are lost, only to reappear in strange forms.[74] The 'great reservoir of *somewhere*' into which such things disappear is both that 'separate chamber in [the] brain – holding [. . .] some horrid alien nature' and the source of what the Opium-eater identifies as 'that inner eye and power of intuition for the vision and the mysteries of our human nature' that 'our English poets have possessed in the highest degree'.[75] These mysteries include the retired realities of the past, which are preserved, in uncanny forms, in the deepest chambers of modern subjectivity. Those who are most in touch with the wellspring of Englishness recognize that it is a 'nature repeated': a phenomenon with no self-same origin, but rather, being the effect of repetition – especially in and through a rotating inventory of accoutrements – a diffused, disorganized, and dislocated 'nature' that is as little at home in the 'inviolable sanctuary' of the individual self as that self is in a global material world.

While the idea of being polluted by foreign matter forms the premise of the *Confessions*, the text's more frightening insight is what happens to the self when material things become thoroughly familiar. Ultimately, what is strange about tea in the cultural landscape De Quincey depicts is how apparently *English* it is – how relentlessly English culture insists on identifying with tea even as, in other ways, it becomes increasingly invested in virulent anti-Chinese orientalism. In a material as well as figurative way, attaching these orientalist specters to opium serves to secure the intimacy of British subjects and their tea. But by teasing open the whole problem

---

[73] According to Locke, 'The Senses at first let in particular *Ideas*, and furnish the yet empty Cabinet: And the Mind by degrees growing familiar with some of them, they are lodged in the Memory, and Names got to them [. . .] In this manner the Mind comes to be furnish'd with *Ideas* and Language.' John Locke, *An Essay Concerning Human Understanding*, ed. Peter H. Nidditch (Oxford: Oxford University Press, 1975), p. 55.

[74] For example, when, under opium's influence, the narrator finds himself in the internal 'reservoir of *somewhere*' to which all the tea-things of earlier times have disappeared, he finds these objects – what Charles Lamb calls 'old china' – in horrifically mutated form: 'I ... found myself in Chinese houses, with cane tables, &c. All the feet of the tables, sophas, &c. soon became instinct with life: the abominable head of the crocodile, and his leering eyes, looked out at me, multiplied into a thousand repetitions: and I stood loathing and fascinated.' De Quincey, *Confessions*, p. 126. See Lamb, 'Old China', *London Magazine* (March 1823), pp. 269–72.

[75] De Quincey, *Confessions*, p. 55

of assimilation – the question of how someone or something comes to inhabit the form of the familiar – De Quincey unravels the whole premise of selfhood around which Englishness and orientalism alike are organized. The theory of the self that emerges through De Quincey's writing about opium refers us, compulsively, to the figure of tea, which refuses to uphold the abstract opposition of England and China, instead revealing their involuted intimacy in the everyday practice of English selfhood.

Binding and Unbinding Chinese Feet in the Mid-Century Victorian Press

ELIZABETH CHANG

In the January 1858 issue of *Tait's Edinburgh Magazine*, a broadly titled survey entitled 'Woman and Womankind' sketches a picture of the conditions, abilities, and limitations of Englishwomen in the century's middle decade. After several opening pages set in dreary ballrooms, the author decides to '[...] call a fact in illustration, and remove our scene to China'; an apparently advisable detour given that '[d]uring the last two years, China and the Chinese have been peculiarly brought before our notice, and thoughts of China have been floating through our minds'.[1] As a part of the subsequent catalogue of depredations of female existence in China, the author takes care to emphasize that '[t]he crippled feet of the high-class Chinese women typifies their mental condition',[2] a double crippling that supports the article's ultimate conclusion: 'The women of China, and the women of England, occupy positions far removed. The former need commiseration, for their's [sic] is a helpless state of physical and moral dependence,' while the women of England, at least the middle and upper classes, 'are free' and yet still insist on choosing the meta-phorical crippling of a 'vapid mind and useless life' of their own volition.[3] Far from the domestic social scene that began the piece, the reader finds herself concluding the article with China, and China's crippling negative difference, as the lasting example to direct her understanding of British women's self-determination.

This was neither a new nor a distinctive position for a reader of mid-century periodicals to be in. Each of the assumptions reviewed in *Tait's* are common to writings of the era – that Chinese bound feet constituted a mental as well as physical disability, that such disability was externally imposed, and could, theoretically at least, also be reversed by external means, and, most of all for the purposes of this essay, that 'thoughts of China' were floating, ungrounded, through the minds of British periodical

---

[1] 'Woman and Womankind', *Tait's Edinburgh Magazine*, 25 (1858), 17–24 (p. 21).
[2] 'Woman and Womankind', p. 22.
[3] 'Woman and Womankind', pp. 17, 23.

readers as a shaping condition of their own self-conception.[4] For China had been an object of interest in periodical culture since the beginning of the First Opium War. Already in 1843, the *Saturday Magazine*, mouth-piece of the Society for Promoting Christian Knowledge, was making the same assumptions of English interest and correspondence in its overview of 'Chinese Feet', writing that:

> Among the customs peculiar to that remarkable people, the Chinese, whose history and manners are now so interesting to us, there is none, perhaps, more universally known than that which forms the subject of our present notice. Yet although we have repeatedly heard the fact stated, that the ladies of China are in the habit of compressing their feet into the smallest possible dimensions, it may not be so well known *how* this is done, and what are the results of such an unnatural practice. ... [W]e would at the same time caution our female readers, not to look with contempt on Chinese ladies on account of these instances of vanity and folly; but to remember that even here, notwithstanding the superior light and knowledge in which we live, too many instances occur of as great an absurdity, and often a more fatal one, – in the compression of the waist, and the consequent injury done to the vital powers by tight clothing.[5]

In this essay I will examine Victorian prose attention to Chinese bound feet in the century's middle decades to investigate these gaps in narrative remembrance – between awareness of foot-binding as a fact and form, ignorance of the physical and material efforts that produced a body with a bound foot as well as the further dispositions of that body, and atten-tion to the domestic parallels of the supposedly foreign practice of foot-binding. I will argue that to draw on the trope of the bound foot is not *only* about confronting a physical effect deemed gruesome by Victorian Britons, although it certainly *is* that. It is also about a confrontation with imported and assimilated ideas of movement, freedom, and the power of narrative intervention. This, I argue, was a confrontation that lays the groundwork for later more specific reform efforts, and one that could

---

[4] As multiple scholars of Victorian literature have pointed out, the history of disability as a categorical term underwent significant revisions and refinements in this era; see, as a starting point, Martha Stoddard Holmes, *Fictions of Affliction: Physical Disability in Victorian Culture* (Ann Arbor, MI: University of Michigan Press, 2010).

[5] 'Chinese Feet', *The Saturday Magazine*, 23 (1843), 4–5 (p. 4).

not have occurred without the particular literary conditions of that mid-century moment.

Because I especially want to highlight the complexities of this confrontation, I am focusing in this essay on the multiple and contradictory effects achieved when Victorian serial periodicals joined with older kinds of descriptive practice, usually provided by volume travel narratives, to write about the ongoing and ever-expanding Sino-British global exchange and to emphasize that exchange's effects on the life and language of home. Recent scholarship considering the global reach of Victorian explanatory prose has noticed the significant differences in content and form when periodicals and volume works are taken together as registers of international conditions.[6] But 'charting' the global 'golden stream' of Victorian periodicals would be overwhelming even if geography and era were not limited, as here, to China in the 1830–1860 period.[7] Serial publications add many hundreds of articles on China – appearing in sources as far distant as the liberal *Westminster Review* and the illustrated periodical of the working-class *The Penny Magazine* – to the burgeoning bibliography of 'Books on China'.[8] This was both because these mid-century decades starkly expanded the territorial and material reach of British writers and readers of China, and also because all kinds of periodical writing expanded greatly in this period. I choose the bound foot as a site of encounter not merely to curtail this multitude, however. In ways that I will sketch

[6] For recent general efforts by the field to confront these conditions, see Tanya Agathocleous, 'Imperial, Anglophone, Geopolitical, Worldly: Evaluating The "Global" In Victorian Studies', *Victorian Literature and Culture*, 43 (2015), 1–8; Lauren M.E. Goodlad, 'Cosmopolitanism's Actually Existing Beyond; Toward a Victorian Geopolitical Aesthetic', *Victorian Literature and Culture*, 38 (2010), 399–411; Ayşe Çelikkol, 'Form and Global Consciousness in the Victorian Period', *Literature Compass*, 10 (2013), 269–76, and Sharon Marcus, 'Same Difference? Transnationalism, Comparative Literature, and Victorian Studies', *Victorian Studies*, 45 (2003), 677–86.

[7] Kay Boardman, 'Charting the Golden Stream?: Recent Work on Victorian Periodicals', *Victorian Studies*, 48 (2006), 505–17. See also Linda K. Hughes, 'SIDEWAYS!: Navigating the Material(ity) of Print Culture', *Victorian Periodicals Review*, 47 (2014), 1–30.

[8] Of these, see P. P. T., 'ART. 1.-China: Its Early History, Literature, and Language; Mis-Translation of Chinese Official Documents; Causes of the Present War', *Westminster Review*, 34 (1840), [261]–287; and the thirteen-part series of articles beginning with 'CHINA.-No. I', *Penny Magazine* (4 August 1835), pp. [297]–299. Finally, for a contemporary bibliography of 'Books on China', see the appendix to William Mayers, Nicholas Dennys, and Charles King, *The Treaty Ports of China and Japan* (London: Trübner, 1867).

out in the main portion of this essay, I argue that the 'tropifying' of the bound foot during these mid-century years helpfully makes plain the complications that periodical dissemination brings.[9] Elijah Bridgman's 1835 assertion of the Chinese that 'Not only the minds of the people, but their bodies also, are distorted and deformed by unnatural usages' takes on new implications when the unnatural usages of foot-binding become common knowledge to the minds of domestic British readers, and even more so when those unnatural usages are returned, implicitly or explicitly, to Britons' own rhetorical practice.[10]

My limiting of historical period will make more sense to scholars of Victorian prose, however, than to historians of Chinese foot-binding. For most histories of British engagements with foot-binding in China focus on the post-1870 period when activists like the novelist Alicia Little (A. E. N. Bewicke) and the London Missionary Society delegate John MacGowan (author of the anti-foot-binding treatise *How England Saved China* [1913]) were most active.[11] Angela Zito's work has critically engaged with the chronologies of modernity marked by foot-binding's ascendance and abolition during the later nineteenth century, and I intend this essay to give some preliminary history of her engagements. In particular, I seek to investigate her suggestions that '[f]or Europeans, the Chinese woman's bound foot operated ambiguously in a late nineteenth-century universe in a way that tended constantly to evacuate social and cultural problems into the "natural" physical body' in the specific context of the mid-century

---

[9] The term is Srinivas Arvamudan's. See his *Tropicopolitans: Colonialism and Agency, 1688–1804* (Durham, NC: Duke University Press, 1999).

[10] 'Small Feet of the Chinese Females; Remarks on the Origin of the Custom of Compressing the Feet; the Extent and Effects of the Practice; with an Anatomical Description of a Small Foot', *The Chinese Repository*, 3 (1835), 537–42 (p. 537).

[11] See John Macgowan, *How England Saved China* (London: T. F. Unwin, 1913). For more on Alicia Little, her work with the Tian Zu Hui (Natural Foot Society) and more general missionary efforts to abolish foot-binding, see Julia Kuehn, 'Knowing Bodies, Knowing Self: The Western Woman Traveller's Encounter with Chinese Women, Bound Feet and the Half-Caste Child, 1880–1920', *Studies in Travel Writing*, 12.3 (2008), 265–90; Shanyn Fiske, 'Asian Awakenings: Alicia Little and the Limits of Orientalism', *Victorian Literature and Culture*, 37.01 (2009), 11–25; and the work of Susan Schoenbauer Thurin, including 'Travel Writing and the Humanitarian Impulse', in *A Century of Travels in China Critical Essays on Travel Writing from the 1840s to the 1940s*, ed. Douglas Kerr and Julia Kuehn (Hong Kong: Hong Kong University Press, 2007), pp. 91–103, and *Victorian Travelers and the Opening of China, 1842–1907* (Athens. OH: Ohio University Press, 1999).

Victorian press.[12] This results in several absences from my argument. My attention to works written in English and mostly published in England sets aside the complex Chinese response during this period, particularly by members of the so-called Taiping Rebellion, and thus is meant as a supplement to the important social histories of Chinese foot-binding practices produced by scholars like Dorothy Ko and Christena Turner.[13] I also give little attention to the physical and social conditions surrounding the initial binding of the feet in childhood, also attended to in detail by Ko, Turner, and Patricia Ebrey, so that I can instead trace the later circulations of the bound foot from action to metaphor and from object to concept.[14]

In following these circulations, we see a different version of prose writing's inversion of ethnography to auto-ethnography that James Buzard has identified as occurring in British fiction of the nineteenth century.[15] To describe China through its bound feet is in some way to train nineteenth-century readers to take details of Chinese bodies and histories out of course and out of context, rendering these figures free from agency and even subjectivity, in the manner Zito has described. But it is also to allow this disembodied metaphor to enter into British domestic discourse. To understand how and why this happened specifically, we need to attend to the many forms and contexts within which foot-binding appeared as

[12] Angela Zito, 'Secularizing the Pain of Footbinding in China: Missionary and Medical Stagings of the Universal Body', *Journal of the American Academy of Religion*, 75 (2007), 1–24 (p. 16). See also her 'Bound to Be Represented: Theorizing/Fetishizing Footbinding', in *Embodied Modernities: Corporeality, Representation, and Chinese Cultures*, ed. Fran Martin and Larissa Heinrich (Honolulu, HI: University of Hawaii Press, 2006), pp. 21–41 (p. 25).

[13] See Dorothy Ko, *Cinderella's Sisters: A Revisionist History of Footbinding* (Berkeley: University of California Press, 2005), and Christena L. Turner, 'Locating Footbinding: Variations across Class and Space in Nineteenth and Early Twentieth Century China', *Journal of Historical Sociology*, 10.4 (1997), 444–79. Other key sources include Ping Wang, *Aching for Beauty: Footbinding in China* (Minneapolis, MN: University of Minnesota Press, 2000), and C. Fred Blake, 'Foot-Binding in Neo-Confucian China and the Appropriation of Female Labor', *Signs: Journal of Women in Culture and Society*, 19.3 (1994), 676–712. In addition, foot-binding has also been considered in the context of global ethics in such works as Kwame Anthony Appiah's *The Honor Code: How Moral Revolutions Happen* (New York: W. W. Norton & Company, 2011) and made a controversial but influential part of arguments for global feminism in works like Andrea Dworkin's *Woman Hating* (New York: E. P. Dutton, 1974).

[14] See Patricia Buckley Ebrey, *Women and the Family in Chinese History* (London: Routledge, 2003).

[15] See James Buzard, *Disorienting Fiction: The Autoethnographic Work of Nineteenth-Century British Novels* (Princeton: Princeton University Press, 2005).

a trope. The extreme compression that allows John Stuart Mill to refer glancingly to 'a Chinese lady's foot' in order to supply for his audience a range of physical, cultural, historical, and ontological conditions, each with its own complex forms of representation, has its own Victorian literary history that has not yet been fully explored.

What sets the bound foot apart as a mid-century trope worthy of further investigation, then, are two distinguishing rhetorical characteristics. First, the practice of binding women's feet is simply more distressing and memorable than other Chinese customs, and so for that reason alone has persisted well into the postcolonial present as a condition 'bound to be represented', as Zito has explained. My focus in this essay, however, will be on what I think is the second distinguishing characteristic: that the bound foot, itself understood as a troubling imposition of immobility on helpless and dependent Chinese women in the manner the *Tait's* article explained, also becomes an increasingly mobile trope even as its circulations served mainly to delineate the limits and consequences of immobility for British subjects as well as Chinese. The more common the references to Chinese bound feet became in mid-nineteenth-century British writing, that is, the less substance the reference needed to put forward to achieve its associative ends, and, consequently, the more capacious its figurative compass of repression, restriction, and constraint became. The image could move anywhere in literary culture to show immobility everywhere. This makes it of unique interest to literary scholars interested in Victorian global form.

In the subsequent sections of this essay, I will review two histories of the circulations of the bound foot as image and trope in nineteenth-century writings. The first section will detail the evolution of the bound foot both as a narrative moment and as a nascent metaphor within the larger evolution of British writing on China during the period of the Opium Wars. This section will attend to the effects on such writing from the constant mid-century exchange between volume narratives and periodicals. With both expanding genres working cooperatively and at times competitively to sketch out the details of global cultural differences, readerly apprehension of foreign bodies and spaces depended ever more completely on not only the content provided by these publications, but also the conceptual organization offered by their narrative and rhetorical form. When conceptual structures came into conflict, as when a periodical extracted a volume narrative for its own purposes, then the rhetorical import of the bound foot expanded and changed. The second section is far briefer, but, I hope, allusive of a broad range of possibility. This section gives the cursory beginnings of the broad-scale dissemination of the bound foot as trope of immobility in other forms of literature in order to suggest the deadening of metaphor that this dissemination begins to (but cannot ever fully) impose. This conclusion is meant to suggest how the bound foot expands broadly but shallowly throughout British literary culture, even as active work for the abolition of the practice by British missionaries and others was deepening and strengthening in China during the same period, making actual bound feet appear to be rhetorically reformable disabilities.

My argument across both sections is that the figure of the bound Chinese foot occupies a strikingly hybrid place in mid-century British writing. It did not exclusively designate foreignness, although it certainly still marked the exotic Chinese body, but neither did it exist only as a dead metaphor whose physical and cultural referent was forgotten. Instead, the trope of the bound Chinese foot was written out between these two positions, promising both the possibility of real social reform while also inscribing the hypothetical and conditional contours of Chinese bodies for British readers. Other body modifications – the compression of 'heads of Indians' or the corseted waists of European ladies – occupied some similar space of overlapping conceptual and physical constraint, as *Chambers's* claim that '[d]eformity of the person is not always congenital, nor the effect of accident: it is often the result of a deliberate attempt to alter what nature has made perfect' demonstrates.[16] But none did so as significantly for a conjoined understanding of the foreign and the domestic as did the bound foot. That prose writers allowed the bound foot to abstract itself into language, but never allowed that abstraction to be fully complete, demonstrates in another way how the imbrications of China's foreignness and difference were reshaping Britain's own culture and literature.

In this section, I will review some of the ways that foot-binding entered into Victorian print culture in an effort to supplement existing chronological histories of this process. Patricia Ebrey, whose comprehensive survey of European attention to Chinese foot-binding comes from the perspective of a scholar of Chinese history interested in the historical conformation of her own field, identifies 'fashion, seclusion, perversity, deformity, child abuse, and cultural immobility' as collective and overlapping approaches to justifying and explaining the practice of foot-binding as observed across the years 1300–1890.[17] Within those categories, however, and limiting myself to a much shorter time frame, I will look at some practicalities

---

[16] 'Artificial Deformities', *Chambers's Edinburgh Journal* (24 April 1841), p. 111.
[17] Patricia Buckley Ebrey, 'Gender and Sinology: Shifting Western Interpretations of Footbinding, 1300–1890', *Late Imperial China*, 20 (1999), 1–34 (p. 11).

of how the bound foot expanded across genre into the huge variety of prose writing that shaped the Victorian reader in ways both ephemeral and non-canonical.

To look at it this way offers different priorities of form from those identifying the travel narrative as a singly narrated work of direct physical experience and observation. Such an identification has never been strictly true, of course; even a seminal travel work like John Barrow's *Travels in China* (1804) reflects prevailing literary conventions by layering together personal observation, historical anecdote, shared reminiscence and more in order to do its descriptive and explanatory work. But especially in the case of the bound foot did prose efforts at contextualization achieve particularly self-referential and self-authorizing ends. By the first decades of the nineteenth century, an introduction to the practice and history of 'small-footed China', as the country was sometimes termed, seemed hardly necessary, given the ample literary precedents of the description. And yet such introductions did occur and recur, establishing their place not only as descriptive and representational but affective and persuasive. Unlike a description of the process of harvesting tea or catching fish with cormorants, foot-binding as cultural practice evolved quickly into foot-binding as cultural metaphor.

In most cases this evolution began as part of a larger effort to tell the history of the Chinese empire as a proposed remediation of the static immobility and consequent resistance to historical progression that China was held to maintain. Not only elite literary reviews but also periodicals aimed at middle-class, often female, readers worked to tell and retell the history of foot-binding as a practice in keeping with developing historically situated understandings of cultural difference – 'It is worthy of remark, that this political custom should still subsist among the Chinese at this day; as it originated with the inhabitants of China more than a thousand years antecedent to the Christian era,'[18] explains the *Lady's Monthly* in 1815, while in 1873 *All the Year Round* asserts that the custom '[...] is of comparatively modern origin, and owes its existence to the whim of Li Yuh, the licentious and unpopular prince of Keang-nan [...(who)] ruled from A.D. 961 to 976'.[19] The sixty-year lapse between these demonstrates the difficulty felt in drawing China into European chronology. In the same manner, though on the opposite side of the coin, evocations of the practice also often professed their utter inability to historicize a baffling

---

[18] 'Origin of a Chinese Custom', *The Lady's Monthly Museum*, 2 (1815), 19 (p.19).
[19] 'Ladies' Feet in China', *All the Year Round*, 10 (1873), 571–2 (p. 572).

custom that resulted in 'a foot, which for singularity at least, may challenge the whole world', as Barrow puts it.[20] The *Quarterly Review*, in a joint treatment of narratives by Amherst embassy members Henry Ellis and John Macleod (McLeod), insists 'How so unnatural, and, to us at least, so disgusting a practice could ever have been introduced, much less established, we cannot pretend to conjecture.'[21]

But even as these familiar Victorian efforts at ordering and historicizing the custom were ongoing, other modes of writing about feet and their movements were also developing. In accounts like those written by government agents like Barrow, Ellis, and Macleod, or by missionaries like Karl Gützlaff, Walter Henry Medhurst, William Lockhart, or George Tradescant Lay, or by military men like John Bingham, Granville Loch, or Arthur Cunynghame, or colonial administrators, like John Francis Davis, or other professionals like the doctor Charles Downing and the plant-hunter Robert Fortune, readers gained information not only about the cultural history of the custom of foot-binding but also details of the practice and effects of the binding itself. This was despite the fact that most travelers to China in the first decades of the nineteenth century had very limited ability to encounter women with bound feet in the course of their travels, and, as my catalogue of respondents makes plain, even fewer of the travelers publishing accounts of foot-binding in the mainstream press were female.

One recompense to this scarcity was the republished work. The publisher John Murray's 1844 issuance of the eighteenth-century Jesuit missionary Father Ripa's *Memoirs* both allowed a more intimate view of the court of China than any previously afforded by British travelers, but also enabled, through the work of periodical review, a further confirmation of readerly expectations. To read reviews of republished works was to be imbricated even further in the circle of authentication and observation, as readers were trained to expect that periodical extracts would set out and identify accounts of the practice in their reviews, re-authenticating the republished narrative of travel through alignment with the preparatory travels of the trope itself. The republication of Ripa's memoirs in particular of course also allowed British readers to sublimate French activity in China as an activity of the past, in counterpoint to the activity of the British present. Thus when Ripa opines that: 'From their inordinate

---

[20] John Barrow, *Travels in China* (London: T. Cadell and W. Davies, 1806), p. 73.

[21] 'Art. VIII. – Journal of the Proceedings of the Late Embassy to China…', *The Quarterly Review*, 17 (1817), 463–505 (p. 497).

jealousy arose the custom of crippling the feet of the women, in order to render walking a torment, and induce them to remain at home,'[22] the family magazine *The Critic* can assert the memoir 'spirited, graphic, and doubtless truthful' before republishing a selection of anecdotes including 'Origin of Small Feet in Chinese Ladies'.[23] Other periodicals could go further; The *Dublin Review*, for one, savours Ripa's image of the emperor '[...] sending his ladies hobbling off to gather some fruit [...] designedly, that he may have a laugh at their many and oft-repeated falls'[.][24] If movement can be regulated as a marker of intellectual or emotional freedom, it can also be comedically amplified, at least within the palace walls.

By the time of Ripa's republication, of course, the so-called First Opium War, as well as the subsequent Arrow War and the internal conflict of the Taiping Rebellion, had already occasioned a number of soldiers' narratives that brought a new and grislier attention to the forms of Chinese women's bodies. Reviews of these narratives joined with the increasingly more substantive sequences of articles published in periodicals across the ideological spectrum seeking to contextualize the events of the war and the war-ending treaties, but they also shared space with an ever-growing number of pieces in middle-class general interest magazines on foot-binding as a specific aspect of Chinese culture, such as The *Saturday Magazine*'s 'Chinese Feet' (1843) and *Chambers's Edinburgh Journal*'s 'Artificial Deformities' (1841) and 'The Chinese Foot Torture' (1843). At the same time, the well-respected *The Chinese Repository*, a periodical published variously in Canton, Macao, and Hong Kong and largely comprised of missionary contributions (and so highly critical of foot-binding), was sent back to England to circulate across the desks of domestic periodical editors, influencing and directing content in ways both implicit and significant, as Elizabeth Malcolm has described.[25] Missionary society rhetoric not always admitted directly into mainstream discourse thus gained entry through treatment of a particular secular topic of interest to general readers. Thus in many cases, writings from China

---

[22] Matteo Ripa, *Memoirs of Father Ripa, During Thirteen Years' Residence at the Court of Peking* (London: John Murray, 1844), p. 58.

[23] 'Father Ripa's Residence at the Court of Peking', *Critic*, 1 (1845), 389.

[24] 'ART. IV.–Memoirs of Father Ripa, during Thirteen Years' Residence at the Court of Peking, in the Service of the Emperor of China; with an Account of the Foundation of the College for the Education of Young Chinese at Naples', *The Dublin Review*, 18 (1845), 112–28 (p. 127).

[25] Elizabeth L. Malcolm, 'The Chinese Repository and Western Literature on China, 1800 to 1850', *Modern Asian Studies*, 7 (1973), 165–78.

entered into the serial sphere through several directions, with a striking divergence in tone and treatment of the same events.

One example of this is the writing of Granville Loch, aide-de-camp to General Sir Hugh Gough during the First Opium War, whose affecting accounts of the sufferings of Chinese women were especially remarked upon in reviews of his narrative *The Closing Events of the Campaign in China* (1843) – its 'details must long haunt the mind', claims *Tait's Edinburgh.*[26] Loch's narrative repeats the story of a 'clever young naval surgeon' whose young patient dies when her mother insists on rebinding the girl's feet after the surgeon has removed the wrappings to treat infection, claiming that 'her daughter had better die than remain unmarried' as unbound feet would certainly ensure.[27] In republishing as an extract this sad story of the 'little coffin in which he discovered the body of his poor young patient' under the title 'The Chinese Foot-Torture', *Chambers's Edinburgh Journal* adds a lengthy parenthesis arguing that 'All will feel the monstrous character of this madness of the Chinese females; but is the waist-constriction of our own any better? [...] there can be no doubt that it also causes coffins to be laid down a doors for "young patients".'[28] Similarly *The Athenaeum* includes this same anecdote with the prefatory remark that '[i]t reminds us forcibly of tight lacing and its consequences [...]'.[29] These digested versions achieve their domestic relocations by excising the volume narrative's longer musings by Loch on the process by which deformity can transform into pleasure – 'I must confess that I began to think, with many others, that a Chinese lady would appear to want some peculiar grace without the deformity of the crippled feet, – so much does custom guide and regulate what is commonly called taste,' writes Loch.[30] Excised too is the context of treaty negotiation that afforded Loch the leisure to share stories with naval surgeons in the first place.

In much the same manner, the invasive military encounters described in John Bingham's *Narrative of the Expedition to China* (1843) find their way not only into assessments of the Anglo-Chinese War itself, but into considerations of the fate of Chinese women's feet when the *Saturday*

[26] 'The Closing Events of the Campaign in China', *Tait's Edinburgh Magazine*, 10 (1843), 425–31 (p. 426).

[27] Granville G. Loch, *The Closing Events of the Campaign in China: The Operations in the Yang-Tze-Kiang and Treaty of Nanking* (London: John Murray, 1843), p. 92.

[28] 'The Chinese Foot-Torture', *Chambers's Edinburgh Journal* (1843), p. 248.

[29] 'The Closing Events of the Campaign in China', *The Athenaeum*, 818 (1843), 605–6 (p. 605).

[30] Loch, *Closing Events*, p. 90.

Magazine reprints his story of offering a Chinese girl a '"new and very bright loopee"' to unwind her bandaged feet.[31] The Christian family magazine, however, demurs from printing the whole of Bingham's intrusive engagement, which continues:

> By signs we expressed a wish to see the *pied mignon* of a really good-looking woman of the party. Our signs were quickly understood, but, probably, from her being a matron, it was not considered quite *comme il faut* for her to comply with our desire, as she would not consent to show us her foot; but a very pretty interesting girl of about sixteen was placed on a stool for the purpose of gratifying our curiousity.[32]

Bingham's narrative is by no means singular in this regard: Arthur Cunynghame, aide-de-camp to Lord Saltoun at the same period, describes helping his ship's doctor remove a foot from a young female corpse as a medical sample and souvenir. '[H]er friends must have been not a little surprised to see that the feet, which so seldom walked before, should, upon our approach, have trotted off, leaving the body behind,'[33] jests Cunynghame, a recounting that is presumably one of the 'amusing personal adventures' praised by the *Foreign Quarterly Review*'s treatment of his work.[34]

Not only military men, of course, but also other kinds of travelers were active in China in the years leading up to the Anglo-Chinese war. Among these Charles Downing takes advantage of the 'lively interest directed at the present moment to China'[35] to pen his *The Fan-Qui in China* (1838). Downing, basing his observations on his experience in Canton and Macao, writes critically of the 'curious Chinese custom of forcing the feet of the members of the fair sex into their distorted and unnatural shape [...] very ridiculous to European eyes'.[36] This criticism and a column of reprinted quotation makes its way into the *Chambers's* review of Downing's work, complete with the magazine's disclaimer that, 'as we do not profess here

---

31 'Chinese Feet', p. 4.
32 John Elliot Bingham, *Narrative of the Expedition to China from the Commencement of the War to Its Termination in 1842* (London: H. Colburn, 1843), p. 357.
33 Sir Arthur Augustus Thurlow Cunynghame, *The Opium War: Being Recollections of Service in China* (Philadelphia: G. B. Zieber, 1845), p. 92.
34 'ART. X-1. The Chinese Repository ...', *The Foreign Quarterly Review*, 34 (1845), 432–49 (p. 433).
35 Charles Toogood Downing, *The Fan-Qui in China, in 1836–7*. 3 vols (London: H. Colburn, 1838), 1. vi.
36 Downing, *Fan-Qui*, 2. 41.

to give any connected view of the contents of Mr. Downing's numerous observations, we may now quote his remarks on the much famed feet of the Chinese ladies'.[37] Yet while *Chambers's* repeats Downing's critique of the 'old lady, verging into dotage, believing all eyes are turned on her in admiration, because her feet are no larger than a child five or six years of age',[38] the magazine does not reprint his narrative's subsequent lapse into the second person, which continues, 'You feel a great temptation to go up and offer the old lady the use of your stick to help her along, as she seems in danger of falling every moment.'[39] Periodical readers, then, receive a narrative closure on the meeting that those perusing the volume text could not achieve, even if their imaginative participation in the scene was itself curtailed.

But periodical readers also often miss the emotional engagement that the volume narrative uses to contextualize a descriptive scene. Readers of the *Bentley's Miscellany* review of the plant-hunter Robert Fortune's third travel narrative, *A Residence Among the Chinese* (1857), could find reprinted Fortune's description of a scene of 'gaily dressed ladies, limping along on their small feet' as well as the quotations Fortune provides from the London Missionary Society medical missionary William Lockhart on the 'barbarous custom of deforming the feet of Chinese ladies, and [...] the serious inconveniences which result from it'.[40] Not reprinted, however, are moments that reimpose the filtering emotional interventions of the foreign observer – both the volume narrative's appreciation of the 'joyous ringing laugh' given by the passing gaily dressed ladies but also its acknowledgment that the 'limping uncertain gait of the women is, *to a foreigner*, distressing to see'.[41]

At work in Downing, Bingham, and Fortune are clearly the cross-currents of sexual desire, racial privilege, and the gendered operations of power that Ebrey, Zito, and other critics of this literature have identified. I also want, however, to point to the distinction between placing the bound foot on display, as Bingham does, and the imaginative or conditional physical involvement with the actual movements of foot-bound women that other travelers hoped to achieve in fancy if not in fact, attention to which is often amplified through the periodical republication. Downing's 'temptation' to help the elderly women is echoed later in James Powers's

[37] 'Chinese Sketches', *Chambers's Edinburgh Journal*, 351 (1838), 310–11 (p. 311).

[38] 'Chinese Sketches', p. 311.

[39] Downing, *Fan-Qui*, 2. 41.

[40] 'China and the Chinese', *Bentley's Miscellany*, 42 (1857), 48–58 (pp. 57–8).

[41] Robert Fortune, *A Residence among the Chinese* (London: John Murray, 1857), pp. 248, 250, emphasis mine.

reprinted composite account, in the *London Journal*'s 'Chinese Women', of his encounters with single 'unprotected' woman falling from her small feet:

> To rush to her assistance was the natural impulse, but the approach of the monster was a signal for the most tremendous shrieking [...] It was a disagreeable dilemma, but it invariably ended in my walking on and leaving the lady to scramble out of the mud in her own way.[42]

Whether fiction or fact, the 'invariable ending' of the narrative paved the way for the bound foot to become itself a patterned story, one that readers would retain as an ongoing internal supplement to any later invocations of the form.

At the same time, there is an increasing internal division in the rhetoric between the language describing the 'macerated' foot itself and the description of the movements of women who possessed such feet. The former frequently resists description entirely, as a *London Saturday Journal* author suggests in a recounting of the display of a patient's 'naked deformity': 'The native handmaid blushed and turned her face, as if ashamed of the discovery. It was not a foot that we saw, neither was it health or disease, but a strange and indescribable compound of them all.'[43] The latter, however, receives a surfeit of accounting. Authors of both periodical and volume narratives were eager to describe the hypothetical identifications necessary to accomplish movement on bound feet. *Chinese Repository* editor Elijah Bridgman explains that:

> In walking, the body is bent forwards at a considerable inclination, in order to place the centre of gravity over the feet; and the great muscular exertion required for preserving the balance is evinced by the rapid motion of the arms, and the hobbling shortness of the steps.[44]

Fellow missionary Walter Henry Medhurst concurs that the Chinese women 'hobbled along, and even managed to run, with their bodies bent forward, much better than we could have expected'.[45]

---

[42] 'Chinese Women', *The London Journal, and Weekly Record*, 18 (1853), 29–30 (p. 30). See also William Tyrone Power, *Recollections of a Three Years' Residence in China: Including Peregrinations in Spain, Morocco, Egypt, India, Australia, and New-Zealand* (London: Richard Bentley, 1853), p. 177.

[43] 'China and the Chinese, No. IX, Conclusion of the Series. Women in China', *The London Saturday Journal*, 3 (1840), 392–5 (p. 394).

[44] 'Small Feet', p. 538.

[45] Walter Henry Medhurst, *China: Its State and Prospects* (London: John Snow, 1838), p. 490.

George Tradescant Lay, a naturalist, missionary for the British and Foreign Bible Society, and consul in several southern treaty ports, goes even further to bring together his reader and the mobile Chinese body. He writes in his much-cited *The Chinese as They Are* (1841) that, '[i]n walking, the knee-joint does not bend, so that any one may imitate the much-admired mincing gait of the country, by stepping with only a rotatory movement of the hip-joint, and keeping the knee and ankle stiffly in one position'.[46] The prospect of English readers of the *Saturday Magazine* or the *Monthly Review*, both of which repeat these directions, actually physically imitating the mincing gait stands in compelling contrast to the static images of small shoes and distorted feet on display in the pages of the periodicals and the display cases of Chinese exhibitions.[47]

This mirrored a larger division in popular evocations of China and the Chinese meant for general readers. On the one hand, authors assessing China's land and people took an increasingly personal approach, facilitated by the series of unequal treaties that opened broad space for travel in the interior of China. These travelers invariably insisted that their explorations revealed truths unavailable to those confined to more familiar treaty ports; for example, Thomas Blakiston, army officer in the Second Opium War who parlayed his service in China into an adventure piloting a steamship up the Yangtze, insists on correcting 'an error into which people in England have been led by taking the accounts of persons who have only visited Canton as descriptive of China', asserting that he 'passed through the breadth of China on the Yang-tsze Kiang' and can therefore be sure that foot-binding was not merely an upper-class but a 'universal' custom.[48] On the other hand, however, descriptions of footbinding were hardening into singular form – '"We have all known from childhood how the Chinese cramp their women's feet",'[49] writes *Bow Bells* in 1864 – and middle-class family periodicals continued to rely on such stereotyped mass-culture images of the 'Flowery Land' to advance their

[46] George Tradescant Lay, *The Chinese as They Are: Their Moral, Social, and Literary Character* (London: W. Ball and Co., 1841), p. 32.

[47] 'Shoes for ladies having small feet' occupy several cases in the catalogue for Nathan Dunn and William Langdon's Chinese Collection; see Nathan Dunn and William B. Langdon, 'Ten Thousand Chinese Things': A Descriptive Catalogue of the Chinese Collection in Philadelphia (London: Printed for the proprietor, 1842), p. 95.

[48] Thomas Wright Blakiston, *Five Months on the Yang-Tsze: And Notices of the Present Rebellions in China* (London: John Murray, 1862), p. 203.

[49] 'How the Chinese Make Dwarf Trees', *Bow Bells*, 5 (1864), 103.

work. In 1875, *All the Year Round* is still able to begin its treatment of 'Ladies' Feet in China' with a quotation from John Francis Davis's 'interesting and instructive work on the Chinese',[50] first published in 1836, condemning the 'folly and childishness of a large portion of mankind [...] displayed [...] in those [...] modes in which they have departed from the standard of nature and sought distinction even in deformity'.[51]

This suggests that the Victorian periodical reader, whether or not she was also a reader of volume travel narratives, was able, by the time of the destruction of the Summer Palace in 1860 if not well before, to hold in concert multiple and conflicting conceptions of the Chinese bound foot. It was an object – to be depicted and circulated in image and a material souvenir, either referentially, as a shoe, or more gruesomely, as a severed piece of flesh and bone.[52] It was at the same time a function of motion, propelling Chinese resistance, effective or not, to the imprecations of British military intervention, but also admitting British imitation of a Chinese walking style that could allow a specific and brief moment of trans-racial identification. And finally, as I will discuss in the next section, it was an increasingly effective entry into metaphor, available both for the purposes of comedy and reform. It was through this final classification that the bound foot has entered the most intimately into Victorian literature. But it has been my argument throughout that the glancing reference to the bound foot cannot be separated from the longer, earlier history that told and retold the conditions and consequences of the binding of a Chinese foot. That earlier literary chronology moves narrative focus and form from histories of foot-binding, to descriptive personal encounters with the bound foot as an object, to observation and engagement with a woman moving on bound feet, while at the same time shifting and evolving to meet the particular needs of each literary genre of publication. Thus a bound foot is never a static or a stable verbal or visual image – it carries with it, as consequence of its potential unbinding, both historical and proleptic encounters with agency curtailed and restored. Periodical and volume authors with a range of professional and religious affiliations could use the bound foot as a universal provocation requiring rhetorical compensation and

---

50 'Ladies' Feet in China', p. 571.

51 John Francis Davis, *The Chinese: A General Description of the Empire of China and Its Inhabitants* (London: C. Knight, 1836), 1. 256.

52 See Bransby Blake Cooper and Peter Mark Roget, 'Anatomical Description of the Foot of a Chinese Female', *Philosophical Transactions of the Royal Society of London*, 2 (1829), 255–60.

restoration. In my final section, I will take up a few slight references to a Chinese lady's foot and argue that the narrative range I have described remains embedded in the metaphorical bound foot even as the context of the actual bound foot falls away.

'What form do Chinese feet assume when denied their proper development?'[53] asks Florence Nightingale as an amplification of her essay 'Cassandra''s central and best-known exhortation – 'Why have women passion, intellect, moral activity – these three – and a place in society where no one of the three can be exercised?'[54] Both of these questions – concerning Chinese feet and women's unexercised passion – survive the many revisions of this influential essay, first begun in early 1850s and privately printed in 1860. The never-given answer is both obvious and also, it seems, not meant to lead readers any further into the actual forms and conditions of Chinese bodies. Indeed Nightingale does not bring in the gender of the possessors of the Chinese feet until several pages later, when she writes of English 'women [who] could not make use of leisure and solitude if they had it! Like the Chinese woman who could not make use of her feet if she were brought into European life.'[55] Nightingale's hollow reference to a seemingly specific Chinese woman whose potential useless-ness remains nevertheless hypothetical depends on the improbability of Chinese women ever being 'brought into European life'. And yet in both cases, the activity and usefulness of the bound foot as a metaphor repudi-ates the inutility of China and the Chinese implicitly proposed. In the same way, when, as I described above, John Stuart Mill makes a slight aside in *On Liberty* to refer to the damaging forces of public opinion that seek 'to maim by compression, like a Chinese lady's foot, every part of human nature which stands out prominently [...]',[56] the confusing agency of his aside – is the lady's foot doing the maiming or being maimed? – shows how easily he expects his readers to catch the metaphor of suppressed individualism. Theorizing the loss and gain of female activity through the binding and unbinding of Chinese feet becomes generally possible

---

[53] *Florence Nightingale's Suggestions for Thought*, ed. Lynn McDonald, *The Collected Works of Florence Nightingale. Volume 11* (Waterloo, ON: Wilfrid Laurier University Press, 2008), p. 549. On this reference, see also Lee Anna Maynard, '"Bound Women: The Plight of the Other in Florence Nightingale's 'Cassandra'", *Nineteenth-Century Prose*, 26 (1999), 63–72.

[54] Nightingale, *Suggestions*, p. 548.

[55] Nightingale, *Suggestions*, p. 574.

[56] John Stuart Mill, *On Liberty* (London: Ticknor and Fields, 1863), p. 134.

precisely because the metaphor of the bound foot is so generally and broadly disseminated – and, indeed, so helpful to capturing a particular understanding of constraint as a physical restriction on mobility. Amherst embassy member Henry Ellis's 1817 critique that, in China, '[t]he mind would seem to be treated [...] like the feet of the women, cramped by the bandages of habit and education, till it acquires an unnatural littleness', has here been carried home to the imperial metropole.[57]

A further look at Nightingale's essay in particular reminds us that her initial question about what form of Chinese feet may assume is not necessarily historically or rhetorically divorced from the main content of Nightingale's essay, which also depends on central contentions about collective and individual mobility. Yet significantly these contentions are reversed from what we might expect: the abstract qualities of passion, intellect, and moral activity suffer from lack of *exercise*, a term that carries heavy physical connotation, while the feet themselves, physical agents of mobility, are held in a more static and abstract construction to *assume a form*. Thus in order to mentally align Nightingale's question about this assumed form with her question about the exercise of passion, intellect, and moral activity (which she clearly intends the reader to do), we must willfully shift the thrust of her query away from the static image it suggests and towards an imagined exploration of the possibilities of movement in general. That is to say it is not the bound foot itself as an object that is our endpoint here, but rather the bound foot's metonymic relationship to a developmental narrative describing the possibilities of movement, not only for Nightingale's readers but also for nineteenth-century subjects more generally. Without ever making the assertion plain, Nightingale's figural use of the bound foot depends on an implicit knowledge of the bound foot's movement as well as its compression.

By way of conclusion to this essay, I want to suggest that thinking about the developmental narrative – both proper and improper – that the bound foot contains forces us to consider not only the internal constraints imposed when an improper form is assumed but also the range and limits of social exercise as externally defined. If we grant with Nightingale that liberty resides in the individual body and that individual mobility manifests liberty's instantiation, then we begin to get at why bound Chinese feet – and considerations of their unbinding – appear in so many places in Victorian writing, in ways both literal and

---

57 Sir Henry Ellis, *Journal of the Proceedings of the Late Embassy to China* (London: John Murray, 1817), p. 197.

figural. To propose the Chinese woman's bound foot as the antithesis to a fully liberated mobility, as opposed to, say, an English domestic subject's congenital disability, is to propose that disability can be denied and mobility can be reinstated through the tenets of reform. This has obviously quite broad implications for both domestic reform possibilities and ideas about Chinese subjectivity and sovereignty, but it is also easily equally appropriated for other efforts towards freedom. When Daniel Deronda's mother, the Princess, recounts to him the suffering imposed by religious and paternal constraint in George Eliot's novel, she likens the 'slavery of being a girl' to '[...] hav[ing] a pattern cut out [...] a woman's heart must be of such a size and no larger, else it must be pressed small, like Chinese feet'.[58] In so doing she too draws upon the overlap between form and movement that the trope of bound feet provides.

British reactions to the curtailed female mobility occasioned by the binding of Chinese feet takes the binding bandages as a form of reverse-prosthesis: spotlighting the deliberate denial of female bodies the possibilities of movement that would grant them subject-status. What is significant is that, like other artificial prostheses, the bandages can theoretically be removed – but with the happy result of increased, rather than decreased, mobility. In the final part of the narrative of the Chinese woman's bound foot, the natural state of movement is to be achieved once external, and frequently colonial or Christian, conditions of environment have been supplied. Building on the kinds of expansions and refigurations that I have describing in this essay, later British activists allowed the dual processes of unbinding Chinese women's feet and unfettering Chinese international development to be inextricably linked throughout reformist rhetoric, and helped to make claims of sovereignty dependent most of all on claims of free and easy movement. This helps us understand the triumphant exultation of the titular character, herself an anti-foot-binding activist, in Sarah Grand's 1888 novel *Ideala*: '[Chinese women] do a wonderful thing. When they are taught how wrong the practice is, how it cripples them, and weakens them, and renders them unfit for their work in the world, they take off their bandages! Think of that!'[59] Grand's fantasy of a reformable disability, in which crippling immobility can be removed by personal choice, stems directly from mid-nineteenth-century formulations

---

[58] George Eliot, *Daniel Deronda* (New York: Harper & Brothers, 1876), p. 214.
[59] Sarah Grand, *Ideala: A Study from Life* (New York: D. Appleton and Company, 1893), p. 254.

of foot-binding itself as a practice predicated on individual movement as well as physical form, as well as the rhetorical circulations that allowed foot-binding to be so widely heard and taught in mid-century Victorian prose.

Elective Affinities? Two Moments of Encounter with Oscar Wilde's Writings

ZHANG LONGXI

Reading Wilde as a Thinker

'Life imitates art far more than Art imitates life,' declares Oscar Wilde.[1] 'Life holds the Mirror up to Art, and either reproduces some strange type imagined by painter or sculptor, or realizes in fact what has been dreamed in fiction.'[2] These witty, antimetabolic propositions of the aesthetics of art for art's sake may have lost their effectiveness or freshness in contemporary western societies, where much of modern, avant-garde, anti-mimetic, and abstract art has drifted so far away from life that it no longer seems to have any bearing on the reality of life. When I first read these words almost forty years ago under very different circumstances, however, they were absolutely powerful, refreshing, and electrifying! I was reading 'The Decay of Lying' in a Chinese translation at a time when a most repressive and hypocritical doctrine of 'socialist realism' dominated what counted as discourse on art and literature in Mao's China. That discourse was repressive because it was the only orthodoxy dictating that art or literature should be a 'reflection of life' – not just any life, but life of the 'peasants, workers, and soldiers'. That discourse was at the same time hypocritical because it was not really a 'reflection of life' at all, but reflection of the Party line only or what the Communist Party ideologues thought art and literature should be, namely, a maidservant attending on the needs of the Party. When the official discourse appropriated such concepts as 'realism', 'life', 'reality', and 'truth', and harping on the necessity of art and literature serving the interest of the Party, and when many people, particularly the young and rebellious, were completely tired of the political propaganda and fed up with such a Party line, reading Wilde could be a revelation, an epiphany of a totally new and different way of looking at art for its own sake.

---

[1] Oscar Wilde, 'The Decay of Lying: An Observation', *Intentions* (New York: Brentano's, 1905), p. 32.

[2] Wilde, 'The Decay of Lying', p. 39.

I recall this personal moment of my first encounter with Wilde's writings because at such a moment, art for art's sake became a gesture of resistance to the official discourse and the orthodoxy, offering a politically subversive understanding of what art and literature could or should be. Wilde's wit, as Regenia Gagnier well puts it, is 'the linguistic subversion of the status quo'.[3] That was exactly what 'The Decay of Lying' came to be in my reading at the time, and its 'subversion of the status quo' was extraordinarily powerful and intellectually liberating, even through the mediated text of a translation. There was of course Wilde's wit, the way he articulated his ideas in wonderful turns of phrase, in brilliant epigrams, parallelisms, and antimetaboles, with such acid humor and elegance, but first and foremost it was the debunking of orthodox ideas, the witty 'linguistic subversion', that appealed to me and made me interested in Wilde *as a thinker* as well as a writer. Max Beerbohm is quite right to say that with regard to Wilde, 'wit was the least important of his gifts. Primarily, he was a poet, with a life-long passion for beauty; and a philosopher, with a life-long passion for thought.'[4] It was the philosophical thought couched in a poetic language that made Wilde a favorite thinker and writer of mine.

It was by pure chance that I first read Wilde, and I cannot now remember how I came to read the translation of 'The Decay of Lying', what book contained that essay, or who was the translator, but reading that essay has left an indelible impression in my mind. Given the condition at the time, when the official discourse was the only one and all writings and publications were censored and controlled, the effect of reading Wilde was not only an experience of aesthetic pleasure, but also a political intervention. Against the repetitively preached idea that art and literature should be a 'reflection of life', it was particularly refreshing to hear Wilde's outrageous statement that 'Lying, the telling of beautiful untrue things, is the proper aim of Art.'[5] Many scholars have criticized art for art's sake as apolitical and escapist, but they have probably never contemplated the possibility of the very politics of resistance such a theory may offer to artists, writers, and intellectuals living under a repressive social and political environment, in which art does not have an independent status, but is subjected to

[3] Regenia Gagnier, 'Introduction', in *Critical Essays on Oscar Wilde*, ed. Regenia Gagnier (New York: G. K. Hall, 1991), p. 5.

[4] Sir Max Beerbohm, 'A Lord of Language', *Vanity Fair*, 2 March 1905; quoted from Appendix C, in H. Montgomery Hyde, *Oscar Wilde: The Aftermath* (New York: Farrar, Straus, 1963), p. 205.

[5] Wilde, 'The Decay of Lying', p. 55.

censorship and ideological control. Under such circumstances, to escape from repressive politics is in itself a political action, and the appeal of 'The Decay of Lying' could be a radical and political one.

That was how I read Wilde's essay in my first encounter, which led me to read his other works later and read them in English when I had the opportunity to study for my graduate degree in the US. I never quite agreed with the widely spread opinion that regarded Oscar Wilde and the famous American painter James Whistler, as Beerbohm reported, 'merely as clever *farceurs*'.[6] I was disappointed to find that even in twentieth-century criticism, Wilde was for a very long time not taken seriously as a critic, and in spite of his brilliant and witty expressions, or perhaps *because of* his wit and brilliance, 'what will be quoted as his', says Richard Ellmann, 'will turn conventional solemnities to frivolous insights'.[7] But in my reading, I always detected a serious purpose in what Wilde had to say behind or beyond his witty and sometimes counter-intuitive remarks, deliberately meant to shock, amuse, or outrage. I agreed with the intelligent comments a great writer, Jorge Luis Borges, made on Oscar Wilde. 'Reading and rereading Wilde through the years,' says Borges, 'I notice something that his panegyrists do not seem to have been suspected: the provable and elementary fact that Wilde is almost always right.'[8] Wilde was of course controversial and provocative, but his mannerism, the mask of a fop, seems to me a mechanism of resistance, a disguise under a repressive moral regime of the Victorian society, which eventually destroyed him in condemnation of his homosexuality. In a way Wilde may be seen as exemplary in proving the Freudian insight that art is the sublimation of repressed sexual instincts, that 'what an artist creates', as Freud argues, 'provides at the same time an outlet for his sexual desire'.[9] My reading of Wilde, however, concentrated on his critical arguments collected in the volume called *Intentions*, and I tried to understand his ideas in the context or lineage of the western critical tradition.

Once I had read Wilde's *Intentions* as well as his other works, it became my strong belief that Wilde should be taken seriously as a critical thinker,

---

6   Beerbohm, in Hyde, *Oscar Wilde: The Aftermath*, p. 205.

7   Richard Ellmann, *Oscar Wilde at Oxford* (Washington, DC: Library of Congress, 1984), p. 5.

8   Jorge Luis Borges, 'About Oscar Wilde', in *Other Inquisitions, 1937–1952*, trans. Ruth L. C. Simms (Austin, TX: University of Texas Press, 1964), p. 80.

9   Sigmund Freud, 'Leonardo da Vinci and a Memory of His Childhood', trans. Alan Tysan, *The Standard Edition of the Complete Psychological Works of Sigmund Freud*, 24 vols (London: Hogarth Press, 1953–74), 11. 132.

though he was not in much of the literary criticism of the 1980s. Thus I tried to argue for the significance of Wilde's critical insights and their relevance, and to establish a sort of systematic aesthetic theory out of his critical thinking with the claim that his ideas presented in the 'dialogues on art and criticism in *Intentions* have a coherent and symmetrical structure'.[10] First, 'The Decay of Lying' puts forward the bold creed of the aesthetics of art for art's sake, which turns the usual understanding of art as mimesis on its head and declares that life imitates art more than art imitates life. It actually means that art shapes our ways of seeing and understanding life and the world. Wilde illustrates this idea by looking at romantic landscape paintings, particularly works of the Impressionists, arguing that it was through wonderful landscape paintings that the Europeans learned to discover the beauty of nature, and that in comparison with art, the natural scenery of a glorious evening sky one saw outside a window was but 'a very second-rate Turner'.[11] Life is chaotic and crude, but art imposes form on the chaos of life and turns its raw material into things eternally beautiful. Then 'The Critic as Artist' establishes a similarly structured relationship between criticism and art like that between art and life, arguing that if we understand life through art, then we understand art through criticism, for 'the critic occupies the same relation to the work of art that he criticises as the artist does to the visible world of form and colour, or the unseen world of passion and of thought'.[12] Criticism, says Wilde, 'treats the work of art simply as a starting point for a new creation'.[13] The dual structure of Wilde's argument about life, art, and criticism shows a more systematically organized theory of aesthetics than most critics have given him credit for, which must be fully acknowledged in our understanding of literary theory and its history.

Wilde claims that 'the highest Criticism, being the purest form of personal impression, is in its way more creative than creation'; that it is 'the only civilised form of autobiography'.[14] In his idea of creative criticism, Wilde fully acknowledges the critic's subjectivity, the specific insight into the nature of life and art from the critic's own perspective and imaginative vision. The idea of 'creative criticism' became the most contended concept in Wilde's critical thinking, and indeed, he may well have characteristically

---

[10] Zhang Longxi, 'The Critical Legacy of Oscar Wilde', in Gagnier, ed., *Critical Essays on Oscar Wilde*, p. 160.

[11] Wilde, 'The Decay of Lying', p. 42.

[12] Wilde, 'The Critic as Artist', in *Intentions*, pp. 136–7.

[13] Wilde, 'The Critic as Artist', p. 142.

[14] Wilde, 'The Critic as Artist', pp. 138, 139.

overstated his case; but we should not forget Wilde's insistence on the self-discipline of the critic, for he argues that 'criticism demands infinitely more cultivation than creation does'.[15]

Putting Wilde's ideas in the perspective of contemporary critical theories, I tried to relate his emphasis on subjectivity and creativeness to a number of philosophical and theoretical arguments from Giambattista Vico's principle of *rerum factum*, the idea that 'the human mind does not understand anything of which it has had no previous impression [...] from the senses', to the ideas and concepts proposed by contemporary critics such as Northrop Frye, Roland Barthes, Edward Said, Harold Bloom, and finally to H. G. Gadamer's rehabilitation of 'prejudice' as the basis of understanding, the realization that 'interpretation begins with foreconceptions that are replaced by more suitable ones'.[16] In tracing Wilde's ideas to such a philosophical and theoretical lineage, are we making an argument that goes beyond what Wilde himself might have intended or anticipated? After all, Wilde called his collection of essays *Intentions*, and indeed, what are his expectations for his argument? What would his intended consequences be? Wilde would probably disregard any effort to reach his *intentio auctoris*, and what matters for Wilde criticism is to appreciate the many insights he had that have gradually revealed their relevance to our own critical understanding today. I am pleased to see the gradual change of Wilde criticism since the early 1990s, to which I have made my humble contribution, which, as an essay first published in 1988, has been acknowledged, together with 'Richard Ellmann's landmark biography of Wilde', as 'among the first to take Wilde's literary criticism seriously and find value in it'.[17] Today we may perhaps say without hesitation that Wilde's critical ideas have been taken more seriously than before, and that his theory of art for art's sake can be seen not as an escape from life, but a positive effort to embrace life, to make it better and more beautiful, and to argue for the spiritual value of art in a world that has put too much emphasis on the worth of material gains.

[15] Wilde, 'The Critic as Artist', p. 126.

[16] Gimbattista Vico, *The New Science of Giambattista Vico*, trans. Thomas G. Bergin and Max H. Fisch (Ithaca, NY: Cornell University Press, 1968), p. 110; Hans-Georg Gadamer, *Truth and Method*, 2nd rev. edn, translation rev. Joel Weinsheimer and Donald G. Marshall (New York: Crossroad, 1991), p. 267.

[17] Melissa Knox, *Oscar Wilde in the 1990s: The Critic as Creator* (Rochester, NY: Camden House, 2001), p. 2.

On Wilde's Reading of Zhuangzi

The encounter between the East and the West has a long history that reaches back to trade on the ancient Silk Road, to Marco Polo's adventurous travel to China in the thirteenth century, and, in intellectual terms, to Matteo Ricci's Christian mission in Beijing in the late sixteenth century and the early seventeenth. The nineteenth century witnessed an increasing interest in Oriental art and thought, which was certainly discernible in Victorian England and found its way into the work of Oscar Wilde as one of the most sentient and quick-minded writers at the time. At the beginning of his novel, *The Picture of Dorian Gray* (1890), Wilde described Lord Henry Wotton as lying on some Persian saddle-bags in a divan and smoking his cigarettes, while the silhouette of several birds in flight, a veritable show of *ombres chinoises*, was unfolding itself in front of his eyes:

> and now and then the fantastic shadows of birds in flight flitted across the long tussore-silk curtains that were stretched in front of the huge window, producing a kind of momentary Japanese effect, and making him think of those pallid jade-faced painters of Tokyo who, through the medium of an art that is necessarily immobile, seek to convey the sense of swiftness and motion.[18]

Here Wilde was portraying what would be an exotic and fascinating Oriental effect in the Victorian English mind, the kind of Orientalist fantasies that could be traced back to earlier forms of *chinoiserie*, a style of literary and artistic representation of the Orient – China and Japan – as the cultural Other in European imagination. The exotic, as the French poet and Sinophile Victor Segalen argues, is the Other – '*qui n'est autre que la notion du différent; la perception du divers; la connaissance que quelque chose n'est pas soi-même*' (it is nothing other than the notion of the different; the perception of the diverse; the knowledge that something is not oneself).[19] For Wilde, as for Segalen, exoticism is an aesthetic attitude, the appreciation of what is different from one's own, and the admiration of beauty that contains the essential and indispensable element of diversity, what Segalen called '*une esthétique du divers*'. At the same time, however, Wilde was perfectly aware that the graceful 'Japanese effect' he created to open

---

[18] Oscar Wilde, *The Picture of Dorian Gray* (New York: The Modern Library, 1992), p. 1.

[19] Victor Segalen, *Essai sur l'exotisme: une esthétique du divers* (Paris: Fata Morgana, 1978), p. 23.

his novel with a sense of elegance and sumptuousness owed more to the fantasy of exoticism than to the reality of an Oriental country. 'The Japanese people are the deliberate self-conscious creation of certain individual artists,' as Wilde puts it in his essay. 'The actual people who live in Japan are not unlike the general run of English people; that is to say, they are extremely commonplace, and have nothing curious or extraordinary about them. In fact the whole of Japan is a pure invention.'[20] Wilde was surely sober-minded in his bold literary imagination, and made a sensible difference between artistic creation and life's banal reality.

This reminds us of a more recent reflection on Japan as 'a fictive nation', a consciously 'invented name' in Roland Barthes's celebrated *Empire of Signs*, in which Barthes declares that

> I am not lovingly gazing toward an Oriental essence – to me the Orient is a matter of indifference, merely providing a reserve of features whose manipulation – whose invented interplay – allows me to 'entertain' the idea of an unheard-of symbolic system, one altogether detached from our own.[21]

The difference is, however, that having acknowledged the fictive nature of his mythical 'empire of signs', Barthes proceeds nevertheless to create a number of myths about the Orient in written text as well as with photographs, as though he was describing Japan as a real Oriental country, whereas Wilde denied any reality of his own literary fiction. For Wilde, of course, art and imagination are far more important than the banality of life, and it is artistic creation that gives us beauty and meaning in life. He certainly prefers the artistic invention of Japan to the banality of Japan as a real country, but he clearly recognizes the difference between literary fiction and mundane reality. Here again we see Wilde at work both as a poetic writer and as a tough-minded thinker.

The second moment of encounter with Wilde is a rare piece of his writing, a review he wrote on a translation of the Chinese philosopher Zhuangzi, or Chuang Tzŭ as spelt by the translator, the English Sinologist Herbert Giles (1845–1935). Giles served as an interpreter and diplomat in China before taking up the position of Professor of Chinese at the University of Cambridge in 1897. He published a translation of the book of *Zhuangzi* in London in 1889, and a year later, Wilde published a long

---

[20] Wilde, 'The Decay of Lying', pp. 46–7.
[21] Roland Barthes, *Empire of Signs*, trans. Richard Howard (New York: Hill and Wang, 1982), pp. 3, 6.

review of this translation. If Wilde's critical essays were for a long time neglected as serious criticism, this review of *Zhuangzi* is even more obscure in Wilde's oeuvre, as it is not readily available in any of the selected works or collections of Wilde's writings currently on the book market. That is surely all the more reason for us to examine it as an important piece of Wilde's writings, so often neglected even by Wilde specialists, because this review of *Zhuangzi*, as we shall see, contains some of his most important insights on social and philosophical issues, and deserves to be taken seriously as a significant work worthy of consideration in Wilde criticism. In fact, even though Wilde is no expert on Chinese philosophy or culture, he has a surprisingly adequate grasp of at least an important aspect of Zhuangzi's philosophy and made some insightful comments on that philosophy, and therefore his review should also be considered a remarkable contribution to cross-cultural understanding between China and the West.

Like Laozi, Zhuangzi is a Daoist philosopher, a great thinker, and the book named after him, which contains a group of texts related to Zhuangzi and his thought, is the most literary and poetic of all ancient, Axel-age Chinese classics. Though not a work of literature as such, Zhuangzi's ideas are expressed in far more elegant and subtle paradoxes, allegories and striking metaphors than one may find in most literary writings. Here is just one example out of many that may demonstrate the literary quality of the book of Zhuangzi, a beautiful passage in which the philosopher recounts a peculiar dream of his:

> Once Zhuang Zhou dreamed of himself being a butterfly, he was really a butterfly fluttering around, happy and comfortable, knowing not that he was Zhou. After a while, he woke up, and he was surprisingly Zhuang Zhou himself. It is not clear whether it was Zhou who had dreamed of being a butterfly, or it was a butterfly that had dreamed of being Zhou. Yet there must be differentiation between Zhou and the butterfly, and this is called the transformation of things.[22]

This 'butterfly dream' is an allegory that articulates Zhuangzi's challenge of the differentiation of all things, the arbitrariness of differentiation as artificial and predicated on a human consciousness at the centre, while as a Daoist philosopher, he advocates the equality or non-differentiation of all things. The dreamy uncertainty is beautifully expressed, and the literary

---

[22] Guo Qingfan (1844–1895?), *Zhuangzi jishi* [*The Variorum Edition of the Zhuangzi*], in vol. 3 of *Zhuzi jicheng* [*Collection of Master Writings*] (Beijing: Zhonghua, 1954), pp. 53–4.

quality of Zhuangzi's allegory is fully recognized by Borges in an interview with Roberto Alifano, in which Borges compares Zhuangzi's dream with several other well-known expressions of the relationship between dream and reality. A common English expression, 'life is a dream', is a plain statement with no metaphorical embellishment or imagery, and therefore not poetic. Shakespeare's line, 'We are such stuff as dreams are made on,' says Borges, is much closer to poetry. When Walther von der Vogelweide cries out, 'I have dreamed my life, was it real?' the poetic depth reaches further than in Calderón or Shakespeare, but Borges gives Zhuangzi the trophy of competition when he says: 'There is poetry in that brief text. The choice of the butterfly is felicitous, since the butterfly has a tenuous quality that is fitting for the stuff of dreams.'[23] There is no doubt that the book of *Zhuangzi* would appeal to Wilde in a way that he would find both ideas and expressions in that book rather congenial.

Wilde's long review, published in *Speaker* on 8 February 1890, is certainly infused with the creative spirit as he argued for in 'The Critic as Artist'. If the mention of a 'momentary Japanese effect' in *Dorian Gray* can be seen as a decorative motif that embellishes the opening of the novel with an Oriental flavor, Wilde's review entitled 'A Chinese Sage' is a serious engagement with the philosophy of Zhuangzi, whom Giles presented as a 'mystic, moralist, and social reformer'. Wilde's review is an important piece that not only gives us a rare opportunity to catch a glimpse of his interest in the thought of an ancient philosopher from the East, but also provides an example of Wilde's criticism that reads Zhuangzi from the perspective of a Victorian critic and uses the Chinese philosopher's ideas to comment on the English society of his own time. Wilde's review is also important because it shows how much interest there was in Daoist philosophy and mysticism at the turn of the century in the late 1890s and the early 1900s.

In his introduction to the translation, Giles describes Zhuangzi as an enemy of the Confucian school and a follower of the mysteries of Laozi (or Lao Tzŭ in his spelling), and also a great debater whose 'literary and dialectic skill was such that the best scholars of the age proved unable to refute his destructive criticism of the Confucian and Mohist schools'.[24] Giles portrays Zhuangzi as a fiercely independent and free spirit, and he

---

[23] Jorge Luis Borges, *Twenty-Four Conversations with Borges. Including a Selection of Poems*, trans. Nicomedes Suárez Araús et al. (Housatonic, MA: Lascaux, 1984), p. 39.

[24] Herbert A. Giles (trans.), *Chuang Tzŭ: Mystic, Moralist, and Social Reformer* (London: Bernard Quaritch, 1889), p. vi.

tells the story of the Chinese philosopher refusing to accept the position of Prime Minister of the State of Chu, saying: 'I would rather disport myself to my own enjoyment in the mire than be slave to the ruler of a State. I will never take office. Thus I shall remain free to follow my own inclinations.'[25] Both Laozi and Zhuangzi are great masters of paradoxical expressions, and Giles samples some of these that articulate what he calls 'the wondrous doctrine of *Inaction*'. For example, 'Do nothing, and all things will be done'; 'The weak overcomes the strong, the soft overcomes the hard'; 'The softest things in the world override the hardest. That which has no substance enters where there is no fissure. And so I know that there is advantage in *Inaction*.'[26] By a strange coincidence, these short and paradoxical sayings sound very much like the epigrammatic expressions we typically relate to Wilde's style, the kind of witty expressions we find in the preface to *Dorian Gray* or in the essays in *Intentions*. Wilde himself must have realized this when he read Giles's translation and found in Zhuangzi a kindred spirit.

Of course, Wilde did not know much about Chinese philosophy or Daoism, and it would be unrealistic to expect from him much expert discussion of Zhuangzi as a Daoist philosopher. What is of interest in Wilde's review, however, is the way in which he read Zhuangzi and found in the Chinese philosopher a congenial style and a sympathetic mind that influenced his own social and political ideas, his conviction of personal freedom and the rejection of all forms of government. In fact, reading Wilde's review and his presentation of Zhuangzi, one may feel confused whether Wilde is quoting Zhuangzi or he is speaking on his own; but that only reminds us of the famous 'butterfly dream' in the *Zhuangzi* we just saw above, the questioning of human subjectivity and differentiation, the uncertainty of identities or differentiations. Thus the way Wilde spoke is in perfect keeping with that spirit of questioning and skepticism, and when we read his review, sometimes we may feel uncertain whether Zhuangzi or Wilde is speaking.

Wilde finds Zhuangzi an anti-social philosopher, and he claims that 'the most caustic criticism of modern life I have met with for some time is that contained in the writings of the learned Chuang Tzǔ'.[27] The English middle class might have seen the portraits of the Chinese sage on porcelain or Chinese screens and found them amusing, but, says Wilde,

25 Giles, *Chuang Tzǔ*, pp. vi–vii.
26 Giles, *Chuang Tzǔ*, pp. viii–ix.
27 Oscar Wilde, 'A Chinese Sage', in *A Critic in Pall Mall: Being Extracts from Reviews and Miscellanies* (London: Methuen, 1919), pp. 177–87 (p. 177).

If they really knew who he was, they would tremble. Chuang Tzŭ spent his life in preaching the great creed of Inaction, and in pointing out the uselessness of all useful things. 'Do nothing, and everything will be done', was the doctrine which he inherited from his great master Lao Tzŭ. To resolve action into thought, and thought into abstraction, was his wicked transcendental aim.[28]

Wilde is here emphasizing the subversive power of philosophical ideas, just like Heinrich Heine did in his treatise on German philosophy and religion. 'Truly, if the citizens of Königsberg had had any premonition of the full significance of his ideas,' says Heine with reference to Immanuel Kant, 'they would have felt a far more terrifying dread at the presence of this man than at the sight of an executioner.' Of course the German citizens of Königsberg, like the English middle class, had no premonition of the terrifying power of philosophical ideas, as Heine continues to say: 'the good folk saw in him nothing but a professor of philosophy, and as he passed by at his customary hour, they gave him a friendly greeting and perhaps set their watches by him'.[29] The significant point is that Wilde saw in the ancient Chinese philosopher Zhuangzi what Heine understood in the philosophy of Kant, and the comparison is quite appropriate as Wilde himself compared Zhuangzi with western philosophers and mystics from Plato, Philo of Alexandria, to Master Eckhart, Jacob Böhme, and Hegel, claiming that 'Chuang Tzŭ may be said to have summed up in himself almost every mood of European metaphysical or mystical thought, from Heraclitus down to Hegel.' But Wilde thought Zhuangzi was even more radical than his European counterparts, for

Chuang Tzŭ was something more than a metaphysician and an illumi-nist. He sought to destroy society, as we know it, as the middle classes know it; and the sad thing is that he combines with the passionate eloquence of a Rousseau the scientific reasoning of a Herbert Spencer.[30]

Bringing the ancient Chinese philosopher closer to the modern world, Wilde's Zhuangzi sounds more and more like Vivian in 'The Decay of Lying' or Gilbert in 'The Critic as Artist', that is to say, personae or

[28] Wilde, 'A Chinese Sage', p. 178.
[29] Heinrich Heine, *Concerning the History of Religion and Philosophy in Germany*, in *Selected Works*, trans. and ed. Helen M. Mustard (New York: Vintage, 1973), p. 369.
[30] Wilde, 'A Chinese Sage', pp. 178, 179.

mouthpieces of Wilde's own ideas, speaking in typically Wildean paradoxical epigrams. Zhuangzi, says Wilde, is not a sentimentalist:

> He pities the rich more than the poor, if he ever pities at all, and prosperity seems to him as tragic as suffering. He has nothing of the modern sympathy with failures, nor does he propose that the prizes should always be given on moral grounds to those who come in last in the race. It is the race that he objects to; and as for active sympathy, which has become the profession of so many worthy people in our own day, he thinks that trying to make others good is as silly an occupation as 'beating a drum in a forest in order to find a fugitive'. It is a mere waste of energy. That is all. While, as for a thoroughly sympathetic man, he is, in the eyes of Chuang Tzǔ, simply a man who is always trying to be somebody else, and so misses the only possible excuse for his own existence.[31]

Zhuangzi's ideal of a Golden Age, says Wilde, is a time

> when there were no competitive examinations, no wearisome educational systems, no missionaries, no penny dinners for the people, no Established Churches, no Humanitarian Societies, no dull lectures about one's duty to one's neighbour, and no tedious sermons about any subject at all. In those ideal days, he tells us, people loved each other without being conscious of charity, or writing to the newspapers about it.[32]

These are obviously Wilde's own ideas disguised as the Chinese philosopher's, but surprisingly they show a remarkably accurate grasp of the core ideas of the Daoist philosophy, its argument against the kind of human intervention, as much represented by modern social institutions as by Confucian teachings, in the natural course of things. As Wilde represents him, Zhuangzi becomes an enemy of social intervention and government, and a champion for individual freedom, which we do find in the original Zhuangzi and in Daoism in general. Wilde's Zhuangzi argues for social and political inaction, which advocates 'leaving mankind alone', for 'there has never been such a thing as governing mankind'.[33] In Wilde's review, Zhuangzi's philosophy becomes mainly a critique of modern life and modern political institutions:

---

[31] Wilde, 'A Chinese Sage', p. 179.
[32] Wilde, 'A Chinese Sage', pp. 179–80.
[33] Wilde, 'A Chinese Sage', p. 180.

And what would be the fate of governments and professional politicians if we came to the conclusion that there is no such thing as governing mankind at all? It is clear that Chuang Tzŭ is a very dangerous writer, and the publication of his book in English, two thousand years after his death, is obviously premature, and may cause a great deal of pain to many thoroughly respectable and industrious persons.[34]

That may be a hyperbole typical of Wilde, but that does not mean it is not sincere, for here we find some basic ideas Wilde develops further into his political essay *The Soul of Man under Socialism*.

As a man of artistic sensibility and a Victorian aesthete, Wilde's idea of socialism may strike us today as fundamentally mistaken and peculiarly quixotic, but it has its connections with the kind of English socialist fantasies of a William Morris, and it constitutes 'an aesthetic utopia', as Krishan Kumar observes.[35] Wilde's socialism is more of a plea for individualism and artistic freedom than a socialist theory. Reading *The Soul of Man* together with his review of Zhuangzi, the connections of ideas are inescapable. The very beginning of the essay reads: 'The chief advantage that would result from the establishment of Socialism is, undoubtedly, the fact that Socialism would relieve us from that sordid necessity of living for others which, in the present condition of things, presses so hardly upon almost everybody. In fact, scarcely anyone at all escapes.'[36] That sounds very much like Zhuangzi's Golden Age when, as Wilde describes it, there were 'no Humanitarian Societies, no dull lectures about one's duty to one's neighbour'; and 'There was no chattering about clever men, and no laudation of good men. The intolerable sense of obligation was unknown.'[37] Socialism is valuable because 'it will lead to Individualism'.[38] It will be the condition of free individuals who follow whatever comes naturally without imposing on others, including for the benefit of others. The personality of man, says Wilde, 'will grow naturally and simply, flower-like, or as a tree grows', and 'it will not be always meddling with others, or asking them to be like itself. It will love them because they will be different. And yet

---

34 Wilde, 'A Chinese Sage', p. 186.
35 Krishan Kumar, *Utopia and Anti-Utopia in Modern Times* (Oxford: Basil Blackwell, 1987), p. 66.
36 Oscar Wilde, 'The Soul of Man', in *The Soul of Man and Prison Writings*, ed. Isobel Murray (Oxford: Oxford University Press, 1990), p. 1.
37 Wilde, 'A Chinese Sage', p. 180.
38 Wilde, 'The Soul of Man', p. 2.

while it will not meddle with others it will help all, as a beautiful thing helps us, by being what it is.'[39]

This reminds us of what Wilde says about Zhuangzi's philosophy in his review, and he more directly refers to Zhuangzi the Chinese philosopher in another passage:

> Individualism, then, is what through Socialism we are to attain. As a natural result the State must give up all idea of government. It must give it up because, as a wise man once said many centuries before Christ, there is such a thing as leaving mankind alone; there is no such thing as governing mankind. All modes of government are failures.[40]

For Wilde, Zhuangzi is a radical thinker that negates all forms of government, a predecessor of modern anarchism. Indeed, as Sos Eltis argues, 'Wilde's individualist doctrine also presented many parallels with Daoist philosophy, a philosophy which itself provided one of the earliest bases for anarchist thought.' He goes on to mention Wilde's review of Zhuangzi and argues that 'The relevance of this doctrine to "The Soul of Man under Socialism" is clear.'[41] If we read Zhuangzi, his witticism and paradoxical expressions indeed suggest some stylistic affinities with Wilde's epigrams in addition to the kind of retrogressive criticism of modern life that Wilde finds attractive and inspiring. Although there are many more ideas and insights in Zhuangzi's philosophy that Wilde did not touch on, the emphasis he put on freedom and individuality in his reading of Zhuangzi does reveal a very important aspect of the Daoist philosopher that deserves our critical attention.

Wilde died as the world moved into the twentieth century, but his interest in Zhuangzi anticipated a similar interest many modernist poets had well into the twentieth century. Both William Carlos Williams and Marianne Moore owned copies of Giles's Zhuangzi translation, and Ezra Pound had most likely read it, too. Giles's *History of Chinese Literature* was popular at the time with the modernists, and 'his version of Zhuangzi's parable about how he dreamed of being a butterfly', as Zhaoming Qian argues, 'may well have appealed to Williams as it had appealed to Pound', as both admired 'the Chinese sage's refusal to make distinctions

---

[39] Wilde, 'The Soul of Man', p. 9.
[40] Wilde, 'The Soul of Man', p. 13.
[41] Sos Eltis, *Revising Wilde: Society and Subversion in the Plays of Oscar Wilde* (Oxford: Oxford University Press, 1996), pp. 22–3.

among worldly things'.[42] Zhuangzi and his predecessor Laozi, along with the Chinese written language and Chinese culture, proved to be a great inspiration for the modernist poets, but these Chinese texts were read differently with different foci and interpretations. What Wilde found in Zhuangzi in the 1890s was a radical critique of middle-class values and modern political institutions, and an advocacy for individual freedom, but what Pound and Williams saw in 'the Chinese sage's refusal to make distinctions' led to the understanding of the Chinese language as a medium that eschewed logical connections and abstract conceptualizations in favor of images and concrete *things* themselves, thus a medium specifically suited to the modernist poetics of immediacy and concreteness. We may also be reminded that roughly at the same time in the 1920s, in *fin-de-siècle* Vienna, Fritz Mauthner appreciated Laozi and Zhuangzi and 'discovered in Tao a primeval critique of language (*in Tao eine uralte Sprachkritik zu entdecken*)'.[43] Understanding of Zhuangzi or Daoism or the Chinese language and culture changes all the time, and Wilde is certainly different from Pound, Williams, and many others. The point is, however, that when we put the different readings and interpretations in perspective, we may realize that the intellectual connections of western modernism with the East are serious and deep, and that Oscar Wilde is one of the predecessors in this respect that still needs to be recognized and appreciated in our understanding of modernist literature.

---

[42] Zhaoming Qian, *Orientalism and Modernism: The Legacy of China in Pound and Williams* (Durham, NC: Duke University Press, 1995), p. 146.

[43] Fritz Mauthner, *Wörterbuch der Philosophie: Neue Beiträge zu einer Kritik der Sprach*, 2 vols (Munich: Georg Müller, 1910), 2. 468, s.v. 'Tao'.

'Lost Horizon':
Orientalism and the Question of Tibet

Q. S. TONG

For all knowledge, one must first direct attention to its sources or origins.

Immanuel Kant, Physical Geography[1]

Mythical space is an intellectual construct. It can be very elaborate. Mythical space is also a response of feeling and imagination to fundamental human needs.

Yi-Fu Tuan, Space and Place[2]

Perhaps more than any other part of China, Tibet has been romanticized and mythologized. In its various forms, Tibet is read, represented, and imagined as the sacred place of Buddhism, the origin of wisdom of life, the abode inhabited by world-controlling masters, the source of superhuman power, an endangered archive of humanity, a Shangri-La, and a timeless utopia where the span of human life could be restored to its imagined longevity. Tibet is a landscape, a fictional space, and an idea. Is it a real place, or is it what Orville Schell has aptly called a 'Virtual Tibet'?[3] Indeed, is there such a place called 'Tibet' as we know it? In thinking about the discursive formation of the idea of Tibet, therefore, we must also consider human consequences of the efforts to fictionalize place, landscape, and geography. Tibet is a historical space to which human dramas have given not just meaning and value, but also a rich range of possibilities for its interpretation, representation, and utilization. In one sense, there is no nature except *human* nature, and there is no place that is not at the same time physical and cultural. Tibet, as we know it, has

---

[1] Immanuel Kant, *Physical Geography* (1802), in *Kant: Natural Science*, ed. Eric Watkins (Cambridge: Cambridge University Press, 2012), pp. 434–679 (p. 445).

[2] Yi-Fu Tuan, *Space and Place: The Perspective of Experience* (Minneapolis, MN: University of Minnesota Press, 1997), p. 99.

[3] Orville Schell, *Virtual Tibet: Searching for Shangri-La from the Himalayas to Hollywood* (New York: Metropolitan Books, 2000).

acquired different identities and manifestations, just as many other places of historical and cultural significance. If Tibet is not just a mark on the map, but a historical invention and geographical imaginary for different contexts, it is not one Tibet, but multiple Tibets that we must consider.

There has been copious critical and historical analysis of how Tibet is invented and transformed into a utopia of spiritual fulfillment by committed missionaries, ambitious adventurers, imperialist agents, and New Age spiritualists.[4] In this collective narrative of Tibet, the British empire played a singular role in the constituting of an official structure of knowledge about Tibet, of what Edward Said has called a 'corporate institution',[5] in which to understand, discuss, represent, and deal with Tibet. Orientalist romanticization of Tibet emerged in the late nineteenth and early twentieth centuries and culminated in the creation of Shangri-La in James Hilton's novel *Lost Horizon* (1933). The idea of Tibet reveals both its limitations and creativities. In the hope of grasping the complex history of the British idea of Tibet, I propose to revisit a set of textual moments that document its genealogical mutations and conceptual changes, including George Bogle's accounts of his mission to Tibet in 1774, Thomas Manning's narrative of his trip to Tibet in the early nineteenth century, and finally, James Hilton's novel *Lost Horizon*. The essay will conclude with brief remarks on the question of Tibet today.

---

[4] Studies of western interests in Tibet are copious, and it would be impossible and unnecessary to provide a full bibliography here. I find the following titles particularly helpful. Gordon T. Stewart's *Journeys to Empire: Enlightenment, Imperialism, and British Encounter with Tibet, 1774–1904* (Cambridge: Cambridge University Press, 2009) is a historical study of the early British missions to Tibet. For a narrative of George Bogle's journey to Tibet, see Kate Teltscher, *The High Road to China: George Bogle, the Panchen Lama, and the First British Expedition to Tibet* (New York: Farrar, Straus and Giroux, 2006). For critical studies of the discursive representation of Tibet, see Peter Bishop's *The Myth of Shangri-La: Tibet, Travel Writing, and the Western Creation of Sacred Landscape* (Berkeley and Los Angeles: University of California Press, 1989), and Donald S. Lopez's *Prisoners of Shangri-La: Tibetan Buddhism and the West* (Chicago: University of Chicago Press, 1998). Orville Schell's *Virtual Tibet* offers a study of popular imaginations of Tibet in Hollywood films. *Imagining Tibet*, ed. T. Dodin and H. Räther (Boston, MA: Wisdom Publications, 2001) assembles twenty essays that cover aspects of Tibetan culture in western representation from the seventeenth century to the present, and Tom Neuhaus's *Tibet in the Western Imagination* (Basingstoke: Macmillan Palgrave, 2012) offers a more focused study of western attitudes toward Tibet since the mid-nineteenth century.

[5] Edward Said, *Orientalism* (New York: Vintage Books, 1979), p. 3.

'Discovery' of Tibet: Colonial Trade and Imperial Knowledge

The British interest in Tibet began to develop in conjunction with its colonial enterprise in India and its global reach for trade.[6] Collectively sponsored and developed by adventurous individuals and colonial institutions, British representation of Tibet, from the outset, was multifaceted, inconsistent, and even contradictory. In the discursive formation of knowledge about Tibet, British diplomatic missions to Tibet were crucial in organizing and consolidating fragmented information for developing an epistemological consensus on Tibet, even though they brought back to the world the image of Tibet not just as a home of spiritual purity, but also as a barren land that must be enlightened or occupied, or enlightened through occupation. During the winter and spring of 1774 and 1775, the Scotsman George Bogle led the first official mission to Tibet, nearly two decades before Lord Macartney's better-known, but failed, mission to China in 1792.[7] Following the establishment and consolidation of its control over India in the mid-eighteenth century, the East India Company (EIC) was keen to expand its territorial and commercial interests beyond the borders of India. The EIC had long desired the opportunities of trade in China. However, Britain lagged behind some of its European counterparts in China trade, such as the Netherlands and Portugal, both of which had strong footholds in China, and it had only limited access to the Chinese market. Its trade with China, though active since the seventeenth century, had mostly been carried out by private traders. The EIC had yet to enter this massive market. Though a latecomer, Britain had its positional superiority, which was its India. Tibet was just next door; its traditional link with the Qing Court in Peking was something to be explored, and it would serve as a backdoor to China. The immediate purpose of Bogle's mission was to 'open a mutual and equal trade communication between the peoples of Tibet and Bengal',[8] but it was evident that the British 'discovery' of Tibet was an imperial project from the outset.

---

[6] Dibyesh Anand argues that the question of Tibet must be considered in conjunction with 'the British imperial legacy'. See Dibyesh Anand, 'Strategic Hypocrisy', *The Journal of Asian Studies*, 68 (2009), pp. 227–52 (p. 228).

[7] Bogle's formal appointment was announced on 13 May 1774. See Schuyler Cammann, *Trade through the Himalayas: The Early British Attempts to Open Tibet* (Princeton: Princeton University Press, 1951), p. 32. The Bogle, Macartney, and Amherst missions were all sponsored by the EIC, and the connections between them have yet to be examined and understood.

[8] Cammann, *Trade through the Himalayas*, p. 32.

The Bogle mission is historically significant for several reasons. First, it was the first British mission to China, or rather to Chinese Tibet. It was a relationship-building mission, and the EIC's goal was to establish a more permanent British presence in Tibet, which could be projected and extended into the interior of China. Although he did not succeed in setting up any institutional/diplomatic presence in Tibet – he did not even manage to get to the capital city Lhasa – Bogle would develop a warm personal relationship with Tibet's second most powerful and influential religious leader, the (Sixth) Panchen Lama, or the Tashi Lama as Bogle called him.[9] The Bogle mission was highly regarded, partly because it was believed that the development of this good relationship with the Panchen Lama would allow the EIC to open up Tibet, which was rich in bullion metal, especially in silver and gold. Though somewhat marginalized and disadvantaged in its competition with the more active western imperial powers in southern China, Britain was hoping to achieve its diplomatic privileges through this mission and, in particular, through Bogle's special relationship with the Panchen Lama. It is said that the Panchen Lama, in his meeting with the Qianlong Emperor in Peking four years later in 1779, spoke favorably of Warren Hastings and the British in India. Given the difficulties in direct trade with the Qing government, 'Bogle's proposed indirect approach, of making friends of the Chinese Emperor's friends', was considered an effective diplomatic policy the EIC should adopt and practice.[10]

Bogle was a shrewd diplomat. His friendship with the Panchen Lama, no doubt the highlight of his journey, was seen as most conducive to the advancement of British interests in Tibet and China. Bogle described this second most important man in Tibet as a gentle, sympathetic, and friendly leader:

I came in soon after Tashi Lama was seated, and having made three profound bows, presented to him my handkerchief, which he always receives with his own hands. He spoke to me for about two minutes, inquiring about my health, what I thought of Tashilhunpo, and how I liked my accommodations.[11]

---

[9] The Panchen Lama was called 'Tashi' Lama, probably because his monastic seat was at Tashilhunpo. It was also spelt as 'Teshu'. See Alastair Lamb, ed., *Bhutan and Tibet: The Travels of George Bogle and Alexander Hamilton, 1774–1777* (Hertingfordbury, Herts: Roxford Books, 2002), 1. 38–9.

[10] Lamb, 'Introduction', *Bhutan and Tibet*, p. 27.

[11] Lamb, ed., *Bhutan and Tibet*, p. 176.

In an audience with the Lama, Bogle was allowed to have tea out of the Lama's own golden teapot, which was 'an honour bestowed only upon Chanzo Cusho, the inferior Lamas, and the vakils of Dalai Lama and the Urga Lama [Taranath]'.[12] Upon Bogle's departure, the Lama gave Bogle as a gift his own three charmed strings of beads, and told Bogle that 'the ladies upon whom he bestowed them would be protected from all evil'.[13] It is said that Bogle may have married one of the Panchen Lama's sisters, with whom he had two daughters, though it is believed that this part of his life was systematically suppressed in both private and official records of his mission.[14]

Second, the Bogle mission was also a fact-finding one for gathering geographical and ethnographical information about Tibet and the neighboring regions, for development of what might be called the imperial knowledge of geography and people in which the British Empire was interested. Bogle's account is the first organized form of knowledge about Tibet, an example of Saidean orientalism that is produced and supported by colonial bureaucracies and government departments, as different from, though complementary to, private individual's accounts such as those by missionaries and travelers.[15] Warren Hastings, the first Governor-General of British India, who proposed the idea of an official mission to Tibet, was motivated by both the possibilities of trade and opportunities to collect useful information about the region of which so little had been known. He had read rather extensively about Tibet, and he hoped that the Bogle

---

[12] Lamb, ed., *Bhutan and Tibet*, p. 177.

[13] 'Bogle gave the lower string, with the pendant ornaments, to his sister, Mrs. Brown [...]. The upper string he gave to his cousin, Mrs. Morehead.' See Clements R. Markham, 'Introduction' to *Narratives of the Mission of George Bogle to Tibet and of the Journey of Thomas Manning to Lhasa* (London: Trübner and Co., 1876), p. cxxxix.

[14] It is believed that Bogle and his Tibetan wife had two daughters, who 'were later educated at Bogle's ancestral home in Ayrshire and there each married a Scottish husband. All reference to Bogle's Tibetan wife seems to have been suppressed when his papers were edited for publication; but his descendants, of whom several survive in Britain, now look back to that ancestry with pride.' See Hugh E. Richardson, *Tibet and Its History* (London: Oxford University Press, 1962), p. 65.

[15] Missionaries had made numerous efforts to visit Tibet. For example, the Franciscan monk Odorico de Pordenone visited Tibet in 1325 during the early period of Buddhist rule in Tibet. Two and half centuries later, the Portuguese Jesuit António de Andrade (1580–1634) traveled to Tibet, and his *The New Discoveries of the Great Cathay or of the Tibetan Kingdom* appeared in 1626. Italian Jesuit Ippolito Desideri (1684–1733) visited Lhasa in March 1716, and his *A Report on Nature, Dress, and Government of Tibet* was written in the years 1712–33.

mission would change the mode of production of knowledge about Tibet. After all, it was the first official attempt to establish reliable and authoritative knowledge about Tibet, which would assist a more conscious formulation of the EIC's policy of trade in Tibet and perhaps in China.

Hastings was meticulous and thorough in his instruction to Bogle about collection of information on aspects of Tibetan life. He told Bogle: 'Any information with regard to the antiquity and to the creed of [its] religion, as well as to the authority, civil and ecclesiastical, of the Lamas, could not fail to be extremely interesting,' He was interested to know, for example, whether indeed one Tibetan lady could have 'several husbands' and 'if this practice obtains in all the ranks of society'. More important, of course, he would like to receive information about the relationship between Tibet, Tatary and China; apart from the history, government, and religions of Tibet, he was hoping that Bogle would find out more about 'its climate, geography and physical characters'.[16] Hastings was a shrewd leader, and he knew the political, diplomatic, and commercial values of such information about Tibet. He told Bogle that thousands of people in England would be interested to listen to the story of an expedition 'in search of knowledge'.[17]

Bogle did not disappoint Hastings. In this short visit of about four months, Bogle produced a substantial amount of writings on Tibet, in his memorandums and letters to Hastings and in personal journals and notes he took during the trip. His political and ethnographical notes on Tibet and Central Asia cover a wide range of topics, including 'Pybas (Tibetans)', 'Demo Jong' [the ruler of Sikkim], 'Kalmuks [Mongols]', 'Kashmiris', 'Yarkand', 'Khampas [from Eastern Tibet, Kham]', 'Dokpas [Tibetan nomads]', 'Nepal', 'Chinese', 'The Twenty-four Rajahs', and Tibetan 'religion, justice and government'.[18] Bogle's reports and journals have few fantastic and imaginative elements; they were factual, almost dry, descriptions of Tibetan life, history, and society. Tibet in Bogle's writings was not yet a place of spiritual power or utopian perfection. Worth noting is that while residing in the Tashilhunpo Monastery, the Panchen Lama's official residence, Bogle began to draft, for the Lama's information, an outline of Europe, with descriptions of the history, government, religion

---

[16] Lamb, ed., *Bhutan and Tibet*, pp. 54–5.

[17] Keith Feiling, *Warren Hastings* (London: Macmillan, 1954), p. 105.

[18] Lamb, ed., *Bhutan and Tibet*, pp. 277–304. 'Yarkand', explains Lamb, 'was long subject to the Mussulmen and governed by its own Rajahs. It was invaded about 12 years ago by the Emperor of China's forces who could make no impression upon it.' Lamb, ed., *Bhutan and Tibet*, p. 289.

and the national character of its major nations. He never finished the work, but what he had written in its Tibetan version was considered for many years to be 'the standard Tibetan account of Europe'.[19]

Hastings thought highly of Bogle's journey to Tibet and considered it comparable to some of the most important adventures and geographical discoveries in the eighteenth century. He was hoping to bring out Bogle's account of the mission, which would have monumentalized not just Bogle, but Hastings himself and the EIC. To this end, he sent Bogle's journals to Samuel Johnson, suggesting that they were comparable to Johnson's accounts of his own trip to Scotland:

> The accompanying sheets [...] contain the journal of a friend of mine into the country of Tibet, which, though bordering on this, has till lately been little known to the inhabitants of it as if it were at a distance of many degrees. The people, their form of government, their manners, and even their climate differ as much from Bengal as Bengal does from England. When I read your account of your visit to the Hebrides, I could not help wishing that a patron of that spirit which could draw so much entertainment and instruction from a region so little befriended by nature, or improved by the arts of society, could have animated Mr. Bogle, the author of this journal, but I flatter myself that you will find it not unworthy of your perusal.[20]

Orientalist knowledge of Tibet had hitherto been left to individuals – missionaries, travelers, and private traders – whose memoirs, accounts of their journeys and personal reflections had been the only source of information about the place. India was an important site of British orientalism; the EIC had an advantage over those individual and isolated efforts, partly because it had access to the religious leadership of Tibet. Its active participation in producing and organizing information about Tibet must be attributable to Hastings whose passion for orientalist knowledge was crucial for the development of modern knowledge about Tibet in the eighteenth century. For instance, Hastings had great respect for William Jones's philological work on the Orient. Jones arrived in India less than two years after Bogle's death, and his arrival was seen as 'a landmark in Indian history'.[21] Hastings and Jones were close friends. Jones's arrival

---

[19] Lamb, ed., *Bhutan and Tibet*, pp. 193–202.
[20] Quoted in Stewart, *Journeys to Empire*, p. 26.
[21] Garland Cannon, *The Life and Mind of Oriental Jones: Sir William Jones, the Father of Modern Linguistics* (Cambridge: Cambridge University Press, 1990), p. 200.

in India on 25 September 1783 was 'a day of rejoicing' for Hastings; welcoming Jones gave him more satisfaction than any other official functions. Jones was also 'drawn to [Hastings], who innovationally wanted the EIC servants to be competent in Indian languages and to appreciate local traditions'.[22] They enjoyed each other's company, and their conversations could be just about anything. Of their literary conversations, Jones said: 'I am always the gainer.'[23] Hastings encouraged and supported Jones's philological studies in India; they together founded the Bengal Asiatic Society in 1784.

The success of the Bogle mission encouraged Hastings to contemplate a second diplomatic mission for the establishment of a permanent British presence in Tibet. Bogle was to set out in April 1779, but the mission had to be postponed, because the Panchen Lama was about to visit Peking. It was then suggested that Bogle meet the Panchen Lama in Peking and accompany him back to Tibet. But the Lama died of smallpox in November 1780 in Peking, and less than half a year later, on 3 April 1781, Bogle died in Calcutta.[24] The EIC's second mission to Tibet led by Samuel Turner would take place two years later in the autumn of 1783.

British interest in Tibet continued to increase throughout the nineteenth century, in conjunction with and parallel to the EIC's more assertive policy and practice in southern China. In the network of trade, Canton

---

[22] Cannon, *The Life and Mind of Oriental Jones*, p. 200.

[23] Feiling, *Warren Hastings*, p. 236.

[24] Markham, 'Introduction', *Narratives of the Mission of George Bogle to Tibet*, p. lxx. At the time of Lama's death, rumours about its cause abounded. George Leonard Staunton, deputy to Lord Macartney, suggested that the Tashi Lama's death might be related to his friendly relationship with the British in India: 'The suddenness of this calamity excited, however, strong suspicions in Thibet. It was there imagined, that the Teshoo Lama's correspondence and connection with the English government of Bengal, had given umbrage to his Imperial Majesty, who yielding, it was concluded, to the suggestions of a policy practised sometimes in the East, drew the Lama to his court with intentions different from those which he had expressed in his invitation.' George Leonard Staunton, *An Authentic Account of an Embassy from the King of Great Britain to the Emperor of China*. 2 vols (London: printed by W. Bulmer and Co., 1797), 2. 52. But this was only speculation. 'Lord Macartney, for whom Staunton was writing, was very bitter at the Chinese after the failure of his mission [...]. Thus it is possible to understand why he might have been willing to disregard the known facts and accept stories of foul play regarding the death of the Panchen Lama.' Cammann, *Trade Through the Himalayas*, p. 77. Macartney's embassy in 1793 was to replace the mission headed by Charles Cathcart whose sudden death before reaching China in June 1788 led to the aborting of the mission. Staunton was being considered as a replacement of Cathcart, but it was decided in the end that a Scottish person was preferable.

(Guangzhou) and Tibet served as the EIC's strategic points of entry, and in both places, its mercantile and commercial enterprises ended in violent conflicts. In case of Canton, Britain engaged in two major wars – the First and Second Opium Wars (1839–42, 1856–60). Much less discussed, but no less violent and bloody, was the British military expedition to Tibet in 1901. Led by Francis Younghusband, the British military campaign against Tibet ended in the capturing of Lhasa and fleeing of the Dalai Lama from the Potala Palace. Like the Second Opium War, this military expedition was not uncontroversial within Britain. Younghusband wrote a vigorous defense of the military operation and his role in his account of the mission.[25] In August 1904, the British troops entered the city of Lhasa. Peter Fleming recreated the historical scene in these vivid words:

Younghusband rode at the head of his Mission through the city-gates. Above them, now for the first time in full view, towered the fabulous bulk of the Potala, golden-roofed, white-walled, taller than St Paul's Cathedral. Its central building, the private quarters of the Dalai Lama, was painted a deep crimson. Sanctuaries were shrouded by yak-hair curtains, eighty feet long and twenty-five feet wide, which cascaded down the precipice-like walls. [...] The Potala was an edifice much bigger, and much stranger, than any of the invaders had seen before.[26]

The Potala Palace was an architectural spectacle, which, however, would quickly deconstruct all the romanticization of Tibet: its sublimity formed a striking contrast with the squalor of the city itself. Quoting Edmund Candler, Fleming continues: 'If one approached within a league of Lhasa, saw the glittering domes of the Potala, and turned back without entering the precincts, one might still imagine it an enchanted city.' But under the glittering golden-roofed palace, Lhasa was 'in fact an insanitary slum [....] In the pitted streets pools of rainwater and piles of refuse disrupted

---

[25] Though of historical interest, Younghusband's account of the military expedition is a pedestrian piece of writing. As far as he was concerned, British 'intercourse' with Tibet had not been satisfactory, and they had made various attempts to improve communication, without, however, achieving the desired effects. Therefore, he wrote, 'the Mission to Lhasa of 1904, was merely the culmination of a long series of efforts to regularize and humanize that intercourse, and put the relationship which must necessarily subsist India and Tibet upon a business-like and permanently satisfactory footing'. Francis Younghusband, *India and Tibet* (London: John Murray, 1910), p. 3.

[26] Peter Fleming, *Bayonets to Lhasa: The British Invasion of Tibet* (Hong Kong: Oxford University Press, 1984), p. 210.

the march-discipline of the Fusiliers. The houses were mean and filthy, the stench pervasive. Pigs and ravens competed for nameless delicacies in open sewers.'[27]

Scholars have noted how the Bogle and Younghusband missions were shaped and influenced by different ideologies. 'When Bogle crossed the Himalayas,' writes Gordon Stewart, 'the Enlightenment played a significant role in shaping British views of geography and of other peoples and cultures; when Younghusband's invasion took place, a popular imperial ideology modulated British views of the world.'[28] However, what is not sufficiently noted or discussed is the convergence of these two views on Tibet, that is, the convergence of the Enlightenment progressive ideology and imperialist and orientalist presentation of Tibet. At the time British imperial impulse drew Tibet into its 'Great Game' with Russia in the late nineteenth century,[29] the discovery or invention of Tibet as the last sanctuary of human civilization presented a contradiction to Britain's imperial modernity. In Britain's global expansion, Tibet was a destination of trade, a gateway to the interior and central part of China, and a subject of imperial geography. Within the geographical vicinity of British India and therefore Britain's sphere of influence, Tibet was an object of colonial conquest, possession and control. And yet, as one of the last frontiers of human knowledge, Tibet was the desired object of knowledge and orientalism. It is also during this period that the question of Tibet as an independent and sovereign state emerged, and its relation with the central government in Peking has remained a controversial issue.[30]

---

[27] Fleming, *Bayonets to Lhasa*, pp. 210–11.

[28] Stewart, *Journeys to Empire*, p. 3.

[29] Tibet became a more prominent international issue when Britain's imperial ambition in Central Asia was rivaled and challenged by the emergent imperial power Russia. In the closing decades of the nineteenth century, the British Empire participated in what was to be called 'the Great Game' to constrain Russia's influence and limit its expansion in Central Asia. For a historical study of 'the Great Game', see Karl E. Meyer and Shareen Blair Brysac, *Tournament of Shadows: The Great Game and Race for Empire in Central Asia* (Washington, DC: Counterpoint, 1999).

[30] In the last decades of the nineteenth century, the Qing empire, after its repeated humiliations in its encounters with the British, was considerably weakened. No longer in a position to manage and govern Tibet, it had to leave the Tibetans more power to deal with the conflicts with the British. This created the impression that Tibet was already an independent state. In 1887, the British Sikkim Expedition was blockaded by the Tibetans. The British made diplomatic protests to Peking; the Qing Foreign Ministry ordered the Tibetans to withdraw, but the Tibetans refused to obey. Their open defiance of the central government's

Adventure and Fantasy: The Invention of Tibet

Indeed, exploration of Tibet was for trade, resources, control and creation of a highland passage to China and its massive market; but it was also for occultic power, transcendence, longevity, and the idea of internal peace. By the mid-nineteenth century, Tibet had remained, by and large, a place unknown to the outside world and waiting to be explored and understood. This does not mean, however, that Tibet had only been an object of imperial knowledge. There had already been indication of its fictionalization in the eighteenth and early nineteenth centuries. Thomas Manning, the first and only Englishman who visited Lhasa and met with the ninth Dalai Lama in the early nineteenth century, produced a limited amount of writing, but his journals written during the trip offered rare insight into the religious life of Tibet. Although Manning's overall assessment of Lhasa was not all that flattering, worth noting, for my purpose in particular, is his description of the Dalai Lama.

On 17 December 1811, Manning had an interview with the Grand Lama, who was only a seven-year-old child at this time. Manning's description of the Lama's appearance, especially his face, is perhaps one of the earliest mystifications and reifications of the Dalai Lama in his childhood:

> The Lama's beautiful and interesting face and manner engrossed almost all my attention. He was at that time about seven years old: had the simple and unaffected manners of a well-educated princely child. His face was, I thought, poetically and affectingly beautiful. He was of a gay and cheerful disposition; his beautiful mouth perpetually unbending into a graceful smile, which illuminated his whole countenance. Sometimes, particularly when he had looked at me, his smile almost approached to a gentle laugh.[31]

Though a child, the Lama Incarnate seemed to command an aura about himself and exerted an uncanny influence over Manning. The very sight of the Lama almost moved Manning to tears: 'I was extremely affected by this interview with the Lama. I could have wept through strangeness of sensation. I was absorbed in reflections when I got home.'[32] Manning

---

instruction further solidified the idea that Peking had no control over Tibet, and the British began to deal with Tibet directly.

[31] Markham, *Narratives of the Mission of George Bogle to Tibet*, p. 265.

[32] After he returned to his residence, Manning wrote: '1st Dec, 17th of tenth Moon. This day I saluted the Grand Lama! Beautiful youth. Face poetically

was so impressed and affected that he began to record visually the Dalai Lama by recalling the child's image in drawing:

> I strove to draw the Lama; and though very inexpert with the pencil, I produced a beautiful face, but it did not satisfy me. I drew another which I could not make handsome, yet there was in some respects a likeness in it which the other wanted. From the two together, and instructions from me, a skilful painter might make a good picture of him.[33]

Manning had served in British India before he decided to make the trip to Tibet as an individual traveler. As Peter Kitson's essay in this volume mentions, he was also one of the interpreters of the Amherst embassy to China of 1816–17, though he left no record of his experiences on that occasion. Given that the EIC's interest in Tibet was focused on the possibilities of trade and diplomacy, Manning's passion for the religious life of Tibet in general and his description of the Grand Lama's 'poetic' beauty in particular were quite remarkable.

There had been awareness of Buddhism in England, but systematic studies of Buddhism only began to appear in the first half of the nineteenth century. Terms such as 'Buddha' 'began to gain currency in the English- and French-speaking worlds'.[34] Manning's trip to Lhasa and his description of the Dalai Lama would no doubt lend support to the idealization and mythologization of Tibet, which, though tenuous and intermittent in formulation, had played a significant part in the long tradition of conjectural history of the world that began to develop in the eighteenth century. Immanuel Kant, for example, insisted that Tibet was key to understanding the history of humanity as a whole, for it might well be the original site of human civilizational activity. He speculated that human beings first lived in the most elevated regions of the globe and later moved to the plains:

> A more precise knowledge of Tibet in Asia would be one of the most important [things to obtain]. Through this we would acquire the key to all history. It is the highest country, it was probably inhabited earlier

---

affecting; could have wept. Very happy to have seen him and his blessed smile. Hope often to see him again.' See Markham, *Narratives of the Mission of George Bogle to Tibet*, p. 267.

33 Markham, *Narratives of the Mission of George Bogle to Tibet*, pp. 266–7.

34 Philip C. Almond, *The British Discovery of Buddhism* (Cambridge: Cambridge University Press, 1988), p. 7.

than any other and may even be the ancestral seat of all culture and sciences. In particular, the learning of the Indians almost certainly originated in Tibet, just as all our arts appear to have come from Hindustan, e.g., agriculture, numbers, chess, etc. It is believed that Abraham dwelt on the borders of Hindustan. Such an original home of the arts and sciences, indeed, I would like to say, of humanity, certainly warrants a more careful investigation.[35]

This speculative global history constitutes a prominent part of Enlightenment thinking about universal humanity and was a crucial aspect of Enlightenment humanism. In his description of the global significance of Tibet, Kant had a special interest in Tibetan religion:

The Fo Sect is the most numerous. By this Fo, they understand an incarnate deity that presently dwells in the great Lama in Barantola, Tibet, and is worshipped in him; after his death it enters into another Lama. The Tartar priests of Fo are called Lamas; those in China Bonzes.[36]

The Lama's spiritual immortality, on which Kant put much emphasis, could be easily turned into a mythological quality:

Missionaries report that they also assert that there is a trinity in the nature of the deity and that the Dalai-Lama is said to administer a certain sacrament with bread and wine, of which, however, no one else eats. This lama does not die, [but rather] in their opinion, his soul lives on in another body which was completely similar to the previous one. Some subordinate priests also claim to be imbued with the spirit of this deity, and the Chinese call such a person a living Fo.[37]

---

[35] Kant, *Physical Geography* (1802), in *Kant: Natural Science*, pp. 434–679 (p. 504).

[36] Kant, *Physical Geography* (1802), in *Kant: Natural Science*, pp. 434–679 (p. 632).

[37] Kant, *Physical Geography*, in *Kant: Natural Science*, pp. 434–679 (p. 652). Johann Gottfried Herder (1744–1803), Kant's student at Königsberg who attended Kant's lectures in 1763–64 on physical geography, recorded Kant's more mystified notion of Fo thus: 'The supreme priest in Tibet (Daleylamma) is a living Fo, sits in the dark like God, underneath lamps; the Lammas are subordinated to him as the eternal father; they have a rite with bread and wine, also incarnation, or more properly enthusiasm [*Begeisterung*] of the Lammae. They believe in transmigration of souls [...].' Quoted in Urs App, 'The Tibet of the Philosophers', *Images of Tibet in the 19th and 20th Centuries*, ed. Monica Esposito. 2 vols (Paris: École française d'Extrême-Orient, 2008), 1. 5–60 (p. 12).

In the imagining of this most elevated region on the earth, Tibet was seen as the 'mankind's arc', where man could protect himself from catastrophic destruction and enjoy incredible longevity and incomparable happiness.[38] Tibet as a world-centre of spirituality and homeland of unalienated humanity began to develop into a major discursive formation in the second half of the nineteenth century, especially in its closing decades, and quite suddenly and quickly, the myths of Tibet began to accumulate.[39] Most consequential of this discursive mystification of Tibet was the development of occultic theosophy, which served as a powerful instrument of anti-modernity. Scholarship on theosophy is copious, and I have no intention to add more to the rich repertoire of historiography on it or its founder Madame Blavatsky, except to note that it is a widely accepted view that Tibet as such was 'discovered' or rather invented in the late nineteenth century as both origin and *telos* of human civilization. It is in the context of high capitalism in the late nineteenth century that the earlier mythological views and formulations

---

[38] The idea of Tibet as 'mankind's arc' was probably associated with the belief that the earth would be catastrophically flooded one day. Geographical discoveries in the nineteenth century showed that the greatest accumulation of ice was in the southern hemisphere, in the Antarctic region, in addition to that in the Himalaya and the Arctic region. There was the theory that 'when the accumulation has reached a certain point, the balance of the earth must be suddenly destroyed, and this orb shall almost instantaneously turn transversely to its axis, moving the great oceans, so producing one of those cyclical catastrophes. [...] [W]hen it occurs, a few just men (and, it is to be hoped, women also) will certainly be left in the upper valleys of the Himalaya.' Andrew Wilson, *The Abode of Snow* (1875) (New York: G. P. Putnam's Sons, 1886), p. v.

[39] To expel the clouds surrounding Tibet, the reprint edition of the French missionary M. Huc's account of his travels in Tibet was issued in 1900 in the hope that a more truthful narrative of Tibet would be sufficient for the reader to remember a 'real' Tibet. The publisher in the Preface wrote: 'Considering the many myths that are now rife about Thibetan Mahatmas and the sensational reports of recent would-be travelers, whose fictitious discoveries are seriously accepted by many readers, it seems appropriate to remind the reading public of a famous but now almost forgotten book, "The Travels in Tartary, Thibet, and China" of the two Lazarist missionaries Huc and Gabet. These gentlemen did not find in Thibet lost manuscripts of the life of Jesus, nor do they describe the Thibetans as savages. Their half-dead servants did not take kodak pictures of them while being tortured on the rack. Nor did they use the powers of hypnotism in their dealings with the Lamas and while being subjected to outrageous tortures. There is, in fact, nothing incredible in M. Huc's story, and yet, perhaps because of this reason, the book is far more interesting than any report that has since appeared.' M. Huc, *Travels in Tartary, Thibet, and China during the Years 1844–5–6* 2 vols. (Chicago: The Open Court Publishing Company, 1900), 2.vii.

of Tibet such as those in the Kantian speculative world history returned as a source of inspiration for the future of humanity.[40] The image of Tibet as a utopia of inner life, a paradise of self-regeneration, and a place of ultimate escape from the evils of modernity was completely destroyed with the People's Liberation Army's entry into Tibet in 1959, which seemed to have only confirmed the perceived needs to preserve its way of life and in particular its religious culture, Tibetan Buddhism, before their disappearance and 'loss'.[41]

Worth noting is the link between the spiritualization of Tibet and the German National Socialist or Nazi movement, which was said to have derived its mythical force partly from 'the world-controlling hidden masters' in Tibet.[42] As mentioned above, Tibet had been thought, at least since Kant, to be the abode of a great king who would descend from the Tibetan heights and come to the rescue of the world from its ruins. Tibet was the last hope of redemption for the whole of humanity. Ernst Schäfer's 1939 expedition to Tibet, sponsored by the Nazi SS, was influenced by the mythological idea of Tibet that it was the place where 'a set of hidden masters' lived and they dwelt in 'two possible realms'.[43] The expedition was therefore partly motivated by the desire to uncover the archeological and ethnographical evidence for corroboration of the Aryan race's origin in Tibet. This connection between Tibet and the Aryans serves as a grim reminder of the dangerous potentialities of mythologizing Tibet.

---

[40] Critical and scholarly studies of occultic Tibet are voluminous, and it is not possible to provide a thorough bibliography in this essay. I mention a few titles that have helped me in thinking about the issues I intend to deal with here. For a study of the popularity of Tibet as a spiritual place, see Ruth Brandon's *The Spiritualists: The Passion for the Occult in the Nineteenth and Twentieth Centuries* (London: Weidenfeld & Nicolson, 1983). Peter Bishop's *The Myth of Shangri-La: Tibet, Travel Writing and the Western Creation of Sacred Landscape* offers a detailed narrative of the transformation of Tibet from physical landscape to mythological space. *The Curators of the Buddha* (Chicago: University of Chicago Press, 1995), ed. by Donald S. Lopez, assembles six studies of Tibetan Buddhism 'under colonialism'. Donald S. Lopez's *Prisoners of Shangri-La: Tibetan Buddhism and the West* (Chicago: University of Chicago Press, 1998) offers a subtle critical analysis of the mystification of Tibetan religion in history and in Western perception.

[41] Donald Lopez, 'Foreigners at the Lama's Feet', in *The Curators of the Buddha*, ed. D. Lopez, pp. 251–5 (p. 251).

[42] Isrun Engelhardt, 'The Nazis of Tibet: A Twentieth Century Myth', in *Images of Tibet in the 19th and 20th Centuries*, 1. 63–96 (p. 65).

[43] Engelhardt, 'The Nazis of Tibet', in *Images of Tibet in the 19th and 20th Centuries*, 1. 63–96 (p. 69).

The Lure of Shangri-La

Mythologization and fictionalization of Tibet must be partly attributable to its geographical remoteness and isolation that had discouraged
and prevented external access to it, and a mysterious Tibet would induce
more explorations, scientific or otherwise, but only to further mystify,
rather than demystify, it. Joseph Rock, one of the most distinguished
explorers in the early decades of the twentieth century, made numerous
attempts to 'discover' the life, culture, and geography of the Tibet–Yunnan
border. Sponsored by the *National Geographic Magazine*, the Austrian-
American explorer made several visits to the Tibetan–Yunnan border; his
accounts and photographs of the life and customs of the region published
in the magazine were widely read and massively influential. In the early
twentieth century, scientific and geographical discoveries which the West
had made during the previous two centuries seemed to have had finally
generated this collective confidence in humanity's knowledge of the
earth: 'To-day the map has no more secrets.' However, Rock, in his long
article 'Seeking the Mountains of Mystery', first published in 1930 in the
National Geographic Magazine, set out to prove the fallacy of this statement by showing that there were places on the Tibet–Yunnan frontier
which scientists and researchers had not yet reached, and which remained
unknown to modern geographical science. It is only ironical that Rock's
scientific explorations, which, organized by the *National Geographic*, were
meant to bring to light the life and culture of the border regions, should
have produced yet more myths about Tibet.[44]

Probably inspired by Rock's reports, James Hilton's *Lost Horizon* was a
crystallization of a utopian Tibet in the creation of Shangri-La. The novel
was the first paperback bestseller in the history of publication, and its
adaptation into a film directed by Frank Capra in 1937 further popularized the book, the story, and most of all Shangri-La. The story is about
a group of four evacuees from the revolutionary tumult in China: two
British diplomats, a fugitive American investment banker, and a missionary; before their plane takes off, however, they are kidnapped by a
mysterious pilot and are flown to an unknown place. It crash-lands in
the mountainous range of the Tibetan boarder; the pilot dies, and the
passengers will be eventually brought to a lamasery, called Shangri-La.

[44] Joseph Rock, 'Seeking the Mountains of Mystery: An Expedition on the
China–Tibet Frontier to the Unexplored Amnyi Machen Range, One of Whose
Peaks Rivals Everest', *The National Geographic Magazine*, lvii.2 (1930), 131–86
(p. 131).

The suffix '*La*', Hilton explains, 'is Tibetan for mountain pass'.[45] They arrive at Shangri-La through the Blue Moon Valley, which is the entrance to the sacred mountain Karakal and the corridor to the mysterious life in Shangri-La. 'About a couple of miles along the valley,' the storyteller says, 'the ascent grew steeper, but by this time the sun was overclouded and a silvery mist obscured the view' (Hilton 53). As four of them continue their journey, almost without knowing it, they hit upon a sharp and brief ascent that 'robbed them of breath':

> Presently the ground levelled, and they stepped out of the mist into clear, sunny air. Ahead, and only a short distance away, lay the lamasery of Shangri-La. To Conway, seeing it first, it might have been a vision fluttering out of the solitary rhythm in which lack of oxygen had encompassed all his faculties. It was, indeed, a strange and half-incredible sight. A group of coloured pavilions clung to the mountainside with none of the grim deliberation of a Rhineland castle, but rather with the chance delicacy of flower petals impaled upon a crag. It was superb and exquisite. An austere emotion carried the eye upward from milk-blue roofs to the grey rock bastion above, tremendous as the Wetterhorn above Grindelwald. Beyond that, in a dazzling pyramid, soared the snow slopes of Karakal. (Hilton 57)

Welcome to Shangri-La! The novel was published in 1933. World War One was still fresh in memory, and the threat of another major world war began to loom large on the horizon. The world had not seen any real and sustained peace for a long time. China's misfortune was manifest; it was a nation torn in conflicts and wars. The story is set in the context of seemingly endless human tragedies.

The kidnapped group of people are flown to Shangri-La against their will, for the British diplomat Conway, who in the film is Foreign Minister designate upon his return to Britain, has been identified as successor to the High Lama of Shangri-La. The most extraordinary story Conway hears about the High Lama of Shangri-La is that he is a Luxembourger called Perrault. Perrault is one of the four Capuchin friars who leave Peking in 1719 and begin an arduous long journey in search of the surviving remnants of the Nestorian faith in the hinterland. Three of them die, and Perrault is lucky to have stumbled into the Blue Moon Valley and is rescued by warm-hearted and hospitable local people. Upon his recovery he works

---

[45] James Hilton, *Lost Horizon* (1933) (London: Pan Books Ltd, 1947), p. 46. Hereafter, this work will be cited parenthetically in the text as Hilton.

to restore a decaying local ancient lamasery and begins to live there. It is the year of 1734, and he is 53 years old. Almost by sheer accident, Perrault finds gold deposits in the valley. Though he is more interested in knowledge and books than money, these deposits of gold prove crucial for sustaining the building and maintenance of the lamasery. In 1789, he is said to be dying. He lies in his room waiting for the final moment. 'He lay for many weeks without speech or movement, and then he began to recover.' He is a hundred and eight at this moment. As if by magic, in his deathbed, 'Perrault had been granted a vision of some significance to take back with him into the world.' He has since lived and worked in Shangri-La. Conway is overwhelmed by this extraordinary story:

> 'It seems impossible', he stammered. 'And yet I can't help thinking of it – it's astonishing – and extraordinary – and quite incredible – and yet not *absolutely* beyond my powers of belief –'
> 'What is, my *son*?'
> And Conway answered, shaken with an emotion for which he knew no reason and which he did not seek to conceal: '*That you are still alive, Father Perrault*'. (120–1)

Father Perrault, the High Lama of Shangri-La, should be more than two hundred years old. It is not by biomedical method or bio-scientific intervention, but through the preservation of mind and body under the natural conditions, that life at Shangri-La is prolonged or rather restored to its natural longevity. In his old age (and partly because of his longevity), Father Perrault is revered as a God in Shangri-La. But he is dying now, and dying at the right time when a successor is identified and successfully brought before him. Conway is moved, and something inside him, something he has not been fully conscious of until now, urges him to think of a form of life different from that to which he is accustomed outside Shangri-La. He decides, as Father Perrault has done two centuries ago, to stay in Shangri-La and to separate himself from the external world, which seems, now more than ever, a theatre of tragedy about man's self-destruction.

In Shangri-La, time no longer has a decisive effect on human life. This timeless Shangri-La is at once Hilton's utopian version of Tibet as a land of purity and his fictional statement on capitalism, modernity, and the modern West. The novel is startlingly prescient in its portrayal of Chalmers Bryant, the fugitive American banker, who, after ruining his bank and losing millions of dollars in speculative investment, is now traveling incognito with Conway. Predatory capitalism, in the figure of this Wall Street broker, is an uncanny foreshadowing of the recent stock-market crash and financial crisis in Wall Street. Speculative financial capitalism might be seen as a Wall Street version of historical adventurous capitalism. And Shangri-La presents a contrast, a different way of thinking about life and reality, and an alternative mode of living and being.

Coda

Tibet continues to be troubled with its multiplicity of identity, and its present predicament expresses that problem of identity. The 'question of Tibet' must be considered in terms of China's influence on its development, even though this influence might take the form of resistance and reaction to what the Chinese government considers to be external orientalism responsible for the creation of the problem of Tibet. However, resonant with historical orientalism that has created a timeless and non-developing Tibet is an indigenous orientalism which, too, identifies Tibetan religion as the last sanctuary against modernity and capitalism. A widespread view held by both the government and its leading academic voices is that the entrenched social stagnation of Tibet is rooted in its religion; religion and social modernity are radically incompatible. The ongoing marketization in China poses a serious challenge to the authority of Tibetan religion and to its control over everyday life in Tibet. Pressures are substantial and multiple on the reforming of religion in Tibet; and it is frequently argued that whether it would survive depends on whether it is ready and willing to reform itself, compromise its control, relinquish some of its power, and attenuate its innate hostility toward modernity's productive and transformative capabilities. Rampant corruption in the religious establishment and among the monks is concurrent and in proportion with the commercialization of Tibetan life. Just as the lure of consumer culture has transformed Chinese society as a whole, the wheel of reform in Tibet would be irreversible.

To conclude, I would bring to attention two issues, which have, I think, significant resonances of the orientalist discourse and practice with regard to Tibet. First, the Tibetan government in exile seems willing to succumb to the discursive orientalist patronization of Tibet by accepting and contributing to the representation of Tibetans as a weak and peaceful people under the rule of external aggressors and of Tibet as a land of spirituality violated by the forces from without. The Dalai Lama in exile has successfully turned Tibet into an international issue under intense global media spotlight. Wang Lixiong, a prominent independent scholar sympathetic toward Tibet, claims in a recent interview that the

Dalai Lama has probably fulfilled his 'historical role'. While critical of the central government's policy on Tibet, Wang believes that the Dalai Lama's strategy 'to get Western people and Western governments to put pressure on the Chinese government so it will make concessions' has not worked. Wang is much less sympathetic toward the new leadership of Tibetan government in exile: 'I think the government in exile hasn't used its brains at all. It's still traveling the world, meeting people, and shaking hands. It's completely useless.' Wang's observation that there are two Tibets – 'One is the Tibet outside the borders and the other is the Tibet inside the borders' – is a sad reminder that historical orientalism continues to influence our understanding of Tibet: 'The Tibet inside the borders has no voice and no representatives. Abroad you have a few hundred thousand people but are they really the representatives of the Tibetan people?'[46] Tibet cannot represent itself; it must be represented, typically in an orientalist idiom adopted and promulgated by those few hundred thousand Tibetans in exile with whom the Tibetans inside Tibet would not identify.

Second, perhaps a more pervasive and consequential problem is what I would call internal racism among the Han Chinese toward the Tibetans. The flipside of the self-orientalized representation of Tibet as peaceful and weak would be the widespread and deep-seated prejudice the Han Chinese harbour toward Tibet, as a backwater on the barren upland where the growth of human life is at the mercy of nature and where the development of civilization would never be possible under its religion. The scope of this internal popular racism among the Han Chinese is staggering. Wang Lixiong demonstrates with compelling evidence that the Han idea of Tibet is radically 'orientalist', and probably more so than that found in the historical orientalist accounts. What is especially disturbing is the widespread everyday internal racism that many Han Chinese would not recognize nor acknowledge. Tibetans are commonly considered second class; even a Han manual worker in Lhasa would think of himself as superior to Tibetans. Long-distance coaches running between Qinghai and Tibet are a movable exhibition of Han racism. Han passengers do not even attempt to conceal their contempt for their fellow Tibetan passengers; Tibetans are openly described as 'dirty and smelly' and are told by the driver or conductor to take rear seats. Once Wang refused to let the Tibetan passenger sitting by him leave and take a rear seat, but surround-

---

[46] Ian Johnson, 'Beyond the Dalai Lama: An Interview with Woeser and Wang Lixiong', *The New York Review of Books* blog, 7 August 2014, <http://www.nybooks.com/blogs/nyrblog/2014/aug/07/interview-tsering-woeser-wang-lixiong/> [accessed 13 August 2014].

ing Han passengers quickly evacuated theirs and moved away, leaving Wang and the Tibetan segregated from other passengers.[47] It would not be possible to think of a Parks trial in the US in 1955 and the Montgomery Bus Boycott in China. For racial segregation is not a state policy, and it should be acknowledged that the Chinese government has done much to eradicate racial discrimination among its cadres, not least because it would be ideologically unacceptable to make that distinction between Tibetans and Han Chinese. It is the popular (and almost unconscious) internal racism that is more unsettling and harder to eradicate. A radical incompatibility between the state's policy over Tibet and this widespread popular internal racism has undermined the central government's efforts to build a Tibet that would be less resentful toward the idea of being part of China.

There might be other problems, but these two forms of orientalism in particular continue to influence our understanding of Tibet. Worth noting is the fact that they articulate the two sides of what I have called internal orientalism – one that exists among Tibetans in exile in collaboration with historical orientalism and the other among Han Chinese in their prejudice toward Tibetans as an other, as a contrast to themselves as more 'civilized'. It is by no means an accident that these two versions of internal orientalism are continuous with the historical views of Tibet discussed above. No one should be so naïve as to assume that historical orientalism would have completed its historical role following the demise of active imperialism and colonialism; on the contrary, it continues to play a significant role in the perception of Tibet and in contemporary politics, especially in the global arena of ideological and regional rivalry among the major powers. The exiled Tibetan government's self-orientalism would have less political potency if Tibet had not been so repeatedly romanticized and violated in history. But how far can such appropriation of Tibet go? It is precisely because the question of Tibet is so deeply entangled with global politics that a quick solution to it does not seem possible or realistic.

---

[47] See Wang Lixiong, *Tianzang: Xizang de mingyun* (Celestial burial: the fate of Tibet) (Hong Kong: Mingjing chubanshe, 1998), esp. Chapter 10, Xinxing zongjiao: minzuozhuyi (Chapter 10, New religion: nationalism).

Index